Using Secondary Data in Educational and Social Research

Conducting educational research

Series Editor: Harry Torrance, Manchester Metropolitan University

This series is aimed at research students in education and those undertaking related professional, vocational and social research. It takes current methodological debates seriously and offers well-informed advice to students on how to respond to such debates. Books in the series review and engage with current methodological issues, while relating such issues to the sorts of decisions which research students have to make when designing, conducting and writing up research. Thus the series both contributes to methodological debate and has practical orientation by providing students with advice on how to engage with such debate and use particular methods in their work. Series authors are experienced researcher and supervisors. Each book provides students with insights into a different form of educational research while also providing them with the critical tools and knowledge necessary to make informed judgements about the strengths and weaknesses of different approaches.

Current titles:

Using Secondary Data in Educational and Social Research

Emma Smith

Open University Press

Open University Press
McGraw-Hill Education
McGraw-Hill House
Shoppenhangers Road
Maidenhead
Berkshire
England
SL6 2QL

email: enquiries@openup.co.uk
world wide web: www.openup.co.uk

and Two Penn Plaza, New York, NY 10121-2289, USA

First published 2006

A catalogue record of this book is available from the British Library

ISBN-10: 0 335 22358 3 (pb)   0 335 22357 5 (hb)
ISBN-13: 9780 335 22358 9 (pb)   9780 335 22357 2 (hb)

Library of Congress Cataloging-in-Publication Data
CIP data applied for

Typeset by YHT Ltd, London
Printed in Great Britain by Bell and Bain Ltd., Glasgow

The *McGraw·Hill* Companies

For WB

Contents

Preface

This is a book about using secondary data in social and educational research. It assumes no prior mathematical expertise and is intended as a practical resource for researchers who are new to the field of secondary data analysis. In particular, the book should be used as a resource for undergraduate and postgraduate students who are interested in using secondary data for the first time as their main or subsidiary research method. Indeed, the aim throughout this book is to encourage researchers to consider the potential for using secondary data as a useful strategy in mixed method designs.

The book comprises three parts. The first contains four chapters that introduce the reader to the role of secondary data analysis as a research method in contemporary social research; it considers the arguments for and against its use and addresses its particular benefit in mixed methods research designs, particularly those in the political arithmetic tradition. Part I concludes by describing some of the practical issues one needs to consider before deciding to use secondary sources in their research. Part II comprises three chapters of worked examples that show the potential for using secondary sources to answer a varied range of research questions. This section provides guidance on accessing, managing and preparing large datasets for analysis. Part III contains the endpiece and three appendices and is devoted to locating sources of secondary data as well as reinforcing the techniques needed for the effective husbandry of large-scale datasets. As the number of sources with potential for secondary analysis are forever expanding and changing, access to existing and new sources will be maintained through the website accompanying this book. This website will act as a portal to all the sources of secondary data that are listed here, as well as providing links to new sources and current developments in the field of secondary data analysis. Access the website by following the links from my staff page at www.education.bham.ac.uk.

Finally, I would like to thank Stephen Gorard, Harry Torrance and Patrick White for their thoughtful help and advice while I was writing this book.

Part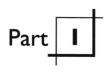

Secondary data analysis: an introduction

All data are the consequence of one person asking questions of someone
else. (Jacob 1984: 43)

This chapter introduces the field of secondary data analysis. It begins by
considering what it is that we mean by secondary data analysis, before
describing the type of data that might lend itself to secondary analysis
and the ways in which the approach has developed as a research tool in
social and educational research. The second part of the chapter considers
the use of secondary data analysis in contemporary social research and
introduces the results of a review of recent research output in the field.

Defining secondary data analysis

Numerous definitions of secondary data analysis appear in the literature,
many with subtle differences which together suggest a lack of consensus
about what is meant by the term. For example, one relatively straightforward definition of the secondary analysis of survey data was suggested
by Hyman (1972: 1), as 'the extraction of knowledge on topics other than
those which were the focus of the original survey'.

Other definitions of secondary analysis have emphasised its usefulness
for exploring new research questions: 'the study of specific problems
through analysis of existing data which were originally collected for
another purpose' (Glaser 1963: 11); or: 'the further analysis of an existing
dataset with the aim of addressing a research question distinct from that
for which the dataset was originally collected and generating novel
interpretations and conclusions' (Hewson 2006: 274). However, such
definitions appear to disregard the potential of secondary analysis in re-
analysing existing datasets with novel statistical or theoretical approaches

in such a way that: 'secondary analysis is the re-analysis of data for the purpose of answering the original research questions with better statistical techniques, or answering new research questions with old data' (Glass 1976: 3). One apparent area of consensus among those looking for a definition of secondary analysis is that it should involve the analysis of someone else's data: 'a collection of data obtained by another researcher which is available for re-analysis' (Sobal 1981: 149). However, this has been disputed as: 'even re-analysis of one's own data is secondary data analysis if it has a new purpose or is in response to a methodological critique' (Schutt 2007: 4127). Other researchers point to the ubiquitous credentials of secondary analysis as 'neither a specific regime of analytic procedures nor a statistical technique, [but] ... a set of research endeavours that use existing materials' (Kiecolt and Nathan 1985: 10). And emphasise its difference from primary analysis: 'which involves both data collection and analysis, while secondary analysis requires the application of creative analytical techniques to data that have been amassed by others' (Kiecolt and Nathan 1985: 10).

Given the rather subtle differences in the definition and interpretation of secondary analysis that we see here, it seems likely that neat distinctions between primary and secondary data will not always be possible (Dale et al. 1988). Such lack of consensus might leave one wishing to adopt a very general definition of secondary analysis such as that offered by Jary and Jary (2000): as 'any inquiry based on the re-analysis of previously analysed research data' (p. 540) or one such as Hakim's:

> [S]econdary data analysis is any further analysis of an existing dataset which presents interpretations, conclusions or knowledge additional to, or different from, those produced in the first report on the inquiry as a whole and its main results. (Hakim 1982a: 1)

Whichever definition one favours, secondary analysis should be 'an empirical exercise carried out on data that has already been gathered or compiled in some way' (Dale et al. 1988: 3). This may involve using the original, or novel, research questions, statistical approaches and theoretical frameworks; and may be undertaken by the original researcher or by someone new.

What are secondary data?

Secondary data can embrace a whole spectrum of empirical forms; they can include data generated through systematic reviews, through documentary analysis as well as the results from large-scale datasets such as the National Census or international surveys such as the Programme for International Student Assessment (PISA). Secondary data can be numeric or non-numeric. Non-numeric, or qualitative secondary data, can include data retrieved second hand from interviews, ethnographic accounts, documents, photographs or conversations. In the UK, an excellent source of archived qualitative data with huge potential for secondary analysis is available through the Economic and Social Data Services (ESDS) Qualidata facility based at the University of Essex. Data available through Qualidata includes in-depth and semi-structured interviews, field notes and observations, as well as personal documents. The service provides support and training, as well as access to contemporary and classic studies of British society, such as the research papers and data for Dennis Marsden and Brian Jackson's 1962 study, 'Education and the Working Class' (see Appendix 1 for details on accessing the ESDS facility). In this book, however, our concern is with numeric secondary data only. (But see Hammersley (1997), Heaton, (1998) and Fielding and Fielding (2000) for further discussion on the methodological and substantive implications of the secondary analysis of non-numeric data.)

The potential for the secondary analysis of numeric data is huge. From a nation's population census to snapshot public opinion polls about the outcome of televised talent show competitions: 'Nearly every important area of activity and attitude in the British population has now been the focus of a major national survey' (Thomas 1996: 3). The range of numeric empirical data that are suited to secondary analysis would include:

- population census
- government surveys
- other large-scale surveys
- cohort and other longitudinal studies
- other regular or continuous surveys
- administrative records.

The next section will introduce these different types of secondary data, although a fuller discussion of specific datasets and data archives is provided in Appendix 1.

Population census

For example, the National Decennial Census or the School Census in the UK.

The National Decennial Census is arguably the gold standard of survey design. The resources needed to develop and administer the process dwarf those of other surveys. For example, the cost of the 2001 UK National Census was around £207 million in a cycle that lasted almost a decade (Office for National Statistics 2005). In 2003 the United States Census Bureau had a budget of $3.9billion and employed more than

860,000 workers in its ongoing data collection efforts (Sales et al. 2006). In England and Wales, an annual school census was introduced in 1997 which gathered data on the aggregate characteristics of young people in school. In 2002, this was extended to an annual *pupil*-level census, which itself became termly (three times a year) from 2007.

Government surveys

For example, the Labour Force Study or the General Household Survey in the UK or the General Social Survey in the USA.

Given the high level of funding and expertise that goes into the development of government surveys, they can often represent the highest quality data that are available. Their scope is generally large and their population can be highly representative, which aids robust inferences (Sales et al. 2006). They are likely to involve skilled teams of survey developers and statisticians and be administered by trained interviewers, so reducing the potential for interviewer bias (Dale et al. 1988). Often these surveys are produced at regular time periods and so can be combined to produce a type of 'synthetic cohort study' (Arber 2001: 276). For example, subsequent waves of the General Household Survey can be used to track a particular birth cohort through time. Although this survey does not track the same individuals, it does track the same cohort and so comparisons between different demographic groups may be made over a 5- or 10-year period, for example. One of the downsides of government-sponsored surveys is that the questions asked may reflect narrow contemporary policy interests, rather than topics that may be of direct interest to the social science researcher. Indeed, the concerns of many social scientists about the use and potential abuse of government-sponsored or 'official' data is well documented, and will be discussed in the next chapter.

Other large-scale surveys

For example, the British Social Attitudes Survey or the Programme for International Student Assessment.

Not all large-scale surveys are produced by the state. However, just like government-sponsored surveys, other large-scale surveys are likely to involve collaborations between professional statisticians and survey designers and are arguably of the best quality available. Their scale can also ensure that they are nationally representative and so enable rigorous comparisons between different social groups, potentially over extended periods of time. The level of resources behind some large international surveys can be quite staggering. For example, the institutes and teams behind the Programme for International Student Assessment (PISA) study include a secretariat, which is responsible for the day-to-day management of the programme, a governing body, international contractors for each of the more than 50 countries involved in the programme, national project managers as well as subject matter and contextual question expert groups. PISA, which is funded by the OECD member countries, accounts for around 30% of OECD's education budget.

Cohort and other longitudinal studies

For example, the British Household Panel Survey and the Millennium Cohort Study in the UK and the High School and Beyond study in the USA.

Longitudinal data enable the researcher to look at continuity and change in behaviour over time, rather than just focusing on brief cross-sectional snapshots of an individual's life (Brooks-Gunn et al. 1991). Panel and cohort studies are forms of longitudinal analysis which are conducted by collecting data at a number of points in time from the same group of people. They share many of the positive features of government and other large-scale surveys but with the additional benefit of enabling researchers to monitor social phenomena over extended periods of time. In the UK, the Centre for Longitudinal Studies, based at London's Institute of Education, is responsible for administering three national cohort studies: the 1958 National Child Development Study (NCDS), the 1970 British Cohort Study (BCS) and the 2000 Millennium Cohort Study (MCS). Datasets from these studies, as well as support and training, are available for secondary analysis from the Economic and Social Data service (ESDS) (see Appendix 1 for more details).

Other regular or continuous surveys

For example, Gallup opinion polls, smaller scale academic studies.

These surveys may be smaller in scale than government-sponsored studies and are likely to have been undertaken perhaps by a small team of academic researchers, by or on behalf of advocacy groups or as a piece of market research or public opinion poll. Their quality may vary, as indeed might their potential for bias and generalisability. For example, they may represent non-random population samples, with the data collection undertaken by novice or untrained researchers or, in the case of some academic studies, by students (Hakim 1982a). Alternatively, commissioned public opinion polls may be of high quality and adopt the latest sampling techniques but may be more susceptible to question bias and, because of their very fast turnaround, poor question piloting. However, results from these ad hoc surveys can also be fruitful sources of data for the secondary analyst. Data of this type are best located from social science data archives or opinion polls archives such as those of the Roper Centre in the USA. In the UK, it is a funding requirement that studies supported by the Economic and Social Research Council (ESRC) make their data available for archiving.

Administrative records

For example, prison or probation records, data on admissions to higher education.

   This category includes data that have been collected as part of routine data management and administration activities, for example, the characteristics of individuals who apply for higher education courses or the number of students who achieve particular examination grades. Often these data are available in aggregate form and require limited re-analysis. However, these data may also take the form of administrative records such as hospital medical records, police and judicial records and so on. With these types of data, issues of confidentiality and access are likely to be paramount, as is the amount of work required to retrieve, prepare and analyse the data. Additionally, these data begin to blur the arbitrary boundary between numeric and non-numeric secondary data. Data retrieved from administrative records can be very powerful, both in the way they can be used and reported by the media, advocates or governments, but also in their potential for understanding social phenomena.

   We will revisit each of these categories of secondary data later in the book; but, first, we consider the development of secondary analysis as a research tool and the extent to which it is currently used in contemporary social science research.

Development of secondary analysis

Secondary analysis has a long pedigree. In 1790 the first national population census was undertaken in the USA, followed in Great Britain in 1801. The potential of these data for secondary analysis and their contribution to the social sciences is exemplified by Booth's work on occupation patterns that were derived from secondary analysis of the 1801–1881 UK Censuses (Booth 1886). By the end of the nineteenth century, the large-scale studies of urban poverty that were pioneered by Joseph Rowntree in York and Charles Booth in London marked the start of the social survey movement and the wealth of opportunities it afforded for secondary analysis. Official records were also put to use for secondary analysis, most notably in Durkheim's important research into the sociology of suicide (Durkheim 1952) which is considered in more detail in the next chapter. In the United States, secondary analysis as a research strategy coincides with the rapid increase in the number of attitudinal surveys before the Second World War. The 'first notable effort' at secondary analysis from a theoretical and methodological perspective was *The American Soldier* (Glaser 1963: 11). *The American Soldier* is part of a collection of around 260 studies of several hundred thousand army personnel that was undertaken during the Second World War. Its four volumes are the accumulation of several years of investigation and include surveys and observations of soldiers' lives before, during and after combat (Lazarsfeld 1949). The work provides a fascinating insight into the lives of service personnel: for example, their relationships with their fellow soldiers and officers, their changing attitudes towards war as a result of experiencing combat and their adaptation to life as civilians. In addition, the collection is seen as a 'fine model indeed for the secondary analysis of a rich archive of data collected for other purposes' (Smith 1984: 196, cited in Williams 1989: 157). The legacy of *The American Soldier* has not just been its contribution to the field of military history. Its theoretical and conceptual developments have found influence in developing theories of class position, of race relations, of 'relative deprivation' and social adjustment; and its methodological applications have led the field in the development of attitude scaling and latent structural analysis (Glaser 1963; Lazarsfeld 1949; Williams 1989).

Other classic examples of secondary analyses include the re-analysis of the Coleman Report during the early 1970s (Mosteller and Moynihan 1972). This re-analysis was in a large part prompted by the huge interest generated by the study *Equality of Educational Opportunity* (Coleman et al. 1966). The original study found that the variation in learner outcomes in schools was strongly related to factors external to the school, such as family background and that the school itself had a relatively small part to play in mediating between different academic outcomes. Perhaps unsurprisingly, given the reception that greeted the original study, a re-analysis of the findings soon followed. Undertaken by faculty members at Harvard University, the secondary analysis identified some discrepancies, errors and issues with the primary study but largely 'affirmed and strengthened' (Smith 1972: 311) the original findings. Another example of important secondary analyses of influential studies is Elashoff and Snow's (1971) re-analysis of Rosenthal and Jacobsen's (1968) study *Pygmalion in the Classroom*.

In the UK, one important use of secondary analysis in the sociology of education is the 1980 re-analysis of the 1972 Oxford Mobility Project dataset by Halsey et al. This study is not only important for its empirical and theoretical contributions, as the subsequent book *Origins and Destinations: Family, Class and Education in Modern Britain* is one of the classics in the sociology of education.

Works such as *The American Soldier*, *Origins and Destinations* and *Suicide* set the standard for secondary analysis in the social sciences, exemplified by their methodological, theoretical and substantive contributions to the development of the field. However, arguably the potential for secondary analysis as an important social science method has never fully been realised in many branches of the discipline, as many of the objections to its use (considered in Chapter 2) attest. While secondary analysis may be more established as a research method in the United States (Hakim 1982), it has remained relatively underused in many areas of the social sciences in the UK. Indeed, the 1988 edition of *The Penguin Dictionary of Sociology* contains no entry for secondary analysis. In the entry for 'official statistics' sociologists were advised to 'approach such data with caution', its use was described as 'perilous' and data collected by government for its own use considered 'meaningless' (Abercrombie et al. 1988: 170). Perhaps some minor rehabilitation of the field has occurred in the intervening years as a definition for 'secondary analysis' was suggested in the 2000 edition and the authors' objections to the use of official statistics have been somewhat mollified in these later editions (Abercrombie et al. 2000).

How widely are secondary data analysis used?

In this section, we broaden our consideration of secondary data analysis to reflect some of the methodological challenges faced by the social science community. The focus begins with a brief discussion about general methodological concerns before considering the implications these may have for the secondary analysis of numeric data.

In education, recent methodological preoccupations in both the UK and the USA have focused on the quality and relevance of research in the field. Educational research is widely viewed as having an 'awful' reputation (Kaestle 1993) of being 'not very influential, useful or well funded' (Burkhardt and Schoenfeld 2003: 3), of following fads (Slavin 1989) and of being of indifferent quality (Hargreaves 1996; Tooley with Darby 1998). While the call in both countries is for a greater unity between research and practice (Burkhardt and Schoenfeld 2003; Hargreaves 1996), there is some divergence in how this might actually be achieved. In the USA, legislation introduced in 2001 stipulates that all federally funded research must adopt scientifically based research methods (Eisenhart and Towne 2003; Olson and Viadero 2002). For some this is seen as an opportunity to elevate educational research to the status of medicine and agriculture (Slavin 2002) and for 'nurturing and reinforcing' a scientific research culture in the field (Feuer et al. 2002: 4). For others, it exemplifies the privileging of certain research methods: namely, experiments and randomised control trials, a failure to understand the complexity of the field and a lack of commitment by the US federal government to promoting true evidence-based practice (Berliner 2002).

In the UK, general methodological concerns centre on a perceived imbalance in the types of research method adopted by educational and other social science researchers (ESRC 2006). Much of this concern is centred on the 'dubious dichotomy' (Payne et al. 2004: 153) that exists between 'quantitative' and 'qualitative' methods. For example, according to the Economic and Social Research Council (ESRC), 'the lack of quantitative skills is endemic in many areas of Social Science and ... there is an urgent need to enhance research quality' (ESRC 2006: 12). The ESRC has demonstrated its commitment to building research capacity in the field of quantitative methods through sponsorship of centres such as the Social Science Research Methods hub at Southampton University, the development of data management infrastructures such as UK Data Archive and its sponsorship of the *European Social Survey* and other internationally renowned longitudinal studies such as the *National Child Development Study* and the *British Household Panel Survey*.

In the field of education, a lack of quantitative skills among researchers is seen as being one of its most significant 'defects' (Gorard et al. 2003a: 19) and, according to key stakeholders, there is a significant lack of quantitative skills in the field:

> There is a widely acknowledged absence of quantitative research of particular kinds, especially, there's a weakness, there's a relative absence and there's no mechanism for addressing that currently. (HE researcher and ESRC Teaching and Learning Research Programme team leader, cited in Gorard et al. 2003a: 13)

In addition to concerns about a lack of quantitative work in education, there are also concerns about the quality of such work:

> I think you can get terrible quantitative work, there are people who just think there's a kind of non-problematic general linear model reality out there and you just tag variables and start with race and that's it ... switch on SPSS, press the buttons with all the defaults on is garbage in garbage out. (chief executive of research funding body, cited in Gorard et al. 2003a: 17)

Thus it can be argued that building research capacity in the use of quantitative methods is not just about increasing the volume of such research but focusing on more basic quantitative techniques. The concern appears to be not only about the relative shortage of quantitative research 'but also a shortage of the quantitative research skills required to be able to understand, and critically review, quantitative research' (Gorard et al. 2003a: 19). The next section considers these concerns in light of a review of publications submitted to the 2001 Research

Assessment Exercise (RAE) and a more recent examination of the published output of eight social science journals.

What evidence is there for a lack of quantitative skills?

In the UK, the funding councils for higher education institutions (HEIs) have highlighted the importance of comparative measures of research excellence. This has resulted in the Research Assessment Exercise (the RAE), the purpose of which is to produce quality profiles for all research activity in UK HEIs. Indeed, the RAE is the principal means by which institutions assure themselves of the quality of research undertaken in the HE sector (RAE 2008). The first RAE was carried out in 1986 with four subsequent exercises prior to the latest RAE in 2008. In *RAE 2001* research quality ratings were based on a range from 1–5*, according to how much of the work was judged to reach national or international levels of excellence. In this way, the quality ratings derived from the RAE provide a single measure of research strength in UK higher education. In this section, therefore, we report the findings from an analysis of the results for the most recently available RAE, *RAE 2001*, and examine the evidence for a lack of quantitative skills in the social sciences and in the field of education, in particular (Gorard et al. 2003b). We begin by looking at the overview reports for the four main RAE social science panels – education, social policy, social work and sociology. Their comments suggest that in some areas of the social sciences, a concern over the paucity of quantitative research does remain:

> The strengths of qualitative, and relatively small scale, research have been complemented by some increase in work that has also drawn on quantitative data. However, there is room for more approaches that use advanced quantitative methodologies and for education to play an active and significant role in methodological innovation. (Education Panel RAE 2001a)

> There was a paucity of quantitative analysis, particularly that combined with qualitative approaches. Quantitative work, while sometimes of very high quality, is rare and not always good when found. (Social Work Panel RAE 2001b)

Note that similar concerns about quantitative work in sociology and social policy and administration were not raised in the RAE 2001 overview documents for these two panels (RAE 2001b). This, of course, does not necessarily mean that such concerns do not exist (and, indeed, some of the evidence presented in the following section argues that, at least in sociology, they well might) rather it may simply be the case that they were just not reported by the *RAE 2001* panels.

Because of the variety of submissions in the field of education, the RAE panel for 2001 required that institutions also provide additional information about the methods undertaken in each submission. This theory/

method field was to be used to classify 'any conceptual framework within which the research may be set, together with a brief indication of the design and/or research method' (RAE 2001c). This means that for education, in addition to providing indicators of quality, the RAE is also able to provide a much more detailed audit of the research methods that were being used (Gorard et al. 2003b).

While the use of the theory/method field to classify research methods is not itself unproblematic, an analysis of the 8700 publications submitted to the education panel in *RAE 2001* does reveal an interesting balance of methodological approaches. Table 1.1 shows the number of times a particular method was reported as being the first or main method used in submissions to the education panel in *RAE 2001*. According to the entries reported in the theory/method field, a large number of submissions (32%) were not clearly empirical: for example, they involved literature reviews or thought pieces. Of the remainder around 14% were largely or wholly quantitative and 28% were largely or wholly qualitative – a balance of around 2:1 (Gorard et al. 2003b). Notice also the relatively lowly position of secondary data analysis, which was listed as the main method for fewer than 1% of the pieces submitted to *RAE 2001*.

The number of *actual* methods used in the sample of work submitted for *RAE 2001* can be compared with a self-reported audit of methods that was undertaken by Gorard et al. (2003b) as part of the same study and reproduced in Table 1.2. This self-audit was completed by 521 researchers who were actively engaged in empirical research in the UK in 2002–2003. They were asked to summarise their knowledge and use of a range of methods taken from a specified list of nearly 300 approaches. The approaches were collapsed into similar categories as used for the theory/method analysis described in Table 1.1. The responses indicate a considerable capacity to undertake quantitative work in the field of education: around three-quarters of the research community reported having conducted a survey and around 65% report having used a secondary numeric source of data.

If we consider the number of times researchers report using quantitative and qualitative methods in their everyday research and the types of method actually adopted in publications that were submitted to *RAE 2001*, we see that while similar proportions of researchers report using quantitative and qualitative techniques (Table 1.2), in submissions to *RAE 2001*, twice as many publications were qualitative in nature than were quantitative (Table 1.1). While this gap is perhaps smaller than expected given the stakeholders' concerns that were explored earlier, it does suggest that perhaps researchers are not quite as eclectic in their use of methods as they might see themselves to be. The differences between those *reporting* using secondary data analysis and those *actually* using this method are more apparent than for the broad area of quantitative

Table 1.1 Frequency of reported first or main method used in publications submitted to Education Panel, RAE 2001

Method	Number	%
Thought piece	1533	18
Literature review	828	10
Survey	697	8
Case study	674	8
Qualitative unspecified	494	6
Comparative	479	6
Policy study/analysis	465	5
Interview	407	5
Textual analysis	392	5
Not classifiable/no method	364	4
Historical/archive	344	4
Quantitative unspecified	271	3
Ethnomethodology	268	3
Action research	233	3
Philosophy	191	2
Observation	190	2
Programme evaluation	131	2
Longitudinal study	121	1
Linguistic/conversational analysis	102	1
Experiment	94	1
Scales/psychometry	80	1
Software for collection/analysis	65	1
Group interview	51	1
Formal tests	46	1
Diaries	37	0.4
Systematic review (meta analysis)	31	0.4
Pictures/sound	29	0.3
Intervention	25	0.3
Secondary numeric data	15	0.2
Total	**8691**	**100**

Source: Gorard et al. 2003b: 44

methods: 65% of respondents to the survey of Gorard et al. (2003b) report using the technique (Table 1.2) but it only features in the theory/method line of only 15 out of 8691 submissions to *RAE 2001* (Table 1.1).

The notion of methodological pluralism (where researchers are tolerant of a variety methods) was further examined by Payne et al. (2004) in their review of 2 years' output from four 'well-regarded mainstream or general' (p. 155) British sociology journals. As in the field of education, concerns have also been expressed in sociology about a lack of quantitative skills (Payne et al. 2004). Indeed, their analysis appears to support

Table 1.2 Frequency of actual methods used in publications submitted to Education Panel, RAE 2001

Method	Number	%
Interview	480	92
Literature review	471	90
Case study	421	81
Sampling	416	80
Observation	415	80
Textual analysis	409	79
Qualitative general	400	77
Quantitative general	393	76
Survey	391	75
Triangulation	370	71
Secondary numeric sources	340	65
Group interview	339	65
Software for collection/analysis	325	63
Pictures/sound	298	57
Evaluation	289	56
Action research	269	51
Systematic review (meta analysis)	254	49
Diaries	239	46
Experiment	212	41
Longitudinal study	199	39
Linguistic/conversational analysis	195	38
Formal tests	194	37
Scales/psychometry	184	35
Ethnomethodology	142	27
Visual/sound sources	91	17
Historical archive	69	13

N = 514 (respondents could list more than one method).

Source: Gorard et al. 2003b: 31

such claims as they found that only about one in 20 published papers used any form of quantitative analysis. Suggesting no evidence of genuine plurality of methods:

> [I]ndividual sociologists – no matter how tolerant, catholic and eclectic – are very unlikely actually to be methodological pluralists ... It is the structure of sociology that became pluralist, not sociologists themselves. (Bell and Roberts 1984: 5, cited in Payne et al. 2004)

Using RAE returns and a self-selected audit survey as a means of identifying the research skills of social scientists can only take us so far. In the next section, we shift our focus back to secondary data analysis to examine the extent to which social researchers are as plural in their use of secondary data methods as their self-reports suggest they might be.

Secondary data analysis in practice

In an approach similar to that undertaken by Payne et al. (2004) and Gorard et al. (2003a), I have undertaken an analysis of the published output of eight mainstream and well-regarded journals in the fields of education, sociology and social work over a 7-year period. The aim of this analysis is to investigate concerns about a lack of methodological pluralism in the use of quantitative methods in these fields and, more importantly for the purpose of this book, for the use of secondary data analysis.

Three journals each in the fields of education and sociology and two in the area of social work were selected. The journals were:

> *Education*: British Educational Research Journal, Oxford Review of Education and *Research Papers in Education*.
> *Sociology*: British Journal of Sociology, Sociology and *The Sociological Review*.
> *Social Work*: British Journal of Social Work and *International Social Work*.

All eight journals are listed in the social science citation index and were targeted at a general audience: for example *The Sociological Review* has 'a flexible approach to both its content and its style. No social topic is considered irrelevant, innovative subject matter and style are welcomed, and articles are always topical and current' (Blackwell Publishing 2005). Similarly *Oxford Review of Education* 'publishes papers on the theory and practice of education from scholars throughout the world in a variety of disciplines: philosophy, political science, economics, history, anthropology, sociology, psychology and medicine' (Taylor and Francis Group 2007). Although each of the selected journals draws contributions from around the world, in particular *International Social Work*, all had editors who were based in the UK. Because of the relatively general scope of the journals there was some degree of permeability across disciplines, for example, papers from the broad field of 'education' appeared in both the 'sociology' and 'social work' journals.

Similarly, the analysis described here does not distinguish between pieces submitted by academic departments and those from other institutions. This might make for a generous interpretation of the output of quantitative and secondary analytic pieces in the field of education where many papers which emphasised secondary analysis in particular were submitted from organisations such as the National Foundation for Education Research (NFER) and examination boards such as the University of Cambridge Local Examinations Syndicate (UCLES), rather than from HE schools of education. Additionally, as we have seen in the

Table 1.3 Use of secondary data analysis and quantitative methods, selected social science journals

Journal	Secondary data analysis	Quantitative methods	Total papers
British Educational Research Journal	34	85	274
Oxford Review of Education	30	56	220
Research Papers in Education	16	51	133
Education total	**80 (42%)**	**192 (31%)**	**627**
British Journal of Sociology	49	58	201
Sociology	26	37	294
Sociological Review	14	24	211
Sociology total	**89 (75%)**	**119 (17%)**	**706**
British Journal of Social Work	15	95	422
International Social Work	18	86	261
Social work total	**33 (18%)**	**181 (27%)**	**683**
All journals	**202 (41%)**	**492 (24%)**	**2016**

introductory sections of this chapter, there is no real clear and unambiguous definition of secondary data analysis. I have, therefore, taken a very inclusive approach to deciding whether or not articles adopt secondary analytic techniques. Selection criteria were limited to numeric empirical pieces which reported aggregate secondary data, as well as those which undertook an analysis of raw data. Bearing these caveats to a rather imprecise art in mind, we now consider the results of the journal search, beginning with the frequency of pieces which adopted quantitative and/or secondary data analysis methods (Table 1.3).

About one-quarter of all the papers that were reviewed adopted some form of quantitative method (492/2016), of these around 41% (202/492) used secondary data analysis. Overall, fewer than 10% of papers (202/2016) involved the analysis of secondary data. The findings for the individual subject areas are considered next.

Sociology

The findings for the 'sociology' journals reflect some of the concerns of Payne et al. (2004) in that only 17% of papers published were quantitative in nature. However, these overwhelmingly used secondary data analysis: 89 out of 119 numeric pieces in the 'sociology' journals adopted some form of secondary data analysis. The range of secondary sources

used in 'sociology' journals was extensive and included the UK population census and government-sponsored surveys such as the *Labour Force
Study*, among many others. Examples of the range of secondary sources
used in the field of sociology include data from the *European Values Survey*
to examine secular beliefs in Europe (Halman and Draulans 2006),
childhood poverty and early parenthood explored through the *National
Child Development Study* (Hobcraft and Kiernan 2001) and the *British
Family Resources Survey* being used to examine the pension prospects of
minority ethnic groups (Ginn and Arber 2001). The use of international
secondary sources was also apparent. For example, the national mobility
surveys in Japan and Israel were used in order to study the relationship
between class structure and social mobility among women and ethnic
groups in these two countries respectively (Shirahase 2001; Yaish 2001).

Education
Around one-third of the papers published in the three 'education'
journals involved some use of quantitative methods. The range of
quantitative approaches varied from relatively small-scale questionnaire
surveys, sometimes combined with other approaches (for example,
Canning 2000; Edwards and Protheroe 2003) to large-scale longitudinal
national cohort studies (for example, Driessen et al. 2005). However, in
contrast to the 'sociology' journals, the papers that used some component
of secondary data analysis comprised a relatively small sub-section of the
quantitative genre. Here only 80 of the 192 numeric pieces used secondary data analysis (see Table 1.3). In the 'education' journals that were
reviewed here, the majority of pieces that included any analysis of secondary data were largely based on the analysis of school examination
data (for example, Goldstein 2001; Strand 2002). Much less use was
made of secondary data from other sources. However, there were some
exceptions. For example, Payne's use of *Youth Cohort Study* data to look at
the impact of part-time work among year 12 and year 13 students (Payne
2003), the use of the *1958 British Birth Cohort Study* to examine the
relationship between family background and school subject choice (Van
de Werfhorst et al. 2003) and the analysis of participation data from the
Higher Education Statistics Agency in an examination of patterns of inclusion among disabled students in higher education (Riddell et al. 2005). A
small number of papers also used secondary data from international
sources. For example, Post's use of the *Hong Kong National Census* to look
at educational stratification and access to higher education (Post 2003)
and use by Williams et al. of the *Programme for International Student
Assessment (PISA)* data to model achievement among 15 year olds in
OECD countries (Williams et al. 2005).

Social work

In common with 'education', less than one-third of publications in the 'social work' journals had a numeric component. As in 'education' a large proportion of these papers reported the findings of relatively small-scale primary surveys, for example Mosek and Adler (2001) and Wardell et al. (2000). Fewer than 20% (33 out of 181) of these numeric pieces involved the analysis or the presentation of secondary data. One reason for this may be the relative paucity of good-quality secondary datasets covering contemporary research areas of interest in the field. However, as the wide range of topics covered in the 'social work' journals attests, social work, like education, is a large multidisciplinary field. Indeed, that there are opportunities in the field of social work for secondary analysis is exemplified by the range of datasets that were reported in the journals included in this study. These include Buchanan and Flouri's (2001) use of the *National Child Development Study* to examine the relationship between parental background and familial emotional support in adulthood and Bertera's (2003) use of United Nation's data on life expectancy to explore social services for the aged in Cuba. There were also studies that combined a range of secondary sources, such as Ji's examination of the effects of risk factors on rates of homelessness in the USA which used secondary data from the US Census Bureau, the National Low Income Housing Coalition, the Department of Housing and Urban Development, the Urban Institute and the Interagency Council on the Homeless (Ji 2006).

This quick analysis of the frequency of use of numeric and secondary analytic techniques in three areas of the social sciences to some extent reinforces the view of the Gorard et al. (2003a) stakeholders that quantitative methods are underused in social science research, although the finding that around one-third of the papers in the 'education' journals used numeric methods perhaps gives some cause for optimism. However, in the 'sociology' journals, where fewer than 20% of papers adopted quantitative techniques, the concerns of Payne et al. (2004) about a lack of methodological pluralism appear to remain true. With regard to secondary data analysis, although a relatively large proportion of papers in the 'sociology' journals adopted this approach, the same cannot be said of the 'social work' and 'education' journals. Indeed, in the field of education, although the results of the Gorard et al. survey (2003a) might suggest that UK education researchers report using secondary data analysis, relatively few actually use the technique in their research – further evidence perhaps of a lack of methodological pluralism.

Summary

This first chapter has sought to introduce the reader to the field of secondary data analysis. It is a field with a long pedigree that extends back to the pioneers of the Victorian social surveys through to the opinion polls, censuses, administrative records and international surveys of today. Despite the huge potential of secondary data analysis methods, there is limited consensus on a definition for the term, although commentators tend to agree that it involves some form of re-analysis or reporting of existing data. Such flexibility in its definition perhaps reinforces its suitability to involve any analysis involving the re-interpretation of existing data which bring new methodological and theoretical perspectives or which adopt the original or novel research questions and which are undertaken by the original researcher or individuals new to the data. It is also important to emphasise that the analysis of secondary data need not involve the manipulation of complex and large datasets. Indeed, much of the data that are available for secondary analysis are in the form of aggregate data – that is, data that have already been analysed and are presented in summary form.

The second part of this chapter considered the extent to which secondary data analysis is currently used in social research. It took as its starting point contemporary concerns that quantitative methods are underused in the field and, by focusing specifically on the field of education, examined the disparity between the type of methods researchers claim to use and their actual published output, which indicates what methods they actually do use; an examination that points, in particular, to a lack of methodological pluralism in the use of secondary data in education research. One of the reasons why secondary data analysis is relatively underused in social research can perhaps be attributed to the wide range of criticisms and concerns that the field attracts. It is these potential pitfalls of secondary analysis that form the focus of the next chapter.

2

Pitfalls of secondary data analysis

> In this country, perhaps more than in any other, figures aren't very
> popular anyhow. A lot of people are badly taught mathematics. They're
> slightly doubtful about figures anyhow. It's too easy to make jokes about
> statistics and all that is a sort of underlay of public opinion. But in
> addition to that, there is a feeling that there's too much spin linked with
> government figures. (Sir Claus Moser, former chief statistician, BBC
> 2007)

The promises of secondary data analysis are many. It can allow
researchers to access data on a scale that they could not hope to replicate
first hand, the technical expertise involved in developing good surveys
and good datasets can lead to data of the highest quality, it can enable
data to be analysed and replicated from different perspectives and, in this
way, provides opportunities for the discovery of serendipitous relationships not considered in the primary research. Secondary data analysis is a
perfect complement to mixed method approaches and, most crucially
perhaps, it is an approach that can truly enable social scientists to 'stand
on the shoulders of giants' (Dale et al. 1988; Gorard with Taylor 2004).
There are also many pitfalls. And it is these perhaps that have contributed
most to the somewhat limited role of secondary data analysis in social
science research and the 'exaggerated suspicion of social measurement
... and excessive distrust of officially-produced numeric data' (Bulmer
1980: 505) among the social science community.

The very nature of secondary data leaves them particularly susceptible
to criticism. For example, it often involves the analysis of data that have
been collected with a very different purpose in mind, such as data from
the PISA study being used to measure patterns of inequity across Europe
(Gorard and Smith 2004). In interview-based survey data, such as the
IEA Civics Study, the secondary data analyst is far removed from the
source of the data and may be unaware of, or unconcerned with, the

context in which the research took place and the nuanced relationship between the interviewer and respondent. Other issues revolve around data quality and concerns that rather than being tailored to the needs of the researcher they require much adaptation and compromise to be of any use (Bryman 2004).

But four main objections to the use of secondary data in social research stand out: that it is full of errors; that it cannot be used to make useful comparisons; that secondary data, and official data in particular, are not value neutral but are controlled by those in power; and that because of the socially constructed nature of social data, the act of reducing them to a simple numeric form cannot fully encapsulate their complexity. However, as I shall try to demonstrate in this chapter, the concerns and caveats we attach to the preparation, analysis and interpretation of secondary data are no different from those we should apply to any other type of data: numeric or qualitative, secondary or primary.

Secondary data are full of errors

'When you are a bit older', a judge in India once told an eager young British civil servant, 'you will not quote Indian statistics with that assurance. The government are very keen on amassing statistics – they collect them, add them, raise them to the *n*th power, take the cube root and prepare wonderful diagrams. But what you must never forget is that every one of those figures comes in the first instance from the *chowkydar* [village watchman], who just puts down what he damn well pleases'. (in Huff 1973: 84)

The notion that official data are so 'vitiated with error' (Bulmer 1980: 508) as to render them unusable for research is widely held. However, this view also suggests that those who do use official statistics are unaware of the potential pitfalls: one cannot assume that 'the world is made up just of knowledgeable sceptics and naive hard-line positivists' (Bulmer 1980: 508). In the UK, the 'gold standard' of survey research is arguably the national census, which has taken place every decade since 1801. Huge amounts of resources and expertise are invested in developing census questions and analytical techniques. Of course, the census is not without its limitations. There are conceptual problems involved in placing people into categories: social class is a good example of this, as is ethnicity. There are also practical problems in ensuring that everyone is counted: how do we account for tourists, for the homeless or transient, for people with multiple nationalities or those who simply refuse to be counted? (Jacob 1984). In the 1991 census, it was estimated that around 1.2 million people, or 2% of the total number of residents, were uncounted (Dorling and Simpson 1993). Nevertheless, it is important not to forget that individuals are routinely excluded from research anyway. Consider the research into widening participation in post-compulsory education, which focuses only on those actually in education; the research into exclusion, which surveys only those pupils who are present in school; or the research into IT usage, which relies on internet survey methods. To preclude the use of all official data simply on the basis that they may contain error is unrealistic, as Bulmer (1980) suggests; the patterns and trends revealed by interrogating these data can be so striking that if the data were so flawed then what could account for such regularity? Indeed, alongside concerns over the reliability of large-scale data is the almost tacit assumption that other data are somehow error free; as with all data, numeric or otherwise, an awareness of their limitations and a 'healthy scepticism' (Bulmer 1980: 508; Gorard with Taylor 2004) about their technical and conceptual basis is essential.

One important example of how we regard the presence of error in official data comes in the interpretation of examination results. When reading the education columns of the national, and even the local, newspapers, it is difficult not to come to the conclusion that we have, in this country, an examination system that lurches from crisis to crisis (Jeffs 1999; Warmington and Murphy 2004). There have been concerns about examination boards manipulating grade boundaries (Henry 2002; Smithers 2001), timescales so tight that new examinations could not be piloted properly so increasing the likelihood for errors (Mansell and Clark 2003), errors in the printing of exam scripts (BBC 2002a), as well as errors in instructions and the wording of questions (BBC 2002b, 2002c). The power of the media in shaping policy and public opinion in the education system is not to be underestimated (Jeffs 1999; Warmington and Murphy 2004). For example, concerns that unqualified teachers were being used to mark exams prompted a recent QCA-commissioned study into marker reliability in Key Stage 3 English. Despite the newspaper headings that preceded the report, it found that there was no difference in marker accuracy between experienced markers and those with no teaching or marking experience and therefore no reason why trainee English teachers or even English graduates could not be used to mark Key Stage 3 English tests (Royal-Dawson 2005). The summer of 2002 will be remembered by many in education for the crisis in the regrading of A-level exam scripts (Education Guardian 2002). The examination results reported that summer came at the end of the first full cycle of the *Curriculum 2000* A-level reforms. These reforms meant that A-level assessment would now be spread over a 2-year period with candidates typically sitting AS-level examinations in year 1 and A2 examinations in year 2. The practical consequence of this was that candidates who failed to score well in their AS examination were either less likely to continue with their studies into the second year of A-level or would be able to resit AS modules during their second year when they had had the opportunity to further develop their knowledge and skills in their subject. This meant that A-level results were likely to improve and leave the examination system open to criticism of falling standards and 'dumbing down'. In response to this fear, examination boards set about adjusting grade boundaries to the extent that the education media could report examples of students who had received A grades at AS but had been awarded grade U at A2. Outcry and scandal ensued and prompted the government to order an inquiry into the allegations, chaired by the former Chief Inspector of Schools, Mike Tomlinson. One salient message to emerge from the inquiry was that the complexity of the assessment arrangements for the new A-level will 'continue to undermine the extent to which A-level results are understood and trusted, even though the actual outcomes accurately reflect students' achievement' (Tomlinson 2002: para. 40). Nevertheless, newspapers remain sceptical and it is hard to see how public confidence in the reliability of the examination system can remain undented.

But perhaps we should not be surprised that examinations contain errors and inaccuracies: examinations are, by definition, a form of measurement and 'measurement inaccuracy is an inevitable character-istic of measurement' (Kober 2002; Newton 2005a: 436). In this way, perhaps errors in examinations have always existed but prior to July 2002, when the QCA reported 38 errors with that year's GCSE and A-level papers (Henry 2002), no data on these errors had been system-atically collected, so we simply do not know whether or not this current spate of examination errors is a recent phenomenon. Examination errors and inaccuracies are not just restricted to the UK, a review of errors in the scoring of mainly US-based tests identified 103 errors over a 25-year period, with instances of human error increasing rapidly since 1998 (Rhoades 2003). What is crucial, however, is to understand the extent and nature of the limitations and to use the data appropriately. Although according to Newton (2005b), any acceptance that errors or inaccuracies in examination data are inevitable is somewhat at odds with the public's 'mythical image of assessment as a process that can, and ought to, be free from measurement inaccuracy and human error' (p. 471).

Why is it that if examinations have always been or inevitably are susceptible to inaccuracies, there is such limited public understanding and awareness about the limitations of our assessment system? Perhaps it is the case that the public now has greater expectations of our testing system. Arguably obtaining decent A-level grades is as important for university entrance now as it ever was, but entry to A-level examinations increased by around 10% between 1990 and 2004 (QCA 2004) and one consequence of modularisation is that there are now more examinations to be processed and a wider range of subjects and pathways to follow. For example, in 2001 the number of examination scripts and coursework assignments produced at GCSE, AS and A-level totalled 24 million (Tomlinson 2002). On the one hand, this should be applauded as an outcome of a successful and more equitable education system and this might be one of the reasons why errors in school examinations are and should be subject to such huge scrutiny. On the other hand, it could be that we are more concerned about inaccuracies and errors because of the increasingly 'high stakes' nature of the assessments. Since the 1988 Education Act there has been an increased use of accountability and performance management targets in the field of education. This is most obvious in the monitoring of schools in England through league tables and Ofsted inspections. As a consequence, examination results in England have become increasingly high stakes and in addition to their intended function of classifying students according to merit, they have been used variously for school improvement, to assess teacher performance as well as to inform parental school choice (Propper and Wilson 2003). This has increasingly led to an 'obscuring of the learner as the main focus of the examination' (QCA 2002). But can examination data be reliably expected to answer the demands we currently put on them?

It has generally been accepted that 'results on a six or seven point grading scale are accurate to about one grade either side of the one awarded' (Schools Council 1980: pamphlet 5, cited in Newton 2005b). When these results are aggregated to the school level, as they are in the production of school league tables, inaccuracies are compounded so rendering the league tables particularly volatile and unreliable. In the USA, Kane and Staiger (2002) estimate that the confidence interval for an average fourth-grade reading and maths score in a school with a test cohort of 68 students extends from roughly the 25th–75th percentile. The reasons for such a large spread are twofold: on the one hand, it is a likely consequence of sampling variation and regression to the mean. On the other, such variation may be accounted for by one-time factors such as a disruption from outside the classroom on the test day, the presence of a disruptive pupil in the class or a particularly favourable relationship between students and teacher. In schools with relatively small numbers of students, such as a year 6 cohort in an English primary school, tests scores are likely to fluctuate even more, making league table rankings even less reliable. Value-added scores offer little by way of solution. Their intention is to capture a school effect by isolating student progress between two time points in a school career. On the one hand, this is already adding additional complexity to an already imprecise measure: test scores; and, on the other hand, it serves more as an effective proxy for prior attainment than a real measure of difference (Gorard 2006). Indeed, the very notion of 'value-added' is itself problematic. Its use derives from economics where inputs and outputs tend to be defined in standardised monetary units, that is not so in education where inputs and outputs have no absolute scale of measurement (Goldstein and Spiegelhalter 1996).

Of course, concern, even scepticism, over the accuracy of examination scores is certainly valid, but this should stand alongside the recognition that examinations do not and cannot presume to be error free and should be reported and understood with this in mind. Fundamental to this concern is the double standards which some commentators apply to the trust they place in numeric and non-numeric data. Again there is the almost tacit assumption that the quality of numeric data has to be judged against different criteria than those applied to non-numeric data. Is the scrutiny and mistrust of numeric data really balanced by a scepticism of the potential for reporting bias in interview or ethnographic accounts, for example? One illustration of this is the apparent lack of concern about judgement and error that is applied to that other yardstick by which schools in England are measured: the Ofsted inspection. This system allows inspectors to visit schools for increasingly short periods of time and confers on them the power to judge schools as 'requiring significant improvement' or 'giving unsatisfactory value for money' and so on. Judgements such as these are made with limited accountability and scrutiny and with little regard to error, yet can have a very real impact on the way in which a school is perceived. In contrast to the scepticism that is applied to numeric data, the validity and accuracy of these judgements is rarely scrutinised (FitzGibbon 1996).

In conclusion, it would be spurious to assume that all secondary data are error free, but we must not forget that *all data* are likely to contain errors. When applied to all research, not just the analysis of secondary data, it is useful to remember that while 'the risks of error are not trivial but if they are recognised and accounted for by multiple measurement techniques, the error need not preclude use of the data' (Webb et al. 1966: 53).

Secondary data are socially constructed

That social data are socially constructed and cannot be reduced to numeric form is a fundamental concern of those who are sceptical about the use of numeric data in social research. The use of 'mere statistical exercises' in reducing the quality of life to numbers and then assuming that these numbers represent reality is, for some social researchers an anathema. However, without secondary data, and the official data collected by governments and non-government organisations in particular, how would social scientists be able to describe the social world around them, posit theories and test them empirically?

The contentious nature of social statistics has a long history. Indeed Durkheim's work on suicide was one of the very first modern examples of 'consistent and organised use of statistical method in social investigation' (Simpson 1952: 9). In developing his principle that 'social facts must be studied as things ... as realities external to the individual' (Durkheim 1952: 37), Durkheim drew on the records of 26,000 suicides from the different nations and regions of nineteenth-century Europe. In doing this, he sought to control, at least in part, for differences in the definition of suicide; and the consistency of patterns he observed in the data over time and place led him to conclude that suicide was a sociological rather than a psychological phenomenon. In carrying out this systematic and methodical approach to understanding numeric data, Durkheim succeeded in moving beyond a 'crude statistical methodology' (Giddens 1996: 164) and instead began to show relationships between individuals and society and then to develop sociological theory that was linked to empirical research.

However, Durkheim's study of suicide has not been without its critics, many of whom consider that one of the fundamental flaws in his work has been his failure to see official statistics on suicide as subjective and 'organisationally defined' (Douglas 1967; Kitsuse and Cicourel 1963). Views such as these challenge the notion of 'numeric data as objective fact about social reality' (Miles and Irvine 1979: 116) and posit that such data are the 'product of socially organised activities of social structures' (Kitsuse and Cicourel 1963: 136), a conjecture that Douglas extends to his categorisation of death: 'How can one conceivably understand something so immensely complicated as "death" in terms other than those of the actors involved?' (Douglas 1967: 182). Work on suicide is particularly open to such criticisms: in western society suicide retains a stigma, families may attempt to conceal a death as suicide and, as suicides are rarely observed directly, the actual intention to kill oneself might be unclear. But it would be spurious to think that such complexities were unknown to Durkheim; indeed, Douglas suggests that this uncertainty over the social nature of suicide data might be the very reason why Durkheim chose the topic for an exposition of his theory on sociological method.

Hindess (1973) takes a somewhat different view of the challenges of using official statistics in this way. He criticises as 'absurd' those who claim that such data are the 'product of observed events, the background expectancies of the observers and of the processing of the observers' report by bureaucratic apparatuses' (Hindess 1973: 11) and who insist that when reporting and analysing these conversations the researcher must also convey the participants' 'unstated and seen but unnoticed background expectancies'. Such a situation would be akin to having, for every researcher's account, a second account of how his or her background expectancies influenced that account. And for the second account a third and so on. According to Miles and Irvine (1979), these demands for increased levels of complexity attached to social data are all very well, but provide little by way of guidance on how to differentiate one person's perceptions from another's or for 'assessing what construction of social reality is most appropriate for changing that reality' (p. 119). It may be the case that official statistics of suicide and other deviant behaviour suffer from particular problems of reliable and valid measurement that make them more difficult to study as social phenomena (Bulmer 1980), however, it is worth remembering that subsequent re-analyses of Durkheim's approach suggest that his original findings do still largely hold true (Atkinson 1978; Giddens 1996; Hughes et al. 1995).

It is hard to deny that official statistics are inextricably linked to society and as such are social products, indeed the very 'concept of society is in itself a statistical construct' (Porter 1995: 37). Porter illustrates this notion with the example of the Bureau de Statistique in early nineteenth-century France. Following the French Revolution, there was a hope of uniting the country by describing it through the collection of numeric data. Detailed questionnaires were sent to the various départements of the new Republic requesting information on property ownership, land use, wealth and so on. The demand for information proved to be overwhelming and the detailed prose received back at the Bureau de Statistique was of little use in categorising French life at that time. The statisticians had demanded data which only a large and disciplined bureaucracy could supply; in short, French society was not yet able to be 'reduced to statistics' (p. 36). A more recent example of the role of society in shaping official statistics is the inclusion of a question on ethnic background in the UK National Census. The 1991 Census was the first UK census to carry a specific question about ethnic group. Prior to 1991, data on ethnicity was produced from a crude amalgam of data on place of birth and nationality (Fenton 1996). However, not having a question on ethnicity would be unthinkable today, reflecting the demographic changes to British society in the second half of the twentieth century. The concern perhaps for future versions of the National Census may be how to deal with the ever more finely discriminated categories of ethnic group: in the 1991 Census there were nine, in the 2001 Census there were 16. Perhaps there may come a time when a question on ethnicity is superfluous because British society has become so heterogeneous that such questions are no longer deemed necessary.

Further concerns about the social nature of official data have been raised by Vulliamy and Webb (2001) in their research into the support offered to young people who have been excluded from school. In their view, a fundamental problem of using official statistics to measure school exclusions is that the data themselves represent a 'considerable under-estimate' of the actual numbers of fixed term and permanent exclusions. Reasons for this may include administrative errors in the data, the conflation of figures for exclusion and authorised or unauthorised absences, the 'voluntary' withdrawal of pupils by their parents, as well as schools' use of unofficial exclusions in order to avoid the bureaucratic procedures necessary to make a permanent exclusion. They argue that school exclusion data are socially constructed and therefore have to reflect the variety of different meanings that can be accorded to them by the participants and the social context involved. Thus, for example, a black student who has been excluded from one school might be treated very differently had he or she attended a different school where teachers had less stereotypical views of ethnic minority attainment. Indeed, a similar issue arises with exclusions from schools involved the new *Academies* programme where there are fears that some students are more likely to be expelled from an academy than from another local school (Gorard 2005).

However, if these last two scenarios were indeed happening, how would we know whether a disproportionate number of black students or those attending academies were being excluded were it not for the secondary analysis of official statistics? One reason that we do not, in fact, know for sure whether academies have higher than expected exclusion rates is simply because national data on exclusions at the school level are hard to come by for independent academic researchers: they are not available through the DfES school performance tables and their reporting in the National Pupil Database is not unproblematic. In our conjecture that academies are excluding higher than expected numbers of students, we have to rely on anecdote and local reports. Without the official data, we cannot produce the national picture to put alongside these localised reports and, if there are injustices, to enable social scientists to challenge policy and demand equity.

That the social world adds complexity to such data should not in itself be a reason not to use it. The argument that these data are socially constructed and can therefore serve no real purpose in helping understand the social world is simply untenable. Secondary data can provide a window to the social world, they can help identify trends and inequities that further inquiry, often using in-depth research methods, can explore. However, as with all forms of data, numeric or otherwise, secondary data, whether official statistics, survey data or in any other form, have to be treated with an appropriate amount of scepticism and respect for their limitations. Official statistics are far too important not to be included in social research. They cannot simply be left for politicians or even the media to do with what they please. It is surely the role of the social scientist to engage with the data, with full understanding of their limitations and to help establish the link between the empirical data, their social context and the theoretical models that might help explain them.

Of course, perhaps a more fundamental question for our example on school exclusions may be to ask why schools might seek to manipulate exclusion data in the first place. Perhaps it is not so much the nature and the quality of the data that is problematic but rather the use to which we put these data and the explanations we demand of them. This brings us to our third pitfall for using secondary data: that they can be manipulated by those in power.

Secondary data can be manipulated by those in power

Public suspicion of official statistics is not new. While it is important that governments have access to accurate and reliable statistics as a corner-stone of policy development, implementation and evaluation, it is also crucial that the public have confidence in the data themselves (BBC 2007a). The public has a right to be informed about the social and eco-nomic conditions of the country in which they live, but also should have sufficient information and familiarity with the data to themselves eval-uate government policy and ensure accountability (Royal Statistical Society 1991). This cannot happen if they do not trust the statistics. Probably the most nefarious recent example of an erosion of public confidence in the quality and reliability of official statistics in the UK surrounded the publication of unemployment data during the 1980s and early 1990s and the accusations that the data were open to political manipulation (Bartholomew et al. 1995; Gregg 1994).

Changes to the measurement of unemployment from 1982 meant that the number of unemployed people was determined using what was known as the claimant count. This was based on computerised records of individuals successfully claiming unemployment benefit, income support or equivalent (Levitas 1996). The claimant count was purely an admin-istrative account and one that was particularly vulnerable to changes in the definition and administration of unemployment. Between 1979 and 1989, there were around 30 changes to the claimant count, changes which resulted in over 1.5 million people being removed from the unemployment statistics (Gregg 1994). For example, in 1986 the intro-duction of the Restart programme and stricter scrutiny of 'availability to work' status resulted in around 300,000 people being removed from the unemployment statistics. Similarly, the 1988 Social Security Act removed unemployment benefit for the under 18s – the result was around 120,000 people deleted from the unemployment record. The claimant count became widely criticised both because it 'seriously underestimated' the number of people without work and because the large number of changes to its definition meant that any serious estimation of whether the unemployment rate was falling or rising over time was 'virtually useless' (Levitas 1996: 46). A further fault of the claimant count was that it was a purely administrative and inflexible measure in that it took no account of the other social consequences of being out of work (Gregg 1994).

Throughout the 1980s and early 1990s concerns over the unreliability of the unemployment measure grew and steps were taken to consider alternative measures (Bartholomew et al. 1995; Royal Statistical Society 1991). Despite the relatively slow progress of change, pressure on government, notably from the Royal Statistical Society, led to a redefinition of unemployment that was based on internationally agreed definitions and to the collection of unemployment data based on the Labour Force Survey, not the claimant count (Bartholomew 1997). The Labour Force Survey is a quarterly sample survey of households living at private addresses in Great Britain. Its purpose is to provide information on the labour market that can then be used to develop, manage, evaluate and report on labour market policies (Office for National Statistics 2006). It uses internationally agreed concepts and definitions that are independent of government control.

There are many other examples in the literature of concerns over the control that governments and other powerful bodies have over the statistics that describe our lives. One example used by Thomas (1996) is that of the National Food Survey (NFS). The NFS started as the Wartime Food Survey in 1940 and is Britain's oldest regularly conducted survey. Its purpose has been largely to monitor nutritional standards but the NFS is also a very useful source of information for the food manufacturing and distribution industries. The estimates of income, price and demand that accompany the NFS are of particular interest and are sold by the government to commercial users, thus according to Thomas:

> The NFS may have contributed substantially to the efficiency and growth of food manufacturing and distribution industries in Britain. But a healthy food industry does not necessarily mean healthy food. The products of the food industry when translated into diets are producing a population with an increasing tendency towards obesity. (Thomas 1996: 7)

Of course, one area where official statistics have often been accused of manipulation is in the area of crime statistics where much has already been written about the 'dark figure' of hidden or unreported crime (see Riedel 2000, for a fuller discussion on the secondary analysis of crime data).

One interesting example of the potential for the selective use of social data by those with a particular cause to fight or interest to promote is given by Beckett (2005). He describes the misleading use of Swedish statistics on child deaths by advocates of a complete ban on smacking children in the UK. His citations purport to suggest a direct causal link between a ban on corporal punishment in Sweden and an absence of child deaths through maltreatment:

> [N]ot all other countries seem to have the same problems with child abuse as Britain does. The experience in Sweden, for example, which has long outlawed the physical punishment of children, is one in which child deaths from deliberate harm by adults *are now unknown*. (House of Commons Health Committee 2003: 17, para. 55, cited in Beckett 2005: 126) [emphasis in original]

> Since Sweden banned smacking three decades ago, child deaths at the hands of parents have fallen to zero. In Britain, they average one a week. (*Observer*, 7 March 2004, cited in Beckett 2005: 127)

These are powerful and emotional arguments, but, according to Beckett, they are founded on a 'myth', one that is based on research evidence that has been used selectively. Obtaining accurate data on child deaths is difficult. The fortunate rareness of the events and the potential for misclassifying the cause of death only serve to increase the potential for inaccuracy. These difficulties notwithstanding, estimates of child maltreatment death rates do exist: the OECD estimates a death rate of 0.6 per 100,000 children in Sweden, against 0.9 per 100,000 in the UK (Beckett 2005). While the Swedish rate is lower than the British, it is higher than the quotations just examined might lead us to believe. Beckett traces the source of these quotations to research into the effectiveness of Sweden's corporal punishment ban undertaken by Durrant (1999). While Durrant's research does seem to support the claims made by the advocates of a ban on smacking, Beckett's investigations show us that Durrant is working with a fairly narrow definition of child abuse deaths: one that excludes deaths that occur in the context of postnatal depression; are accompanied by the suicide, or attempted suicide, of the perpetrator; are caused by neglect; are intentional; and the deaths of very newborn babies (Beckett 2005). Indeed Durrant's research is concerned only with 'fatal child abuse' which is defined as:

> The killing of a child by one or a series of assaults by a parent or a person with the status of a parent to eliminate a disturbing behaviour of a child without the intention to kill. (Somander and Rammer 1991: 47, cited in Beckett 2005: 130)

If this narrow definition of child abuse deaths were to be adopted, then Durrant's work does indeed suggest that between 1976–1990 'no children died in Sweden as the result of abuse' (Durrant 1991: 441, cited in Beckett 2005). But this interpretation of the findings by the advocates of a ban on smacking does require caution. We are not comparing like with like, the Swedish data are being used to compare a very narrow definition of child abuse deaths in one country with *all* maltreatment deaths in England and Wales. Even if Durrant's figures on child abuse deaths in Sweden are to be accepted, they do not imply a direct causal link between a ban on smacking and an elimination of child cruelty deaths, indeed, the author does not, in fact, claim such a relationship. What this example shows us, from a methodological perspective, is that official data of this type are open to misinterpretation, but, from a social science perspective, what it also shows us is the importance of engaging with the data and, just as Beckett has done, uncovering instances where the data may have been misused or misinterpreted. Clearly, there is an important role for social scientists here.

So as we can see, official data can be laid open to accusations of manipulation by government (and those with an interest in promoting certain outcomes), but the government is, in turn, held accountable by such data. When shortcomings are perceived to occur then the government can be challenged. This is what happened with the unemployment data and happens today, for example with the use of league tables and national targets in education and health. The use of targets and other strategies for monitoring the performance of the public services has risen dramatically through the 1990s and into the new millennium. Done well this increased monitoring can improve effectiveness and allows the public greater scrutiny of government policies. Done badly, it can be ineffective, harmful and give poor value for money (Royal Statistical Society 2005). For such monitoring to work it must be independent of undue political influence and open to independent scrutiny, but if social scientists are reluctant to engage with the data then how can any shortcomings be revealed and remedied? It is not just statistical scrutiny that is required, there is also a role for social scientists in conceptualising social categories, for providing theoretical justifications for the inclusion of social indicators, for ensuring accountability and for collaborating with social statisticians (Bulmer 1980); again, this cannot happen if social scientists do not fully engage with social data. Indeed, as Thomas (1996) writes, 'the message for the social sciences is not that these statistics should be ignored because of the distorted picture they sometimes give, but that these distortions should be investigated and exposed' (p. 10). This brings us to our final pitfall of secondary data: that they do not lead to useful comparisons.

Secondary data do not lead to meaningful comparisons

Secondary data can be used to make powerful and often contentious comparisons between different groups, societies and nations. For example, much of the evidence used to support the boys' underachievement debate in the UK is founded on the inappropriate use of official statistics on school examination performance (Gorard 1999; Smith 2005a). Indeed, the potential of such data to make unwarranted and invalid comparisons is, for some, an important caution against their use. In the field of education policy, one of the most powerful examples of the use of secondary data analysis to generate comparisons has been its use in international comparative tests of academic achievement.

Since the 1950s large-scale international comparative tests have given nations the opportunity to compare the progress of their students with those in other countries. The importance of international comparisons in focusing a nation's education policy cannot be underestimated and reflects the changing role of education in many industrialised countries. While still very much in the 'service' of the nation state, changes to global political and economic geographies have resulted in the education policies of many European, Asian and North America countries losing some of their 'preoccupation with localism and regionalism' (Husen and Tujinman 1994: 13), becoming much more concerned with accountability and efficiency measures and a lot more sensitive to educational trends in other countries. It is not surprising then that the theories, hypotheses and conjectures arrived at by these international studies have traditionally excited much media interest. Cross-cultural studies of academic achievement have been of interest to educators, politicians and the public since the post-Sputnik days of 1950s' America, when anxiety over Russian superiority in the fields of science and engineering led to a rethink of education policy in the USA (Ravitch 1995). Underpinning these comparisons is the assumption that better schools equate to a better economy, so perhaps it is unsurprising that the stakes for 'failure' in these comparative tests are high. As a consequence, and despite the reservations of the test designers, these test outcomes are frequently reduced to a form of international Olympiad, where success is praised and low rankings can equate to a national 'crisis account' of falling standards and failing students. A good example of this is Germany, a country whose education system was once considered 'world class'. Relatively poor performance on the 2000 Programme for International Student Assessment (or PISA) firmly established Germany's own 'crisis account' of school underachievement. National reform of the school system was called for and educational inspectors were sent north to Finland – the PISA success story – to look for remedies (Sharma 2002; Slater 2001), although you don't have to look far for similar concerns in England (*Daily Telegraph*, 9 April 2003; *Guardian*, 30 January 2003).

However, there are other factors that may affect intellectual development and academic achievement, including the cultural bias of tests, student motivation and attitudes towards test taking, as well as socio-economic differences and cognitive and social stimulation, which cannot be assessed by standardised testing alone (Fletcher and Sabers 1995; Hilton 2006). The complexities of achieving cross-nation comparability on the tests also require scrutiny. Indeed, if comparability between different domestic examination boards, different subjects and different cohorts is problematic, then the difficulties faced at the international level must surely be even greater (Gorard and Smith 2004; Nuttall 1979; Schagen and Hutchinson 2006). These difficulties can be compounded by a lack of proportionate analysis of test data, as well as methodological shortcomings in the very design and administration of the tests (Brown 1998; Gorard 2000; Prais 2003; Smith 2005a; White and Smith 2005). International comparative tests are also expensive, they are complex to design and administer and much care needs to be taken with their interpretation. Education systems are changing and evolving all the time, policy focus shifts in its priorities and the different contexts in which education systems operate can also change. These and many other factors have to be taken into account when drawing comparisons in the national and, more particularly, in the international context.

One example of the technical problems that influence the sampling, reporting and curriculum coverage of the large international tests, in this case the Third International Maths and Science Study (TIMSS), is given by Brown (1998). One of the major sampling issues in TIMSS involved the selection of the test cohort. Here, the test designers opted to sample whole classes of pupils, for example those in year 9 (or grade 8). However, it is the practice in many countries to hold children back a school year until they have reached certain minimum competency levels. This meant that in TIMSS, 25% of pupils in these particular countries were not in their age-appropriate year group and also that the groups that did participate in the TIMSS study now comprised the more able pupils, who were of sufficiently high ability to progress academically. The problem of age-related sampling was so acute in 16 out of the 42 participating countries (including Denmark, Germany and the Netherlands) that their results were not thought to allow for fair comparison. The generally linear relationship between age and attainment also meant that countries with older cohorts of students were likely to achieve higher mean scores. This is important, as nearly 30% of the variance in the test's outcome could be explained by differences in mean age alone (Gorard 2000). However, where TIMSS had sampled whole classes of pupils, PISA defined their cohort as those pupils born in a particular calendar year –

1984 for *PISA 2000*. Given the practice in many countries of holding some students back a school year, this strategy ought to have countered some of the criticisms of the TIMSS sampling strategies – all students would now participate in the test whether they were in their age-appropriate year group or not. Prais (2003), however, disputes the validity of this arrangement. He argues that the PISA sample of 15-year-old students would now include the less able students who had previously been excluded from international tests such as TIMSS. Consequently, these countries would have seen their scores in PISA fall compared with previous tests. Although this would not have happened in the UK, where the practice of holding less able students back a year is uncommon and so here scores ought to remain largely unaffected by the change. Contrariwise, sampling older students could also mean that in some countries, where the end of compulsory education is around age 15, large groups of students, conceivably the least able, might have already left school and would be excluded from the analysis – resulting in possible grade inflation.

Avoiding ecological fallacies when generalising the results of student-level data to national policy is also relevant to international comparative studies. The 'virtual absence' of cross-national *educational* variables that predict student achievement suggest that it is difficult to separate the effect of educational policies and instructional practices from the contexts in which they are developed and implemented (Nelson 2003: 6). Even so, links between achievement on these tests and education reform are frequently made. In the UK, the high performance of students in the Progress in International Reading Literacy Study (PIRLS) was attributed to the success of the National Literacy Strategy (Miliband 2004). In the USA, relatively poor achievement in the tests during the 1980s was used as a lever to refocus reform towards the high stakes accountability system we have today (NCEE 1983). The impact of context may also affect the relationship between what students know and how well they actually perform on these tests. For example, Boe et al. (2002) estimate that over half the variance in national mean achievement scores in the TIMSS can be accounted for by 'student–task persistence'. One popular account of the 1995 TIMSS assessments appears to support this. During the administration of the tests, American students were reportedly kept back from their games lesson to complete tests which, they were assured, would not count towards their grades, whereas in South Korea, students were marched in to the hall to the sound of their school band and urged to do their best for their country (Brown 1998).

International comparative tests are not without their technical, methodological and political limitations. However, if we do wish to compare the mathematical knowledge or the school experiences of young people in France with those in Scotland, then the results from tests such as PISA provide the highest quality estimates that are available. As researchers, we have a responsibility to report the data accurately and with full awareness of their caveats and limitations. This does not always happen. For example, in the official reports accompanying *PISA 2000* it is stated clearly that the Netherlands did not meet the minimum sampling requirements for inclusion in that wave of PISA and that results cannot be regarded as representative. Similar caveats apply for England in the *PISA 2003* wave, but the data are still used and reported without regard to these important limitations (Torrance 2006). Why countries might want to compare the academic achievement or school experience of their young people with those in other countries is one issue. Another is what, if anything, can the results of these comparisons tell us about the relative 'health' of our school systems, as well as about strategies that might be adopted to improve any shortcomings. International comparative tests might provide us with a 'gold standard' method of test design but the answers to a nation's educational concerns cannot be gleaned from studying only the rankings of international league tables. Neither should the tests be rejected on this account. Rather, they ought to be used as complements to the close contextual study of a nation's school system and the structures and ethos that are at its very foundation.

Summary

Secondary data analysis remains a relatively underused methodological technique in the social sciences. It is a technique that is open to much criticism. As we have seen in this chapter, numeric secondary data have been censured for reducing the complexity of social experiences to mere quantities, for being susceptible to outside control and for being 'vitiated' (Bulmer 1980: 508) with errors. In defence of secondary data, we have suggested that without them how can social scientists describe the social work around them, posit theories and test them empirically? Official data, as reported by governments, should be used to ensure accountability; within this there is a role for social scientists in informing the collection of social data, for developing social indicators and providing theoretical justifications for the use, or exclusion, of different social categories. Numeric social data can never be error free, neither can the producers of the data prevent their being used to make unwarranted comparisons, but neither should they be disregarded on this account. Rather, they should be treated with the appropriate scepticism and attention to its limitations that we should apply to any social data, be they primary or secondary, numeric or 'qualitative'. What is surprising, however, is that this does not always happen: data that are more 'qualitative' in nature are not always treated with the same cautions that, we are told, apply to numeric data. For example, in the field of education in particular, we do not always treat the findings from interviews or ethnographic accounts with the same amount of scepticism and distrust we confer on numeric reports. We may be concerned about the possibility that one head teacher in one primary school may guess when reporting the numbers of students who receive free school meals, yet we seem to worry less when the uncontextualised findings of small-scale research are generalised to a wider population. This is not to suggest that secondary data should not be scrutinised for bias and error but rather that the same caveats and cautions we apply to numeric data should be applied to *all* data.

Neither should secondary data be seen as a panacea. Rather, they should be valued as complimentary, as a resource that can be used in their own right but also much more powerfully in combination with other methodological approaches from surveys to ethnographies. Surely it is difficult to argue that a study about the challenges facing a small number of bilingual learners would not be made more powerful if it were located alongside census data describing the characteristics of the local population, bilingual or otherwise, or alongside the findings from international or national tests that might further inform the research about the challenges faced by bilingual learners in a larger context? Arguably, perhaps, as far as the data that social scientists use to answer their research questions, whether numeric or non-numeric, the moral should be that 'we should make the most of what we have' (Hyman 1972: 18).

Having reviewed some of the potential pitfalls of secondary data analysis, our attention in the next chapter turns to some of its promises and, in particular, its contribution to political arithmetic approaches that involve combining methods in social research.

3

Promises of secondary data analysis

> Secondary analysis benefits science in many ways, all stemming from one fundamental feature of the method. It expands the types and number of observations to cover more adequately a wider range of social conditions, measurement procedures, and variables than can usually be studied in primary surveys. Thus it produces a more comprehensive and definitive empirical study of the problems the investigator has formulated. Examining the wide array of materials in the course of secondary analysis also expands our intellectual horizons. We are stimulated to think about otherwise forgotten problems and also forced in the direction of higher levels of abstraction. (Hyman 1972: 11)

Much has been made of the potentials of secondary analysis in terms of economies of money, time and personnel (for example, Burton 2000; Dale et al. 1988; Glaser 1962; Gorard 2002; Hyman 1972, 1978). It is a method that is seemingly perfectly suited to 'the research needs of persons with macro-interest and micro-resources' (Glaser 1963: 11). The huge range of topics covered by secondary datasets also adds to its appeal. Indeed, the availability of large-scale high-quality datasets, often free or at nominal cost, are one of the true opportunities presented by secondary analysis. But there is more to secondary analysis than easy access to other people's data for the lazy or impoverished researcher. As this chapter will show, secondary analysis has a range of applications in teaching as well as in its theoretical and methodological contributions.

Social benefits

In addition to methodological and theoretical opportunities, there are also social benefits to secondary analysis. Secondary analysis is an unobtrusive research method. It has the ethical benefit of not collecting additional data from individuals and so protecting their privacy by respecting an individual's right to be left alone 'free from searching inquiries about oneself and one's activities' (Bulmer 1979: 4). This, of course, is of particular benefit for research into sensitive issues and of vulnerable and hard to reach groups (Brooks-Gunn et al. 1991; Dale et al. 1988; Rew et al. 2000). Secondary analysis is also a very democratic research method. The availability of low-cost, high-quality datasets means that secondary analysis can 'restrain oligarchy' (Hyman 1972: 9) and ensure that 'all researchers have the opportunity for empirical research that has tended to be the privilege of the few' (Hakim 1982a: 4). The establishment of data archives, continuing advances in computing technologies and the increasing availability of internet-based resources have opened up the opportunities for secondary analysis as never before. Indeed, as 'it is the cost of data collection that are beyond the scope of the independent researcher, not the costs of data analysis' (Glaser 1963: 12), the very accessibility of the data enables novice and other researchers to retain and develop a degree of independence. Often when researchers are employed on busy projects, there is limited time and resources to apply for grants for other funding and, if successful, there are likely difficulties in securing opportunities for fieldwork. By circumventing the data collection process, secondary analysis can enable novice researchers to gain valuable experience in undertaking research in an area of their own interest, as well as presenting opportunities to publish and present their findings as independent researchers. In this sense, secondary analysis has a valuable role in the capacity building of research skills as well as in developing an early career researcher's theoretical and substantive interests (for example, Smith 2005a; Smith and Gorard 2007; White and Smith 2005).

In a similar way, secondary analysis has an important role in teaching and in research methods teaching in particular. For example, when teaching the methodologies of survey design, questionnaires from large-scale surveys can be examined for good or indifferent practice in question wording, scale construction, question ordering (Sobal 1981) and approaches to data analysis. It is also a useful tool for teaching statistics; students can examine patterns and findings using real data so lending the exercise a degree of relevance. Sampling and issues of generalisability can be taught by comparing the findings from sample surveys with census datasets (Sobal 1981). Encouraging students to undertake their own secondary analysis allows them the opportunity to test their hypotheses on good-quality, large-scale *real* data (Cutler 1978; Dale et al. 1988; Sobal 1981). Additionally, by encouraging students to adopt secondary analysis for at least part of their dissertation research, ethical issues and concerns regarding access to the field and respecting the confidentiality of respondents are reduced or may be avoided entirely.

Moving the field forward: methodological and theoretical benefits

Secondary analysis provides limitless opportunities for the replication, re-analysis and re-interpretation of existing research. It provides researchers with the opportunities to undertake longitudinal analyses, to research and understand past events, to re-analyse primary studies with new perspectives and to engage in exploratory work to test new ideas, theories and models of research design. Secondary analysis can also enable triangulation with data from other sources, for example, by comparing sample survey results with census data or the findings of early studies with more contemporary research. Such analysis can also reveal serendipitous relationships in the data (Dale et al. 1988). For example, the first evidence for a link between lung cancer and smoking was found because doctors in 25 British hospitals were willing to make medical records available to researchers. Similarly the relationship between an early version of the contraceptive pill and blood clotting in a small proportion of users emerged from the scrutiny of death and hospital admissions records (British Association Study Group 1979).

An additional advantage of secondary analysis, and in particular the type of analysis that involves combining data from a range of secondary sources, is that it enables a more robust analysis of subgroups, such as minority ethnic groups or groups of vulnerable individuals who may be undersampled even in a single large-scale study (Brooks-Gunn et al. 1991; Dale et al. 1988). For example, one re-analysis of three large-scale US surveys raised doubts over longheld beliefs about the existence of a 'black matriarchy' among African-American families. Rather, this re-analysis suggested that the differences between the black and white survey respondents were 'small and inconsistent' (Hyman and Reed 1969: 352). The black and white families were much more alike in terms of the extent to which the mother exerted influence over family affairs than previous single surveys, which sampled smaller numbers of black respondents, had suggested. This combination of the data from more than one survey enabled a more robust analysis of the relatively small number of black respondents compared with previous surveys.

Adopting approaches that utilise secondary data can enable the researcher to access data that are usually of the highest quality. According to Hakim (1982a), often the surveys conducted by professional social scientists working in government organisations are more likely to be of better quality, larger scale and more representative of the general population than the 'local and frequently non-random samples that often form the basis of surveys carried out by academic social scientists, with students often used as interviewers' (p. 15). Secondary analysis can allow researchers to gain a second perspective on the data: 'They can ask research questions differently, construct indices differently, analyse the data differently . . . or have different theoretical orientations' (Cook 1974: 162), in such a way it has the potential to uncover errors in the original analysis. As well as challenging the findings of previous research, secondary analysis also has the potential to reinforce the results of the original analysts, as happened with the re-analysis of the Coleman Report in the early 1970s. While this emphasis on re-analysis may be particularly important for policymakers, it might be less useful for the career advancement of the secondary analyst where pressure to stand out as an individual thinker may require one to do more than replicate (Cook 1974).

Of course replicating another's work does not mean that secondary analysis is necessarily atheoretical or merely descriptive. Away from the methodological potential of secondary data analysis, there is also its contribution to theory development, where according to Hakim (1982a), it can 'allow for greater interaction between theory and empirical data because the transition from theory development to theory testing is more immediate' (p. 170). In removing the lag between research design and analysis, secondary analysis can enable researchers to 'think more closely about the theoretical aims and substantive issues of the study rather than the practical and methodological problems of collecting new data' (Hakim 1982a: 16). It is also important to emphasise the role of secondary data in descriptive research. Descriptive studies often have lower status in academic circles than research that tests a model or tries to substantiate a prediction and often they are viewed as less scientific or as not leading to useful generalisations. This tendency to rush to explain phenomena before determining whether or not they actually exist means that 'many important . . . phenomena are under-described and poorly measured . . . there is too quick a tendency to jump to theory testing and prediction' (Campbell et al. 1982: 78). In the field of education, two examples spring to mind: concerns over a shortage of teachers and the apparent underachievement of boys (Gorard 1999; Gorard et al. 2007; Smith 2005a). In both, the rush to theory testing has occurred before the phenomenon itself had been adequately measured and described and, in both, it was secondary data analysis that was used to question the misperception and suggest possible alternative accounts.

In Chapter 2, we discussed one potential pitfall of secondary data analysis, and numeric research more widely – that of reducing social data

to numeric form. One of the examples used was data on school exclusions, the concern being that school exclusion data are socially
constructed – if a student who was excluded from one school had
attended a different school with a more tolerant inclusion policy he or
she might not have faced exclusion. The argument to counter this is that
if we did not have social statistics on phenomena in school exclusion,
however difficult to measure, then how would we know whether school
exclusion was a particular concern among certain groups of students?
Secondary data analysis can tell us which groups of students are excluded
or at risk of exclusion, from which types of school and over which particular period of time. Similarly the data from social surveys and
government administrative records can tell us which families are living in
poverty, the extent of such poverty, whether it has been reproduced over
generations, the effect that it has on wider society, for example through
educational attainment and health status, and also the impact of government policies to reduce poverty. While secondary data analysis can
tell us *what* is happening in society, they cannot tell us *why* these
inequalities exist – that requires combined approaches of the sort
described later.

Political arithmetic in the social sciences: a role for secondary data

The importance of secondary analysis in describing inequalities in society
shows it to be a fundamental component of the political arithmetic tradition of social research. This section considers a role for the secondary
analysis of numeric data in the political arithmetic tradition.

What is political arithmetic?

There is a long established tradition of using a 'political arithmetic'
approach to social research in the UK. The term was first applied to social
research in the eighteenth century with William Petty's treatise on
economic and social measurement (Hogben 1939). The tradition was
named 'political' as it sought to influence government, a forerunner
perhaps of evidence-based policymaking; and 'arithmetic' because it
utilised numbers, usually through the interrogation of large-scale datasets. In particular, the tradition sought to reinforce the place of social
measurement in government policy and planning, as well as in wider
public debate (Heath 2000), at its heart was a concern for equity and
issues of social justice were made implicit (Power and Rees 2006).

The call to adopt a political arithmetic approach to social research was
reiterated in a lecture given at the London School of Economics in May
1949 by D.V. Glass in which he set forth a plea for the closer involvement

of social researchers in lending a scientific justification to the formulation, testing and ongoing evaluation of social policy (Glass 1950). Notwithstanding the obvious problems with applying social research to social policy, namely the complexity and changing objectives of social policies, their restricted and shortened lifespans and the potential ignorance and prejudices of government administrations, Glass argued that provision for social research should be an integral and essential part of government legislation. In more recent jargon, A.H. Halsey has argued for a role for political arithmetic as a means of ensuring accountability (Halsey 1994).

However, this promise of a political arithmetic tradition in which social research was integral to social policy proved to be short lived. One reason for this was the advent, in the late 1960s, of phenomenological and ethnomethodological approaches to social research which challenged the orthodoxy of social statistics – the heart of political arithmetic approaches – and questioned the place of numerical data as 'objective fact about social reality' (Miles and Irvine 1979: 116). Unlike disciplines such as economics and geography, sociology, in particular, fared badly during this paradigm shift, one consequence of which is that as a discipline it has been left with a reputation for 'practical utility at an historic low and ... (is now) regarded as the least developed of the social sciences in terms of the rigour of its methods' (Wiles 2004: 31). This should not, however, represent an overly simplified or negative role of the place of political arithmetic in the social sciences, there have been exceptional examples of work in this field, most notably in the field of social mobility and equality of opportunity (for example Goldthorpe et al. 1980, Halsey et al. 1980). But it is certainly true that Glass's vision of a policy sociology did not materialise and arguably one of the fundamental reasons for this was the mistrust and suspicion with which many social researchers hold the secondary analysis of numeric social data.

The new political arithmetic: a role for secondary data?

Very recently, attempts have been made to reclaim the ground of political arithmetic for sociology. In a debate in the 2004 issue of the *British Journal of Sociology*, Lauder et al. set out their vision for a policy-oriented sociology which links sociological theory with empirical data to inform, challenge and hold government accountable (Lauder et al. 2004). This notion is set out explicitly when applied to combining methods in education research by Gorard (2002). Here is what he terms a '*new* political arithmetic' model, which in its simplest form would allow research findings to be combined in a two-stage process:

In the first stage, a problem (trend, pattern, or situation) is defined by a relatively large-scale analysis of relevant numeric data. In the second stage, this problem (trend, pattern, or situation) is examined in more depth using recognised 'qualitative' techniques with a subset of cases selected from the first stage. (Gorard 2002: 351)

In the spirit of the political arithmetic approach, the numeric techniques adopted in this model would be relatively straightforward and largely descriptive, the combination and integration of smaller scale in-depth work would encourage inter-disciplinarity and the exchange of ideas, theories and perspectives between researchers of different methodological and substantive persuasions. It is an approach that seeks to transcend the traditional 'qualitative' and 'quantitative' paradigms (Gorard 2002) and one that is sympathetic to the central role of quality and application in educational and social research. It is also one that holds secondary data analysis at its centre. One of the particular advantages of secondary analysis is that 'the secondary analyst does not have to embrace any particular epistemological position', there is no conflict between using survey methods and other, less structured techniques to solve a research problem' (Dale et al. 1988: 2). And as the 'dominant mass' of social science research is based on questionnaires and interviews, combining secondary data analysis with depth approaches serves to enhance the 'insight and understanding gained from less structured forms of interviewing or from ethnographic work' (Dale et al. 1988: 2) and help avoid 'over-dependence on a single fallible method' (Webb et al. 1966: 1).

However, none of this is new. While the combination of 'quantitative' and 'qualitative' approaches advocated by the new political arithmetic approach may be being made more explicit in this round of the debate, as we saw in Chapter 1, it is still the case that secondary data, and official statistics in particular, are underused in much social research.

Secondary analysis in the new political arithmetic tradition

There are many useful examples of secondary data being used in the new political arithmetic tradition within the sociology of education. Here we consider only three. The first cites a widely application of political arithmetic: *Origins and Destinations: Family, Class and Education in Modern Britain*, the classic study from Halsey et al. (1980). The second is an example of the new political arithmetic approach being applied to a medium scale research council-funded study, while the final example is taken from my own PhD.

Origins and destinations

One of the most important and widely known recent examples of a political arithmetic approach to empirical research in the sociology of education was the secondary analysis of the 1972 Oxford Mobility Project dataset (Halsey et al. 1980). This dataset consisted of life history interviews with 10,309 men aged between 14 and 64, living in England and Wales in early summer 1972. As we shall see later, this study is not only important for its empirical and theoretical contributions; it is also a classic example of the secondary analysis of survey data. The data used in the study was not collected by the researchers themselves, neither was the research instrument designed with their own specific project in mind: indeed, the original survey design was for a study of mobility (Goldthorpe et al. 1980) and not for a study of educational experience. As a consequence, the data contained certain limitations which had to be accounted for by the authors; the most important limitation was that the survey included only men – there were no data collected from women; additionally, the organisation of education in England and Wales meant that it was desirable only to include men younger than 60 years of age and who were resident in England and Wales at the age of 14. These adjustments resulted in an achieved sub-sample of 8529 men. Another limitation was that the data were largely objective, rather than subjective. This meant that they contained a great deal of information on an individual's educational, familial and occupational background but nothing about their psychological attitudes and attributes. Nevertheless, this study from Halsey et al. (1980) and the subsequent book, *Origins and Destinations: Family, Class and Education in Modern Britain*, is one of the classics in the sociology of education.

By adopting a political arithmetic approach to their work Halsey et al. sought to answer the important question of whether education can change society. Their approach to analysing their dataset was, again in the political arithmetic tradition, relatively straightforward: involving simple arithmetic procedures such as frequency counts, percentages and ratios before proceeding to more complex statistical analysis such as regression modelling and path analysis. Yet, despite this relative simplicity, the impact of their findings was huge. Not only were they able to follow the expansion and progress of the education system in this country in the years after the First World War, they were also able to chart the class differences therein and challenge the notion that the 1944 Education Act and the tripartite system of schooling that followed had brought the country closer to its ideal of a meritocratic society. Their contribution through this study was not only empirical, the data also allowed for the testing of theoretical notions of class, society and schooling. For example, by challenging Bourdieu's theory that education serves mainly to reproduce the distribution of cultural capital, with the view that rather than reproducing the education system has succeeded in disseminating cultural capital and they provide the empirical evidence to support their claim. Thus, in *Origins and Destinations* we have a classic example of a political arithmetic approach that uses large-scale secondary data to produce empirical and theoretical advances in our understanding of the role of education in our society.

Schools, markets and choice policies
Our second example is taken from a more recent study funded by the Economic and Social Research Council, which examined the long-term impact of market forces in public policy provision, specifically in education (Gorard et al. 2003b). The impetus for the study was the increasing application of market principles in education since the 1988 Education Reform Act. In particular, the increase of parental choice to the extent that it could create conditions where schools were competing for students. This effectively meant that the school 'catchment area' system, where children were simply allocated to their local school, was abolished and families now had the right to apply for admission to their chosen school. The underlying principle behind this being that successful schools would receive greater numbers of applications and so expand and attract more and more students, while less successful schools would be forced to improve in order to survive. One of the concerns about such policies would be that schools, in order to survive, would be under pressure to recruit the most able students and schools that were unable to do this would lose students and become 'sink' schools edging towards a 'spiral of decline'. This study was intended to test the extent to which the introduction of market forces, in particular parental choice, since the 1988 Education Act had caused either scenario to occur.

The study employed a combination of large-scale secondary data analysis with in-depth case studies of local authorities and schools. This combination of large-scale and small-scale methodologies makes the study an important example of the '*new* political arithmetic' approach to social research. In order to test whether schools had become more socially stratified since the 1988 Education Reform Act and the introduction of market principles to choice in education, the study used a combination of approaches from geography, sociology and economics to measure segregation between schools at different levels of aggregation. Using official data on every secondary school in England and Wales, the authors of the study were able to combine data on school organisation (such as size and sector), school outcomes (such as GCSE scores), local contextual factors (such as population density) and student composition in schools (such as figures for free school meals and ethnic group). This was combined with documentary analysis of school admissions material and interviews with officials in around 40 LEAs and, in the final stage, case studies of 21 schools in nine contrasting LEAs.

One key finding to emerge from this investigation was that market-oriented principles have had 'minimal impact on the social ordering' of schooling (Gorard et al. 2003b: 183). Their conclusions are of importance, not just because of the scale and rigour under which the research was undertaken, but because they contrast with 'more conventional narratives of increasing "polarisation" and "stratification"' (p. 184) that characterise much of the work on education markets in this country. This research, just like the work of Halsey et al., is an important example of the political arithmetic approach to social research. It has adopted relatively straightforward numerical and statistical techniques to shift its focus from the aggregate large-scale study of every secondary school in England and Wales towards the small-scale in-depth focus on the individual school. In doing so it has made a lasting contribution to educational policy as well as sociological theory. However, in combining the large-scale with the in-depth, it takes a clear step forward from the traditional political arithmetic approach of the origins and destinations research towards one which arguably constitutes a 'new political arithmetic' and one which is ideally compatible with the use of secondary data.

Analysing underachievement in schools
The final use of secondary data in the new political arithmetic tradition is a brief example taken from my own PhD work. While not proposing it as a textbook PhD by any means, this example is simply to demonstrate that small-scale, largely unfunded research undertaken under a restricted timescale (I was working as a full-time teacher at the time) can still aspire to the political arithmetic tradition. The aim of the research was to understand patterns of differential attainment in the secondary school by developing a model for identifying underachievement. This involved collecting and measuring 30 variables that are linked to achievement from over 2000 year 9 pupils in 12 secondary schools: variables included academic attainment, family background, pupil motivation, school attendance and so on (Smith 2002). These variables were used as 'best possible' predictors of success in national examinations and the resulting model enabled students to be identified who had performed significantly below their prediction (the 'underachievers') as well as those who achieved better results than expected (the 'overachievers') (see Smith 2003). Exploratory focus group interviews were then conducted with groups of 'underachieving' and 'overachieving' pupils in order to try to ascertain any underlying differences that might distinguish these two groups (Smith 2007). This more in-depth work was preceded by an initial stage, which used the secondary analysis of examination data to reflect

on the changing nature of academic achievement over a 30-year period and to establish long-term patterns of differential attainment between male and female learners. The use of large-scale secondary data in this way did not only stimulate the theoretical basis for the entire PhD, it also provided a theoretical and methodological context for the in-depth survey and interview work that followed. This is another example of research aspiring to the new political arithmetic tradition: large-scale data were used to describe a phenomenon that had strong links to equity and social justice, which was then followed by in-depth work seeking to examine more closely and then explain the patterns to emerge in stage one.

Missed opportunities?

This section considers some potential missed opportunities for undertaking secondary analysis alongside in-depth research. In doing this, I take three examples of very small-scale research projects, some based on PhD work, where the authors rely on the responses of only a handful of subjects in order to generate their finding and formulate their hypothesises. It is not the intention of this section to criticise this work per se, but simply to suggest that had the authors taken into account some of the huge range of data on their topics which already exist, it could have added context and rigour to their findings.

Bilingualism in primary schools
This study is an ethnographic account of the experiences of a small number of bilingual learners as they pass through the final phases of primary education. The children are all of Pakistani Muslim heritage, they are successful learners, their families speak English to a 'high degree of fluency' and many are professionals; but the study argues that despite the advantages that bilingualism conveys on these young people, they are still condemned to failure and underachievement in school. The study is potentially problematic for several reasons: it has no suitable comparison group against which to compare the experiences of these young learners and neither does it differentiate the impact of bilingualism and culture, for example by comparing the children's experiences with those of first-language Welsh speakers. Finally, the study presents no evidence to support its central thesis that the cultural and linguistic divide between teachers and their bilingual pupils is the underlying cause of their underachievement.

So, do bilingual children underachieve in school? As the author of this study does not consider the various problems with using the term 'underachievement' in this context, it is reasonable to assume that the author is referring to low achievement and *not under*achievement, so instead we need to consider the evidence about whether bilingual children are low achievers in school (Smith 2003). We know from official examination statistics that young people from certain ethnic minority groups, such as those from Pakistani and Bangladeshi heritages, achieve at the lowest levels in National Curriculum tests in school (DfES 2003). But we also know that this has strong links to poverty and that not all ethnic minority children are bilingual. So, what is the evidence to support the author's central claim about bilingualism and low achievement?

One potential source of evidence, which could add context and rigour to this study, comes from the Progress in International Reading and Literacy Study (PIRLS). The study is described in detail in Appendix 1, but briefly it is an international comparative study of the achievement, reading habits and attitudes of pupils aged 9–10 years. At the time of writing, the most recent sweep of PIRLS, *PIRLS 2001*, surveyed 3156 pupils in 131 schools in England (Joncas 2003). In addition to assessing pupils on their literacy and reading skills, PIRLS also collected a great deal of contextual information on the pupils, their schools and their families. Examples of the stems of the *PIRLS 2001* questions, which may be useful in a study of home language and bilingualism, are shown in Box 3.1.

Box 3.1 *PIRLS 2001* student questionnaire: selected background questions

---

- What languages did you learn to speak when you were little?
- How often do you speak English* at home?
- How often do you speak English* with *adults* living in your home?
- Were you born in England*?
  If no...
- How old were you when you came to England*?
- Was your mother born in England*?
- Was your father born in England*?

---

* Depending on test language and country.
Source: PIRLS 2001

Comparing the attainment of students in the *PIRLS 2001* literacy tests with certain home background characteristics that might impact on test language development reveals the patterns shown in Tables 3.1 and 3.2. On average, students who came from families where neither parent was born in the country of the test, scored lower on the *PIRLS 2001* literacy tests. The achievement gaps between families where one parent was born in the test country, or both were, do vary across countries tested: the gap is relatively small in England, compared with the USA.

Table 3.1 Literacy attainment for selected countries, according to whether students' parents were born in test country

Country	Father and mother born in test country		Father or mother born in test country		Neither parent born in test country	
	% pupils	Average attainment	% pupils	Average attainment	% pupils	Average attainment
England	67 (1.8)	559 (3.8)	21 (1.0)	553 (4.9)	12 (1.5)	536 (6.4)
France	70 (1.7)	533 (2.8)	16 (0.7)	526 (4.3)	15 (1.3)	503 (3.9)
Germany	75 (1.2)	553 (1.8)	10 (0.4)	530 (3.9)	15 (1.0)	498 (2.9)
Scotland	80 (1.0)	537 (3.4)	15 (0.8)	520 (6.1)	5 (0.5)	506 (11.4)
USA	68 (1.8)	556 (4.1)	15 (0.8)	530 (5.3)	17 (1.7)	522 (6.9)
International	77 (0.2)	506 (0.7)	13 (0.1)	491 (1.1)	9 (0.2)	476 (1.6)

( ) standard errors.

Source: Mullis et al. 2003

Table 3.2 Literacy attainment for selected countries, according to whether student speaks language of test country at home

Country	Always or almost always		Sometimes		Never	
	% pupils	Average attainment	% pupils	Average attainment	% pupils	Average attainment
England	88 (1.0)	559 (3.4)	11 (0.9)	510 (5.9)	1 (0.2)	~
France	87 (0.9)	532 (2.5)	12 (0.8)	494 (3.6)	1 (0.2)	~
Germany	90 (0.7)	547 (1.8)	9 (0.7)	487 (3.6)	1 (0.1)	~
Scotland	89 (0.9)	533 (3.8)	9 (0.7)	502 (5.1)	2 (0.4)	~
USA	85 (1.1)	551 (3.7)	14 (1.1)	506 (6.1)	2 (0.3)	~
International	79 (0.2)	508 (0.7)	16 (0.2)	474 (1.4)	6 (0.1)	424 (2.7)

( ) standard errors; ~ insufficient data to report.

Source: Mullis et al. 2003

Internationally, most students (79%) reported always or almost always speaking the language of the test at home, a figure which was higher in the five example countries given in Table 3.2. In most countries, and the five shown here were no exception, students who regularly spoke the language of the test at home were more likely to achieve higher scores in the *PIRLS 2001* literacy tests.

This quick analysis of the results from *PIRLS 2001* suggests that in England, students who only sometimes speak English at home were, on average, achieving lower scores on literacy tests. Similarly, students whose parents were both born outside England also achieved lower scores. The attainment gap between those students who had both or only one parent born in England was very small. Further analysis of the *PIRLS*

2001 datasets would be able to tell us more about these patterns and reveal for example, whether families who did not regularly speak English at home were more likely to have an active reading culture where children were read to regularly or about the socioeconomic relationship between family characteristics and reading habits, attitudes and attainment.

This example shows just one possibility of how secondary data can add context and authority to a small-scale in-depth study. Of course, there are other possible sources of data on bilingualism and language use which might complement this study more than data from international comparative tests: the data collected on English as an additional language (EAL) as part of the Annual School Census in England would be a good place to begin (for example, DfES 2007a).

Higher education choice

The second example is a two-year longitudinal case study of the decision-making process of young people as they choose their route into higher education. The focus of the study is 15 young people attending one sixth-form college. Broadly, the research examines the role that family and friends play in helping shape higher education choices, as well as the relationship between these choices and a young person's occupational (specifically 'middle-' or 'working-class') background. The findings suggest that although families have a strong influence on young people's understanding of the higher education sector and on the subsequent choices that they make, their friends also have an important role to play. While this study offers a theoretical framework to account for its findings, it does, by its own admission focus on a very small number of individuals. One opportunity for developing the study to understand the factors that influence HE choice more widely might have been to consider the findings from the Youth Cohort Study. This use of secondary data could provide a clearer indication of *what* the influences that help shape young people's HE decisions are and, when used alongside the in-depth work, would help understand *why* these factors might be important.

To illustrate the usefulness and the potential of secondary sources for providing the context to a smaller scale study, I have carried out a quick descriptive analysis of one question from the latest wave of the Youth Cohort Study. The Youth Cohort Study (YCS) is a series of surveys of 16 to 19 year olds which 'monitors their decisions and behaviour in making the transition from compulsory education to further or higher education, employment or another activity' (Jarvis et al. 2003: 6). More information on the Youth Cohort Study and details of how to access the datasets and related reports are given in Appendix 1. Here we use one question from the YCS to explore the different sources of advice for young people who are considering participating in higher education.

This secondary analysis involved data retrieved from the second sweep of YCS 11 which surveyed young people who were eligible to leave compulsory schooling in summer 2001. Data collection for this sweep of the YCS took place during the spring of 2003 (Jarvis et al. 2006a). The young people included in this short analysis are those who achieved higher grades at GCSE and who were in the process of considering whether or not to continue to higher education. Among the many questions which asked young people about their plans for higher education was a question about who they might talk to for advice about whether or not to apply for university:

Did you ever talk to these people about whether or not you should apply to university?

Respondents were then asked about each of the following groups of people in turn:

- school teachers
- careers service advisers or Connexions advisers
- parents
- siblings
- other relatives
- friends.

Table 3.3 shows the results of this quick analysis for male and female students and gives the percentage of students in each group who answered 'yes' to this question (the total number of students asked the question in each of the three groups shown in Table 3.3 is given in the last line of the table). As you can see, around 90% of male and female students had asked for advice from their teachers, parents and friends. Gender differences were not particularly strong here but slightly more girls spoke to their friends about their choices.

Table 3.4 looks at the responses to the same question, this time according to occupational group. The results for three occupational groups are shown here: *large employers and higher professionals* and *semi-routine and routine occupations* plus *lower supervisory occupations*. To account for the differences in numbers between the *large employers and higher professionals* and the *semi-routine and routine* plus *lower supervisory occupations*, the last two groups have been collapsed. Parents, teachers and friends are still the groups who are most asked for advice, but young people from the *semi-routine and routine* and *lower supervisory* occupational groups were less likely to ask for advice, compared with those from the *large employers and higher professionals* group. For example, 86% of

Table 3.3 Percentage of students who answered 'yes' to question on asking for advice when applying to university, according to sex

	Male (%)	Female (%)	All students (%)
Teachers	90	89	89
Advisers	60	57	58
Parents	93	94	93
Siblings	35	39	37
Other relatives	42	44	43
Friends	89	93	91
Total number asked	**871**	**1267**	**2138**

Source: Jarvis et al. 2006a

Table 3.4 Percentage of students who answered 'yes' to question on asking for advice when applying to university, according to selected occupational groups

	Large employers and higher professionals (%)	Semi-routine and routine plus lower supervisory (%)	All students (%)
Teachers	93	86	89
Advisers	57	59	58
Parents	97	90	93
Siblings	39	35	37
Other relatives	46	41	43
Friends	94	89	91
Total number asked	**557**	**298**	**2138**

Source: Jarvis et al. 2006a

students in the *semi-routine and routine* plus *lower supervisory* occupational groups asked their teachers for advice about university, compared with 93% of those from the *large employers and higher professionals* group.

The final analysis presented in Table 3.5 shows how asking for advice about HE varies according to sex within the two occupational categories we have selected for this example. Male students from the *semi-routine and routine* plus *lower supervisory* occupational groups were the group least likely to ask for advice. In particular, they were much less likely to ask advice from parents and friends. However, the number of cases is beginning to get rather small (i.e. n = 40 for cell*) and so differences need to be interpreted with some caution.

This example has tried to illustrate how the simple analysis of one question from a representative national survey can provide a context to

Table 3.5 Percentage of students who answered 'yes' to question on asking for advice when applying to university, according to sex and selected occupational groups

	Large employers and higher professionals (%)		Semi-routine and routine plus lower supervisory (%)	
	Male	*Female*	*Male*	*Female*
Teachers	94	92	84	87
Advisers	59	55	58	59
Parents	98	96	₍ 84	94
Siblings	37	39	32*	37
Other relatives	46	45	38	42
Friends	93	94	86	91
Total number asked	**248**	**309**	**123**	**175**

Source: Jarvis et al. 2006a

more in-depth work. Rather than relying on the views of a handful of individuals, using the responses from several hundred young people can help researchers begin to understand how representative their work is and help construct a framework for exploring the reasons behind why such patterns might emerge from the data. The resources needed to undertake such a study are in no way considerable and would not be out of the reach of a lone researcher undertaking small-scale work.

Racism in schools

Several recent studies have focused on the issue of racism as a 'potent and detrimental force within British schools' (Archer and Francis 2005: 387). While the topics covered in research of this nature are undoubtedly important and timely, many of the studies are small scale and often lack a suitable comparison group making it difficult to generalise beyond the sample being studied (for example, Archer 2002; Archer and Francis 2005). So, what additional information can secondary data analysis provide on the issue of racist behaviour in schools? One source is the data derived from the Young People's Social Attitudes Survey (YPSAS). The study is described in more detail in Appendix 1, but, briefly, the YSAS is a survey of the views of young people on a range of topics including problems at school, politics and decision making and prejudice and morality (National Centre for Social Research 2005a). At the time of writing, the most recent YSAS was undertaken in 2003 and achieved a sample of 663 young people aged 12–19. While the number of questions asked in the survey about prejudice are rather limited, they do provide an interesting context for a study about young people's views on prejudice in wider society. This quick analysis of the YPSAS looks first at the attitudes young people hold about racial prejudice before moving on to examine their beliefs about the treatment of those from less wealthy backgrounds.

Box 3.2 gives an excerpt from the interviewer's question about prejudice towards minority ethnic groups.

Box 3.2 Prejudice towards minority ethnic groups

> Now some questions about racial prejudice in Britain. First, thinking of *Asians* – that is, people whose families were originally from India, Pakistan or Bangladesh – who now live in Britain. Do you think that there is a lot of prejudice against them in Britain nowadays, a little or hardly any?

Source: National Centre for Social Research 2005b: 17

A similarly worded question was asked about black people whose origins were from the West Indies or Africa (National Centre for Social Research 2005b). Of course, these questions are not unproblematic: they do not distinguish between different Asian (or black) groups, do not offer an obvious 'don't know' response and are, of course, based only on a young person's perception of prejudice. However, the results from a descriptive analysis of perceptions of prejudice according to a young person's self-stated ethnic group show that 87% (39% + 48%) of respondents perceived that there was 'a little' or 'a lot' of prejudice against people of Asian origin, with 74% (54% + 20%) perceiving the same amount of prejudice for 'black' people (Tables 3.6 and 3.7). Similar patterns in responses were given for the different ethnic groups, although the small (albeit representative) numbers of respondents from the non-white groups means that these results need to be interpreted with caution.

An additional series of questions were asked of the young people's perceptions of prejudice according to socioeconomic status of the victim, as well as ethnic group. The analysis that follows shows the results from two questions about which groups were more likely to be committed of crimes of which they were innocent. The first asked about the different treatment of black and white people and the second of rich and poor (see Box 3.3 and Table 3.8).

Table 3.6 Responses to question on prejudice against Asian people, according to stated ethnic group

	A lot		A little		Hardly any		Don't know		Total
	N	%	N	%	N	%	N	%	N
Black: African	0	0	5	83	1	17	0	0	6
Black: Caribbean	1	20	3	60	1	20	0	0	5
Black: Other	2	100	0	0	0	0	0	0	2
Black: All	3	23	8	61	2	15	0	0	13
Asian Indian	1	11	4	44	4	44	0	0	9
Asian: Pakistani	5	25	13	65	2	10	0	0	20
Asian: Other	2	33	2	33	2	33	0	0	6
Asian: All	8	23	19	54	8	23	0	0	35
White: European	228	39	287	49	56	10	13	2	584
White: Other	4	40	3	30	3	30	0	0	10
White: All	232	39	290	49	59	10	13	2	594
Mixed origin	10	56	4	22	4	22	0	0	18
Other	3	75	1	25	0	0	0	0	4
Total	**256**	**39**	**322**	**48**	**73**	**11**	**13**	**2**	**664**

Source: National Centre for Social Research 2005a

Table 3.7 Responses to question on prejudice against black people, according to stated ethnic group

	A lot		A little		Hardly any		Don't know		Total
	N	%	N	%	N	%	N	%	N
Black: African	0	0	5	83	1	17	0	0	6
Black: Caribbean	1	20	2	40	2	40	0	0	5
Black: Other	0	0	2	100	0	0	0	0	2
Black: All	1	8	9	69	3	23	0	0	13
Asian Indian	2	22	4	44	3	33	0	0	9
Asian: Pakistani	0	0	16	80	3	15	1	5	20
Asian: Other	0	0	4	67	2	33	0	0	6
Asian: All	2	6	24	68	8	23	1	3	35
White: European	125	21	311	53	134	23	13	2	583
White: Other	2	20	5	50	3	30	0	0	10
White: All	127	21	316	53	137	23	13	2	593
Mixed origin	4	22	9	50	5	28	0	0	18
Other	1	25	2	50	1	25	0	0	4
Total	**135**	**20**	**360**	**54**	**154**	**23**	**14**	**2**	**663**

Source: National Centre for Social Research 2005a

Box 3.3 Treatment in court (1)

Suppose two people – one white and one black – appear in court, charged with a crime they did *not* commit. What do you think their chances are of being found *guilty*?
...the white person is more likely to be found guilty?
...they both have the same chance?
...the black person is more likely to be found guilty?

Source: National Centre for Social Research 2005b: 17

Table 3.8 Responses to question on treatment in court, according to stated ethnic group

	White person more likely		Same chance		Black person more likely		Don't know		Total
	N	%	N	%	N	%	N	%	N
Black: African	0	0	2	33	3	50	1	17	6
Black: Caribbean	0	0	0	0	5	100	0	0	5
Black: Other	0	0	1	50	1	50	0	0	2
Black: All	0	0	3	23	9	69	1	8	13
Asian Indian	0	0	3	33	6	67	0	0	9
Asian: Pakistani	1	5	11	55	7	35	1	5	20
Asian: Other	0	0	4	67	2	33	0	0	6
Asian: All	1	3	18	51	15	43	1	3	35
White: European	31	5	376	64	166	28	10	2	583
White: Other	1	10	7	70	2	20	0	0	10
White: All	32	5	383	64	168	28	10	2	593
Mixed origin	0	0	12	67	4	22	2	11	18
Other	1	25	0	0	3	75	0	0	4
Total	**34**	**5**	**416**	**63**	**199**	**30**	**14**	**2**	**663**

Source: National Centre for Social Research 2005a

In response to this question, just under one-third of young people overall thought that the black person would be more likely to be found guilty than the white, while the majority of respondents thought that they would have the same chance in court. These views do differ within the different ethnic groups, with both black and Asian groups more likely to feel that the black person was more likely to be found guilty, although the number of respondents from these groups is relatively small and the results need to be treated with caution.

The question was repeated, this time asking about the different treatment of a rich and a poor person (Box 3.4).

Box 3.4 Treatment in court (2)

> Suppose two people from different backrounds – one rich and one poor –
> appear in court, charged with a crime they did *not* commit. What do you
> think their chances are of being found *guilty*?
> ...the rich person is more likely to be found guilty?
> ...they both have the same chance?
> ...the poor person is more likely to be found guilty?

Source: National Centre for Social Research 2005b: 17

The responses to this question are interesting: over half of the young
people thought that the poor person was more likely to be found guilty
than the rich person, a pattern apparent across all ethnic groups (see
Table 3.9).

This brief descriptive analysis of some of the results of the Young
People's Social Attitudes Survey suggests that young people perceive
aspects of prejudice across different ethnic groups, a phenomenon
already widely acknowledged by researchers who work in this area, but
what the data also show is that young people also perceive prejudice and
injustice for people of different socioeconomic groups. Further analysis of
the YPSAS data would perhaps tell us more about the extent to which
this perception exists among different groups of young people. The role of

Table 3.9 Responses to question on treatment in court, according to
socioeconomic group

	Rich is more likely		Same chance		Poor is more likely		Don't know		Total
	N	%	N	%	N	%	N	%	N
Black: African	0	0	2	33	4	67	0	0	6
Black: Caribbean	1	20	0	0	4	80	0	0	5
Black: Other	0	0	1	50	1	50	0	0	2
Black: All	1	8	3	23	9	69	0	0	13
Asian Indian	0	0	4	44	5	56	0	0	9
Asian: Pakistani	2	10	7	35	11	55	0	0	20
Asian: Other	0	0	4	67	2	33	0	0	6
Asian: All	2	6	15	43	18	51	0	0	35
White: European	12	2	238	41	324	56	9	1	583
White: Other	1	10	4	40	4	40	1	10	10
White: All	13	2	242	41	328	55	10	2	593
Mixed origin	1	6	8	44	9	50	0	0	18
Other	1	25	0	0	3	75	0	0	4
Total	**18**	**3**	**268**	**40**	**367**	**55**	**10**	**1**	**663**

Source: National Centre for Social Research 2005a

poverty in mediating prejudice is one that does not receive a great deal of attention in research into racism and prejudice, where the absence of comparison groups would make such a phenomenon even more difficult to uncover – but it is, arguably, one that is worthy of further study.

While not providing the detail of in-depth studies, the data from studies such as the YPSAS do provide a useful context for small-scale research. In addition, they have the potential to help researchers understand the patterns underlying some of the phenomena currently of concern in contemporary social research, as well as uncovering potentially overlooked relationships and offering opportunities for further investigation.

Summary

Official information, imperfect and badly adapted for sociological purposes as it often is, generally suffices to show the magnitude, nature and locality of a problem; common knowledge, obtainable by conversation with those who have lived in close contact with its circumstances will place it in fair perspective; while a rapid investigation by sample will give an approximation to detailed measurements. Very often this is all that is wanted. (Bowley 1915: 11, cited in Bulmer 1980: 506)

Secondary data analysis offers social, methodological and theoretical benefits to the social researcher. Arguably, it is most effective when combined with other approaches, most notably in the new political arithmetic tradition of research. Political arithmetic reinforces the place of social measurement in influencing government policy and planning and is at the very heart of an evidence-based approach to policymaking. However, the early promises of this tradition have not been fully realised in the latter half of the last century. One of the reasons for this is arguably long-established concerns about the re-analysis of the large-scale numeric datasets which are fundamental to political arithmetic approaches. Secondary analysis is the perfect complement to a 'new political arithmetic' tradition of conducting social research: its scale aids generalisability, the numeric techniques needed for its analysis can be relatively straightforward and accessible to most social scientists not just statisticians. It can be readily combined with in-depth approaches and the very nature of many large-scale datasets can reinforce the desire for social equity which is at the heart of the political arithmetic tradition. But none of this is particularly new. The call for combining large- and small-scale approaches to social research pre-dates much of the research and methodological debates considered in this book yet secondary data analysis is still an underused technique. It remains to be seen whether there is a role for secondary data analysis in this new round of the political arithmetic debate.

4

Doing secondary analysis

> Perhaps the most important attribute for the user of published data is a large dose of scepticism. (Jacob 1984: 45)

This chapter considers some of the things a researcher needs to think about when using secondary data. There is a misapprehension among some commentators that doing secondary analysis is easy because it by-passes the tricky data collection phase (Glaser 1962). Neither is it necessarily the case that data researchers did not collect themselves are more prone to error than primary data. Rather, secondary data suffer from the same limitations that affect all social data and researchers need to make the same analytic decisions and compromises they would make when preparing and analysing data they collected themselves. It is, of course, true that there are specific things that the analyst needs to think about when using secondary data and it is these that we focus on in this chapter. We begin by considering the need to establish the purpose of the secondary data source being considered as well as its relevance to one's research questions. The discussion then considers practical issues such as the resources need to undertake the analysis and technical issues such as sampling, response rates and the nature of the variables included in the analysis and, in particular, their fit with one's own research questions. These considerations are then brought together in a worked example that explores the potential of the General Household Survey for use in a secondary analysis of household consumption.

What is the purpose of the research?

> The successful secondary analyst must be able to use and interpret the
> data with the knowledge and insight that went into its original collec-
> tion. (Dale et al. 1988: 16)

With this in mind, a good place to start is, rather obviously perhaps, to
find out exactly what it was that the primary research was trying to
achieve. You might begin by examining the research questions or aims of
the research or look at who commissioned and undertook the study: was
the study commissioned by a government department, was it study based
on opinion polls or market research or was it a piece of academic
research? The easiest way to find this out is to examine the research
manuals or other documentation accompanying the study or, if the data
are presented as a report, this information should be located in accompanying appendices.

Because secondary data are not necessarily more objective than data
based on observations or ethnographies, it is important to get some idea
about the concepts that motivated the original research and which may
influence its application to your secondary analysis. If the research was
commissioned or undertaken by an advocacy group, for example, there
may be a particular aspect or interest that the research emphasises. This
narrower focus may be fine for advocacy research but might be insuffi-
ciently objective to be presented as evidence in an academic study. For
example, polls on abortion law reform commissioned by right to life
campaigners and pro-choice groups that have been conducted by the
same polling companies over similar time periods are still able to produce
very different results – results that may reflect the ideology of the particular commissioning group (Finney and Peach 2004: 14).

Another thing to think about when selecting your data is the type of
conceptual or theoretical framework that was used in the original study.
Often this is apparent from reading the manuals or appendices which
accompany the data. Again, caution is needed as apparently very similar
surveys can have subtle but important differences. For example, two
widely cited international studies of student attainment the *Trends in
International Mathematics and Science Study (TIMSS)* and the *Programme for
International Student Assessment (PISA)*, have very different conceptual
frameworks. PISA is concerned with understanding young people's
ability 'to use their knowledge and skills in order to meet real-life challenges rather than how well they had mastered a specific school
curriculum' (PISA 2000: 16), while, in TIMSS, the focus is on the curriculum, on what the curriculum contains, how it is implemented and
what it achieves or, in other words, what students have actually learnt
(Mullis et al. 2004). Although these differences are very subtle – they are

still measuring knowledge and understanding of the school curriculum – the secondary analyst will need to decide which study is closer to their own theoretical or substantive interests.

Once the purpose of the study is apparent, there are a few other preliminary checks that the analyst might wish to make on their chosen study: they concern the method of data collection and the structure of the questions used.

Who collected the data?

Often the data produced by large-scale surveys is collected through face-to-face interviews between the respondent and a professional interviewer who may have no other relationship with the study. Therefore, it is worth finding out who collected the data. If professional interviewers were used, they are likely to have followed a scripted questionnaire. The guidelines that are given to interviewers conducting such surveys can be very precise. For example, in the detailed script for interviewers conducting the 2002 World Values Survey, interviewers were required to show cards at appropriate points, reverse the order of options for question responses and not to read out the 'don't know' options (ICPSR 2005). Contrast this perhaps with academic researchers who might unthinkingly rephrase a question to ensure it has been properly understood (Porter 1995) and so may elicit a different type of response or develop a different relationship with the respondent than an interview that kept to a strict script. Neither way of collecting data is necessarily problematic for the secondary analyst, however, it is still important to know who undertook the survey in order to help gauge how objective the research might be.

How were the data collected?

It is also important to find out how the data were collected. Many of the large-scale surveys that are described in Appendix 1 adopt traditional data collection techniques, such as questionnaire and/or face-to-face interview, but the data collected by market research or opinion poll companies may have employed different methods. Data generated by these companies are not necessarily less methodologically rigorous than academic surveys (Harrop 1980), but they may lack substantive rigour: some polls have an astonishingly quick turnaround, often as short as 24 hours, leaving little time for question development and data analysis (Finney and Peach 2004). In the UK the recent success of online polling companies such as *YouGov*, further underlines the importance of knowing where your data came from. Although claiming validation for their method by recent successes in predicting the outcomes of events as diverse as the 2003 elections to the Scottish Parliament and the first Pop Idol contest (Kellner 2004), 'internet polling is still susceptible to a number of biases and methodological weaknesses' (Finney and Peach 2004: 16). Secondary users of such data will need to be alert to issues such as low response rates, the use of incentives to participate, as well as issues of sampling bias, in particular towards those who have access to the internet and who would choose to register and volunteer to participate in these surveys. In addition, because we know very little about whom in the general population has access to the internet, we cannot draw a probability sample and this limits the generalisability of any findings (Sparrow and Curtice 2004). By the same token, there are also flaws with traditional polling methods: telephone and face-to-face interviews are biased towards those who might be at home at the right time; databases of landline telephone numbers exclude mobile numbers and answer phones and voicemail services enable people to screen calls and choose who they wish to talk to (Kellner 2004). The message for the secondary analyst is that all methods of data collection are prone to inconsistency and error; as ever, it is up to the researcher to be alert to these shortcomings and to exercise appropriate scepticism and caution in their use and reporting.

What types of question were used?

Question design is also crucial. In many large-scale surveys a great deal of resources are invested in designing and developing the questions. While this might eliminate or reduce the potential for leading or biased questions, it is still useful to cast a sceptical eye over the types of question that are being asked and to consider their relevance and fit with your own study. This is particularly important in research conducted by or on behalf of advocacy groups, the media and so on. For example, in surveys commissioned by the media, questions may mirror a headline or newspaper rhetoric or may contain limited options for responses and so potentially bias any results (Finney and Peach 2004). In the days following the 9/11 terrorist attacks, public opinion polls conducted in the United States quickly identified Osama Bin Laden as the country's leading enemy. However, by the first anniversary of the attacks, polls were revealing that the majority of Americans believed that it was Saddam Hussein who was personally responsible. The popular view for this shift of opinions is that it was a consequence of the Bush administration's publicity campaign to prepare the American public for the war in Iraq. This, according to Althaus and Largio (2004: 1) is a 'misperception' – the key reason for the shift in opinion was the wording and format of the poll questions that were being asked. Their review of opinion polls taken in the weeks and years following the attacks suggests that in open-ended questions asked during September 2001, few Americans held Saddam Hussein responsible, but this changed when respondents were given a choice of possible perpetrators in forced-choice questions. The universal switch to forced-choice questions after 2001 served only to compound the misperception (Althaus and Largio 2004).

How relevant are the data to your own research questions?

Once you have selected your data and, to the extent that it is possible to do so, determined its purpose and objectivity, the next thing to think about is how closely the data matches your own research questions and empirical aims. Crucial to this is the fit between the variables that you are interested in studying as part of your own research design and the variables that actually exist in the dataset. Ensuring congruence between variables can be an important challenge for the secondary analyst.

Do the variables match?

One example of the challenges faced by researchers when there is a potential mismatch between one's research questions and the variables available for secondary analysis became apparent in our 2005 secondary analysis of the *PISA 2000* study (White and Smith 2005). The context for this study was current national and international concerns about shortages in teacher supply and retention (for example, OECD 2002). *The PISA 2000 School Questionnaire* gathered the views of school principals about, among other things, their experience of teacher shortages and teacher turnover and the impact this had on student learning. Whereas our interest was in examining the school level factors which impact on teacher shortages and turnover; the questions asked in *PISA 2000* referred to 'teacher shortage/inadequacy' and 'teacher turnover' and school principals' *perceptions* of the extent to which either of these two phenomena 'hindered' the learning of 15-year-old students in their schools. There were several problems with the data generated by *PISA 2000* and their fit with our research questions. First, 'teacher shortage/inadequacy' conflates two different (and perhaps unrelated) phenomena. It is impossible to discern from individual responses whether a school principal's answer relates to shortage, inadequacy or a combination of the two. Second, it is unclear how a school principal would be able to assess whether any of these problems 'hindered' the learning of students in their institutions. This task would be difficult to address in a dedicated research project and may, arguably, be impossible outside a controlled intervention. In view of this, school principals' responses to these questions cannot easily be taken at face value. Finally, of course, these data only relate to school principals' *perceptions* of shortages and turnover, no actual data on teacher vacancies was collected or asked for in the *PISA*

2000 study. Therefore, for the purpose of our study, several conceptual adjustments had to be made. The most fundamental was to accept that the school principals' responses represented perceptions of whether a problem with teacher shortage/inadequacy or turnover exists in their institution. If school principals were worried about teacher supply or quality, it may be reasonable to expect that they would demonstrate this concern in a questionnaire addressing these issues. Therefore in our analysis, the responses were treated as proxies for a general concern regarding teacher shortages/inadequacies.

Even so, the data provided by PISA were arguably the best quality available. The data provided a unique opportunity to examine the views of a large number of school principals from a range of education contexts, making this study a new development on the small-scale work which often characterises research in this area. Our concerns about the match between research questions and variables were explicitly documented in reports emerging from this project and our warrant paid due regard to its limitations (White and Smith 2005).

Do your definitions match?
Another important consideration is the extent to which your definition of a variable matches the definition from the agency which collected the data. Although definitions are vitally important, they can be very vague and very complex. Consider the definitions of 'further study' and 'assumed to be unemployed' which accompany the UK Higher Education Statistics Agency (HESA) data on student destinations at the end of higher education:

> [Further study only] includes those who gave their employment cir-
> cumstances as temporarily sick or unable to work/looking after the
> home or family, not employed but not looking for employment, further
> study or training, or something else and who were also either in full-
> time or part-time study, training or research, plus those who were due to
> start a job within the next month or unemployed and looking for
> employment, further study or training and who were also in full-time
> study, training or research. (HESA 2007)

While 'assumed to be unemployed':

> includes those students who gave their employment circumstances as
> unemployed and looking for employment, further study or training, and
> who were also either in part-time study, training or research or not
> studying, plus those who were due to start a job within the next month
> and who were also in part-time study, training or research or not
> studying. (HESA 2007)

Perhaps it is the (mis)use of punctuation, a desire for precision, or the need to include some reference to further study, but these are not particularly clear and straightforward definitions. Contrast HESA's 'assumed to be unemployed' with the International Labour Organisation's (ILO) definition of unemployment; this is the most widely used definition of unemployment and is the one adopted by the UK government. Although in its fullest form it is quite long and complicated, it is readily summarised as:

> All persons above a specified age who during the reference period were
>
> a. 'without work', i.e. were not in paid employment or self-employment,
> b. 'currently available for work', i.e. were available for employment or self-employment during the reference period; and
> c. 'seeking work', i.e. had taken specific steps in a specified time period to seek paid employment or self-employment. The specific steps may include registration at a public or private employment exchange; application to employers; checking at worksites, farms, factory gates, market or other assembly places; placing or answering newspaper advertisements; seeking assistance of friends or relatives; looking for land, building, machinery or equipment to establish own enterprise; arranging for financial resources; applying for permits and licences, etc. (Rodda 2005)

In short, the 'unemployed' are those people who 'have not worked more than one hour during the short reference period, generally the previous week or day, but who are available for and actively seeking work' (O'Higgins 1997: 1).

In addition to overly complex definitions, the researcher also needs to ensure that the definition that they are working with matches that used in the secondary dataset. For example, does your definition of unemployment match the standard ILO definition? Definitions for the variables used in surveys and other secondary sources are usually to be found in the documents that accompany the data or in the appendices of reports and other publications.

Do you have the resources to retrieve and analyse the data?

Despite the obvious advantages of secondary analysis in terms of economies of time, money and personnel, the scale and complexity of many large studies means that it can take time to develop the skills and expertise needed to use the datasets effectively. For example, working out exactly what the variables represent and how they are coded, cleaning the dataset, deleting variables that may be of less interest, combining variables and recoding variables, all takes a lot of time. The time one needs to commit to preparing and carrying out a secondary analysis is not always realised by other researchers. For example, a colleague and I recently requested a very small amount of pump-priming money to fund an exploratory analysis of the Pupil-Level Annual School Census (PLASC). Although the funding was awarded, the proposal's reviewers did remark that the amount of time requested to carry out the study (6 days) seemed rather extended. The zipped files containing the datasets ran to 22 different documents, one with over 7 million cases. The amount of work required to decide which datafiles were relevant to the study, to clean and retrieving variables, to merge datasets and so on, was considerable and that was before we could begin the analysis.

Therefore, once you have located your secondary sources, it is worth pausing to consider the extent to which the data need re-analysis. Many of the large survey, census and administrative datasets that are described in Appendix 1 will already have been extensively analysed. If you are interested in descriptive data, then they are likely already to have been presented elsewhere and there is no need to download and re-analyse the data further. For example, the publications that accompany the PISA dataset already contain extensive analysis of trends between groups of students with regard to their responses to different questions in different educational contexts. In the UK, the findings from the large national surveys are presented in the range of publications published by the Office for National Statistics: for example, *Social Trends* and *Living in Britain*. This type of data is ideal for researchers who wish to use secondary sources to present a context to more in-depth work or who have limited experience or interest in downloading, preparing and re-analysing some of the other datasets described in Appendix 1. So if you are interested in describing trends in the performance of boys and girls in international literacy tests or reviewing patterns of household expenditure, this kind of data is usually already available in aggregate form (i.e. already analysed) and just needs to be reported and correctly cited. (See Chapter 5 for some worked examples which use aggregate data of this type.)

By the same token, re-analysing data that have already been analysed is not necessarily a waste of time. For novice researchers, it is an invaluable way of becoming familiar with the range of data available as well as with the techniques of data preparation, analysis and presentation: skills that have applications in social science research more widely. Re-analysis can also lend new and original perspectives to existing data, for example, through the use of new statistical techniques or different theoretical frameworks.

Retrieving datasets can be very straightforward. Data from surveys such as PISA and TIMSS can be downloaded directly from the project websites. But access to many other datasets requires the user to register through their institution or for their institution to be part of a wider consortium of data sharers. For example, access to the aggregate data from the UK National Censuses can be obtained via CASWEB provided the user has an ATHENS password. Access to other datasets may require registration and some international datasets can only be accessed if one's institution is a member of a data-sharing consortium, such as the Inter-University Consortium for Political and Social Research (ICPSR). Many archives have certain requirements as to the accessibility, use and storage of their datasets and it is important to read through the terms and conditions of data release and confidentiality.

The internet has made it possible to access data from sources that would previously have been impossible, or at least impracticable, for anyone other than the best connected researcher. Sitting at your desk in the English Midlands it is possible to re-analyse the data from classic American sociological studies, to examine progress towards millennium development goals in sub-Saharan Africa and review immigration trends in the Canadian provinces. However, accessing international datasets can be more complicated that it might seem at first, particularly when the data are presented in a language with which the researcher is unfamiliar. Unsurprisingly, many international archives, although they have English-language versions of their websites, make their datasets available only in the national language.

In deciding on your data, you should also consider whether you have the technical skills to analyse the full dataset. Many datasets require a certain amount of technical expertise and a familiarity with concepts such as statistical weightings and so on. However, fortunately, there are a number of courses available to help researchers with even the most limited skills in data management and analysis. The teaching datasets that accompany several of the large government surveys are also a good place to practice managing and analysing data. Secondary analysis of these large datasets need not be the preserve of skilled social statisticians; with a degree of patience and perseverance even a novice researcher will find much to reward their endeavours in the huge range of secondary sources that are available for analysis. A selection of UK-based training opportunities are introduced in Appendix 1 but it is worth reminding the the reader of the huge range of courses available at the University of Essex research methods summer school, the Cathy Marsh centre at the University of Manchester and the institutions and centres associated with the ESRC Research Methods hub based at the University of Southampton.

Are the data of good quality?

Official statistics categories 'occupy contested terrain, the numbers they contain are threatened by misunderstanding as well as self-interest' (Porter 1995: 41).

Assessing the quality of your selected dataset is crucial. Indeed one of the problems with secondary analysis is that errors that may have been present in the original data may no longer be visible (Kiecolt and Nathan 1985). The difficulty, of course, is in knowing what the errors might be and how they might be remedied. However, the cautions that apply when examining data for errors and checking that they are measuring exactly what you expect them to be measuring are no different those you would apply when assessing the accuracy of any other piece of research.

Another crucial consideration when analysing secondary data is the possibility that the indicators adopted either by the secondary analyst or the original researcher(s) may have tenuous connections to the concepts under study: 'Slippage between concept and indicator is an ever present danger in secondary analysis' (Hyman 1972: 23). One example of this is the PISA indicator of parental wealth. While this indicator ostensibly measures 'wealth' by asking about ownership of consumer items, it does not correlate very highly with other indicators including parental occupation (Gorard and Smith 2004). It is also worth considering whether any reviews or commentaries have already been written about the data. This might unearth existing analyses that may complement your own research but could also reveal methodological shortcomings. Barretta-Herman's re-analysis of the IASSW World Census 2000 points to several limitations of the study, including a lack of clarity in terminology used and a lack of specificity in the aims of the study (Barretta-Herman 2006). (See Chapter 2 for a discussion about shortcomings in international comparative tests.)

What are the sampling strategies and response rates?

Two important questions for when you have identified the dataset are: how was the sample drawn and is it sufficiently representative to allow generalisations to be made to the wider population? Many large-scale surveys employ rigorous sampling techniques to try to ensure that the data that they collect are representative and will support generalisations. For example, in the PISA studies, a sample of schools is drawn from all schools in the participating country. Schools are selected on criteria such as size, to ensure an even spread of different types of institution. For each school sampled, additional replacement schools will also be selected. These replacement schools share the key characteristics of the main sample schools and are substituted for the main schools in the event of

Table 4.1 School response rates, before and after replacement *PISA 2003*, selected countries

Country	Participation rate before replacement	Participation rate after replacement
Canada	80	84
Finland	97	100
France	89	89
Germany	98	99
Japan	87	96
Korea	96	100
Spain	98	100
UK	64	77
USA	65	68

Source: OECD 2005b: 171–172

their non-participation. However, even such rigorous sampling techniques cannot always ensure complete and representative coverage of the population. Table 4.1 shows the response rates for a selection of countries that participated in *PISA 2003*. The first column of figures shows the response rates for schools from the original sample and the second column the rates after replacement schools had been approached. For many countries, the response rates are very robust. In Finland, Korea and Spain almost all the schools selected to be part of the original sample participated in the survey. The use of replacement schools ensured that coverage in these three countries was 100%. On the other hand, the UK and the USA are the two countries with the lowest school response rates even after replacement schools had been contacted. Indeed, these are the lowest rates for all 41 countries participating in *PISA 2003*. The poor response rates for the UK and USA are too low for the findings to be generalised to the larger country population and any results for these countries should be used with caution or even disregarded.

Other studies may also suffer from response rates far lower than the desired 100%. For example, the Youth Cohort Study has seen a steady decrease in its response rate – from over 70% in the late 1980s to 47% in 2004 (Table 4.2). The response rate for the various sweeps of the Labour Force Survey tends to be in the region of 63% (Higgins 2007). Similarly, the response rate for the 2003 Young People's Social Attitudes survey was 66% (Park et al. 2004). The 2000 International Association of Schools of Social Work (IASSW) World Census generated a response rate of only 21% and that was heavily skewed in favour of certain regions (Barretta-Herman 2006).

Response rates for surveys can be found in the technical manuals or appendices that accompany the reports and should always be consulted

Table 4.2 Response rates for the Youth Cohort Survey

Survey year	Initial used sample	Sweep 1 response rate
1985	12,180	69
1986	19,565	74
1987	21,032	77
1989	20,000	71
1991	20,060	72
1992	36,292	69
1994	27,139	66
1996	24,500	65
1998	22,500	65
2000	25,000	55
2002	30,000	56
2004	30,000	47

Note: the survey is not annual.

Source: DfES 2005

before you proceed with your analysis or investigation of the data. One of the decisions the secondary analyst has to make is whether or not they feel that these response rates are sufficiently robust to enable further analysis; this, as with many other things in social research, is a matter of judgement.

Linked to response rate is dropout, particularly in longitudinal cohort studies. One problem with analysing cohort and other longitudinal studies is the absence of substantial amounts of relevant data, often arising through participants dropping out. A cohort study like the 1970 Birth Cohort Study (BCS) uses a group of neonates and seeks permission to follow them through their lives. This study started with 16,695 cases in Britain. By 1999, 2608 were untraced, 246 confirmed emigrated, 109 died and 338 refused, leaving 13,394 cases (Bynner et al. 2000: 31). Unfortunately, the cases dropping out at each 'sweep' are not random, so introducing a substantial bias for subsequent analysis. This potential for bias should be highlighted and taken into account by analysts and their users. For example, Croxford (2006) provides an excellent summary of some of the major problems faced when conducting an analysis over time using a cohort study (in this case the Youth Cohort Study).

How timely are the data?

Another question to ask yourself is when were the data collected? And, additionally, are the data still relevant for today? Data that have been around for a long time are not necessarily of less value to researchers than data collected very recently. One potential limitation to the use of government surveys is their timeliness: they are often at least 2 years old before they are made available for secondary analysis. An exception is the Labour Force Survey whose database is available for analysis within 14 weeks of the data collection period (Arber 2001). However, this general availability does mean that the surveys can be easily downloaded for secondary analysis but, equally importantly, the findings can also be published ready analysed in aggregate form.

It is also worth bearing in mind how relevant data collected some time ago are when applied to contemporary research questions. For example, the 1958 National Child Development Study gathered data on the attitudes and experiences of school-aged children when they were 16 years of age. These children, who were born in the late 1950s, have lived through a very different educational era from young people currently in school, most notably the introduction of comprehensive schooling in the mid-1960s, the raising of the school leaving age to 16 in 1972, the abandonment of the 11-plus examinations in many parts of the country and, of course, the introduction of the National Curriculum in England and Wales in 1988. The lessons for contemporary education research from any secondary analysis of this data are necessarily limited in their application. This is not in itself problematic; it all depends on one's research questions: as a comparative study against subsequent cohorts for example, such data would be invaluable.

Who was the information collected from?

When reviewing your dataset it is important to investigate who the actual information was collected from. In particular it is worth deciding whether the respondents would actually be in a position to answer the question with any degree of accuracy or whether their response was coloured by their own experiences, prejudices or expectations. Our research into school principals' perceptions about teacher shortages, which was described earlier, is a good example of this (White and Smith 2005). No data were collected about *actual* numbers of vacancies and turnover rates and we have only the school principals' *perceptions* about the extent to which a problem actually existed. Again, this is not necessarily problematic but it needs to be recognised in the warrant one attaches to the research. This is also important in studies which collect and then categorise data from different groups. For example, in studies concerned with participation in post-compulsory education, it may not always be clear whether the classification of occupation should be that of the potential student or of their parents. It would seem unreasonable perhaps to base the occupational classification of a student on their own work history when they may never have been anything other than a full-time student. But where the occupations of the two parents differ, which is to be preferred? If one or more of the parents has not lived with the student, does this make a difference? What about more mature students? Should their occupational classification be based on the previous occupation of their parents? Should we use two different classification systems for younger and older students? If so, when should the cutoff point be? (Gorard et al. 2007). There are no straightforward answers to these questions, but the issues they raise need to be considered when you select variables for analysis and when findings are reported.

What categories are used to group the data?

Another important consideration is the type of categories that have been used to group the data. An obvious example of this comes with the categorisation of ethnicity or occupational class, which themselves reveal longstanding issues of classification (Lambert 2002; Lee 2003). The categories themselves are somewhat arbitrary and they interact importantly with each other and with other categories such as sex (Gorard et al. 2007). A further problem comes when examining trends in social categories over time as the variables collected, or the coding used, may also change over time. Consequently, it is often difficult to make genuine and straightforward comparisons over time or between groups. This is true, for example, of the Higher Education Statistic Agency (HESA) datasets in recording the ethnic origin of students in HE. Until 2001/02 there was only one category for 'white' students in the UK. Now a distinction has been made between white, white-British, white-Irish, white-Scottish, Irish traveller and other white. There are now, also, categories for a number of mixed ethnic groups, including mixed white. While this may reflect changes in society, and could increase the completion rate for this question, it makes comparison over time more difficult. The categorisation of socioeconomic groups and young people with special educational needs are two other examples.

How precise are the data?

The secondary analyst needs to be aware of potential issues in the way in which data, in particular aggregate, or summary, secondary data, are presented. For example, the use of rankings can overemphasise differences that are in fact rather small and the inclusion of too many decimal places can suggest an accuracy that is not warranted by the measure being presented. In order to be alert to such specious accuracies, the secondary data analyst will need to pay careful scrutiny to the footnotes and appendices that accompany the data and keep an eye out for guides as to the precision of the data, such as error bars and confidence intervals.

For example, results from international tests are usually presented as

Table 4.3 Progress in International Reading Literacy Study, average scores and standard errors

Country	Average scale score	Standard error
Bulgaria	550	3.8
Canada*	544	2.4
Czech Republic	537	2.3
England*	553	3.4
Germany	539	1.9
Hungary	543	2.2
Italy	541	2.4
Latvia	545	2.3
Lithuania*	543	2.6
Netherlands*	554	2.5
Sweden	561	2.2
United States*	542	3.8

*These countries all have queries next to their response rates.

Source: Mullis et al. 2003: 26

mean scores, often accompanied by a 95% confidence limit (which provide an estimate of the variability of the scores). The size of these bands means that the scores for some countries overlap and that simple ranking of countries can be unhelpful and disguise closely ranked performances. Table 4.3 shows the average scores for a selection of the highest ranking countries in the 2001 Progress in International Reading Literacy Study (PIRLS). Notice that when the standard errors of the mean score are accounted for the rankings in the table are fairly meaningless. This does not prevent much being made of the results, particularly among the media. For example, England's third place success in *PIRLS 2001* was attributed to a return to traditional teaching methods in primary schools (*Daily Mail*, 7 April 2003), the National Literacy Strategy (*DfES Press Release*, 8 April 2003, *Guardian*, 9 April 2003) and Harry Potter (*Daily Express*, 9 April 2003). Whereas the standard error indicates England could be as high as second or as low as fifth.

In checking the precision of the data it is also important to check whether the data distinguish between the groups of interest. The level of differentiation between different ethnic categories is an obvious example of this.

Who is missing from the data?

In other words: are there any groups who have been excluded from the data? This is an important consideration for secondary analysts who will need to consider carefully the nature of any information that might have been omitted during the data collection process. It is not unusual to find that individuals are simply missing from official statistics, a situation made more problematic by not knowing who or how many people are missing. The recent debate on immigration statistics is a good example of this (BBC 2007b; *Guardian* 2007). In England at present, the Pupil-Level Annual School Census does not collect any data on the eligibility of permanently excluded students to receive free school meals, neither does it record their National Curriculum year group. This means that if you wished to study the profile of an institution in terms of individual students who receive free school meals, you would have to omit from the study all students who had been permanently excluded – as students in receipt of free school meals are one of the least successful groups in school, in terms of aggregate examination performance, excluding this group from your analysis leaves a potential bias in the data.

There is one study currently underway in a UK university which is examining the participation of men in higher and further education: this is a group that has apparently not benefited from the current widening participation agenda. But the study is only focusing on men currently undertaking access or foundation courses: that is, men who are *already participating* in education. What about the men who are not participating and who are arguably not benefiting from the widening participation agenda – surely these are the respondents who the researchers ought to be focusing on, surely these are the ones who are best placed to tell us about the barriers to participation in education? This sort of bias in research design is one that the secondary analyst, and arguably all researchers and reviewers, need to be aware of. The research is funded by the ESRC and its datasets will presumably be archived for use by future secondary analysts. This, unfortunately, is not an unusual omission in educational research (Gorard and Smith 2007) and it is certainly not a concern that should only occupy secondary analysts.

Are there any missing data?

An even more common problem for large-scale datasets lies in data missing even from existing cases. These 'missing' data, which can include 'not known', 'information refused', 'information not yet sought', and 'other' non-completed, often account for a large proportion of the responses. Missing data are a particular concern when the data request information on an individual's ethnicity and occupational group. For example, in the 2005 ethnicity data for first-year UK domiciled undergraduate and postgraduate students reported by the Higher Education Statistics Agency (HESA), the ethnic group was missing for around 10% of cases (HESA 2006). Similarly, analysis of the data for applicants to teacher training courses in England and Wales in 2005 showed that other than 'white', 'missing' is officially the largest ethnic group (GTTR 2006). In fact, the unknown cases considerably outnumbered all minority ethnic groups combined.

Often the number of respondents identified as belonging to a minority ethnic group is quite small, leading to the volatility of small numbers when analysing trends over time or differences between groups. Similar issues concern data reported for occupational group. The data presented by UCAS on the occupational group of students applying for and being accepted to undergraduate programmes in British universities consistently reveal around 20% of cases whose social group is unknown (UCAS 2006). This has important implications now that the UCAS will pass these data directly to HEIs as part of widening participation initiatives (BBC 2007c). Of course, we have no way of knowing the occupational group of those students whose data are missing. Consequently, the high proportion of missing cases in an analysis using these variables could significantly bias the results being presented, even where the overall response rate is high. This means that any differences over time and place or between social or ethnic groups, needs to be robust enough to overcome this bias (Gorard et al. 2007).

In our recent secondary analysis of training statistics for initial teacher training in England, we found that around 8% of trainees failed to complete their postgraduate teacher training programme (Smith and Gorard 2007). The reasons recorded for why an individual might not complete their course do vary and are considered to be extremely important for those who monitor participation in teacher training and particularly the use of financial incentives. But the data on reasons for leaving training are missing for over half of the trainees with 'unknown' reasons given for a further 6% (Table 4.4). This leaves reasonable data for only around one-third of trainees and makes reliable evidence for the reasons trainees fail to complete initial teacher training impossible to discern from these data.

Although secondary data analysis has an important strength in enabling researchers to research small and hard-to-reach groups, care does need to be taken to ensure that sample sizes are robust and representative. For example, Connor (2001) used the Youth Cohort Study to try and identify a sample of students who had achieved the required grades but did not continue to higher education. In total, 600 such potential participants were identified, but the achieved sample size for the study was only 176 (29%). The problems in identifying those who opt out completely from post-compulsory education was further highlighted in this study when it emerged that 36% of the students previously thought to be non-participants had actually returned to education, possibly after taking a year out. This meant that this study was able to identify only 63 out of a possible 600 students who so far as the

Table 4.4 Reasons for leaving ITT courses

	N	%
Academic failure	374	4
Transferred to other HEI	21	0.2
Health reasons	186	2
Death	12	0.1
Financial reasons	59	0.7
Other personal reasons	2307	27
Written off after lapse of time	49	0.6
Exclusion	18	0.2
Gone into employment	98	1
Other	426	5
Unknown	482	6
Missing	4450	52
Total	**8482**	**100**

Source: Smith and Gorard 2007

researchers could tell did not participate in higher education in spite of the fact that they had achieved the required grades.

Ethical considerations when using secondary data

One advantage of secondary data analysis is that it doesn't require the researcher to collect new data. In practical terms, it means that it is not necessary to go through the many steps that are increasingly required in order to obtain ethical approval for research, a particular advantage for undergraduate and masters'-level dissertation study. But this does not mean that research involving secondary data analysis is necessarily free of ethical consideration. In particular, there is the notion of informed consent and the problems with using data for a purpose other than that for which they were collected and for which the respondent did not necessarily agree. Although survey data and other secondary data may be anonymised, it does not mean that the moral obligations that would hold for any researcher gathering ethnographic or interview data are absent when secondary data are used. Surveys in particular involve an interviewer entering the home and perhaps asking sensitive questions and establishing a rapport of trust with the respondent. However, the advantage of structured interviews, in this respect, is that the respondent can choose not to answer questions (Dale et al. 1988).

A somewhat broader ethical consideration concerns the type of information that is collected in research, in particular in government-sponsored surveys. Here the questions asked in these surveys reflect issues of political as well as contemporary interest. As Neuman (2003) argues, official statistics are 'social and political products' (p. 328), and such assumptions guide the data collection and categorisation process, and dictate which data we collect. In this way, the collection of official statistics brings new attention to an issue that might not have existed before. But of course, these same processes also dictate *any* data that researchers will collect. While using secondary data can bypass some of the ethical considerations that preoccupy researchers conducing more in-depth work, this does not mean that ethical issues are not relevant. Rather, the secondary researcher has an ethical responsibility to respect the data in their possession and not to misuse them. Of course, on the ethical plus side, secondary data analysis is an unobtrusive research method and its use ensures that no further intrusion into the homes and lives of the respondent is required.

Using the 2005 General Household Survey to examine patterns in the ownership of consumer durables

This section applies the questions we have discussed in the first part of this chapter to a worked example which uses the 2005 General Household Survey to examine the ownership of consumer durable items. We begin by describing how to locate a suitable dataset before considering practical issues such as data collection, sampling and response rates and the management of variables. The questions, definitions and variables that are shown here all come from the files which accompany the GHS dataset.

Locating a dataset

A good place to start your search for a dataset is with the ESRC Question Bank (see Appendix 1 for more details). It is possible to search the Question Bank by looking for a particular survey, or as in the example here, by searching through the topic menu. Using the topic menu leads you to an alphabetic list of topics, clicking on the 'Housing and Household Amenities' link takes you to a list of four potential surveys that contain questions pertaining to the ownership of household durables (Slide 4.1, scroll down to see household durables section). These are the British Household Panel Study, the General Household Survey, the Expenditure and Food Survey and the Family Resources Survey. The example here looks at data from the General Household Survey.

Once you have selected the study on which you will base your secondary analysis, the Question Bank provides links to further information which, in the case of the General Household Survey, is available from the Office for National Statistics and the UK Data Archive. Having located a

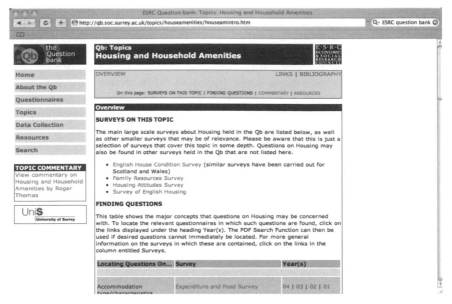

Slide 4.1 ESRC Question bank: Housing and Household Amenities databank

potential dataset, the next step is to find out about the background to the survey: its aims, its sponsors and procedures for data collection, sampling and so on. If you are interesting in looking at the aggregate data for this survey (that is data that have already been analysed and that are presented in publications such as *Living in Britain*) then background details of this nature will appear in the publication's appendices.

For those working with the raw data, more detailed information is available when you download the documentation associated with a particular survey. In the case of the General Household Survey (GHS), you will need to log onto the Economic and Social Data Service website (see Appendices 1 and 3 for an introduction to this facility and guidance on setting up an account) and download the data files and documentation associated with the GHS (Slide 4.2).

There are around a dozen files associated with the 2005 version of the GHS. Downloading these files will provide you with all the information you need in order to assess the suitability of using the GHS to help answer your research questions. The documents available for download include the GHS questionnaire, summary report, response rates, as well as the actual dataset (see later for more details).

If you decide to download the data yourself, a useful place to start is with the GHS teaching datasets. Further details about the range of support available for users of the GHS are introduced in Appendix 1. Otherwise have a look at the ESDS GHS website (ESDS 2007a, 2007b).

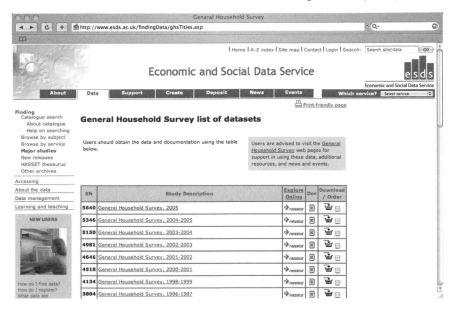

Slide 4.2 Downloading the General Household Survey datasets from ESDS

When you download the 2005 GHS datasets you will receive a large file containing folders which have the following documents:

- Two datafiles in the format of your choice (e.g. SPSS or Stata), one containing the household dataset only, the other the combined household and individual (client) data.
- GHS 2005 Overview Report.
- GHS 2005 Appendix A: Definitions and Terms.
- GHS 2005 Appendix B: Sample Design and Response.
- GHS 2005 Appendix C: Sampling Errors.
- GHS 2005 Appendix D: Weighting and Grossing.
- GHS 2005 Appendix E: Questionnaires and Show Cards.
- GHS 2005 Appendix F: Summary of Main Topics Included in GHS Questionnaires 1971–2005.
- EXCEL file containing Table of Questionnaire Changes 2004–2005.
- GHS 2005 Coding Frames.
- GHS 2005 Derived Variable Specifications.

The following section will use these documents to introduce the GHS and take you through the steps needed to prepare it for analysis. Although the discussion is focused mainly on the steps needed in order to analyse raw data from the GHS datasets, an understanding of variable names, questionnaire items, response rates and so on, is still important even if you are looking at the summary data from publications such as *Living in Britain*.

Background to the survey

The General Household Survey (GHS) is a continuous national survey of people living in private households, conducted annually by the Office for National Statistics (ONS). The main aim of the survey is to collect data on a range of core topics, covering household, family and individual information (ESDS 2007a, 2007b). It is sponsored by several government departments including the Department of Health, the Department for Work and Pensions and the Scottish Executive. The main GHS comprises a household questionnaire completed by the household reference person (see later for a definition) and an individual questionnaire completed by other members of the household who are aged 16 and over.

Data collection

Information for the 2005 GHS was collected by face-to-face interview with trained interviewers using computer-assisted personal interviewing (CAPI). Interviews were sought with all members of the sampled household aged 16 and over; proxy information for children was also obtained. To help maximise response rates for the GHS, a letter was sent in advance of an interviewer calling at an address. The letter briefly described the purpose and nature of the survey and prepares the recipient for a visit by the interviewer (Office for National Statistics 2007).

Sampling and response rates

In GHS 2005 16,560 addresses were sampled. The GHS aims to interview all adults aged 16 or over at every household at the sampled address. It uses a probability, stratified two-stage sample design. The main sample is drawn from postcode sectors, which are similar in size to wards and the secondary sampling units are addresses within those sectors (Office for National Statistics 2007: 1). Table 4.5 shows the outcome of visits to the addresses selected for the 2005 survey. Out of the 18,695 addresses that were selected, 17,184 were eligible and this produced a sample of 17,310 eligible households (as some addresses contained more than one household). Interviews (including proxy interviews) were carried out with every member of 11,980 households. In a further 291 households, interviews were conducted with some, but not all, members of the household. This produced a total of 12,271 full or partial interviews (Office for National Statistics 2007: 6).

Table 4.5 Sample of addresses and households, GHS 2005

Selected addresses	18,695
Ineligible addresses	
Demolished or derelict	
Used wholly for business purposes	1511
Empty	
Institutions	
Other ineligible	
No sample selected at address	
Address not traced	
Eligible addresses	17,184
Number of households at eligible addresses	17,310
Number of households where all individual interviews achieved (including proxies)	11,980
Number of households where some but not all individual interviews achieved	291

2005 data include last quarter of 2004/5 data due to survey change from financial year to calendar year.

Source: Office for National Statistics 2007: 7, Table B2

Variables and questionnaire items

The variables of interest in this example are ownership of consumer durables such as a home computer, a washing machine, a car, a colour television and a telephone. As well as selected household characteristics, namely, employment status, occupational group, gross annual income and number of school-aged children in the household. The best place to find out how these variables are measured is in the questionnaire that is available as an appendix in the documentation accompanying the dataset. In the GHS the questionnaire is available as *Appendix E: Questionnaires and Show Cards*. This document describes the questions and prompts that the interviewer used to elicit information from the respondents. Box 4.1 shows the questions associated with ownership of a home computer; similar questions were used for the other variables linked with consumer durables, although the car ownership questions are more detailed. The items in bold are the variable names as they appear in the datafile as this enables one to know exactly which question the variable is linked to.

Box 4.1 Use of home computer, GHS 2005

Now I'd like to ask you about various household items you may have – this gives us an indication of how living standards are changing.

Does your household have any of the following items in your (part of the) accommodation?

INCLUDE ITEMS STORED OR UNDER REPAIR.

INCLUDE ITEMS OWNED, RENTED OR ON LOAN.

IF ANY MEMBER POSSESSES AN ITEM, THE HOUSEHOLD POSSESSES IT.

Ask all households

47 Computer Home computer?

EXCLUDE: VIDEO GAMES

Yes 1
No 2

Ask if household does not have a home computer

(Computer = 2)

48 CompWhy (You said your household doesn't have a computer). Is that because you . . .

don't want one 1
would like one but cannot afford it 2
or is there some other reason? 3

Source: Office for National Statistics 2007: 10–12

The questions here are retrieved from the section of the household questionnaire which focuses on consumer durables. Extracts from the script are shown in Box 4.1, beginning with the interviewer reading a preamble.

A similar structure was used for questions relating to other consumer durables.

Definitions of variables
As indicated earlier, there are two datasets available for the 2005 GHS. The first contains information relating to the household and is derived from interviews with the household reference person (file name **ghs05_client_hhld**) and the second contains data derived from interviews with other household members (here labelled the **ghs05_client** file). A household is defined as: 'a single person or a group of people who have the address as their only or main residence and who either share one meal a day or share the living accommodation' (McCrossan 1991, cited in Office for National Statistics 2007: 6).

Similarly, the household reference person (HRP) is defined as the following:

- in households with a sole householder that person is the household reference person
- in households with joint householders the person with the highest income is taken as the household reference person
- if both householders have exactly the same income, the older is taken as the household reference person (Office for National Statistics 2007: 7).

In the Household database, the data that relate to an individual (for example, their economic activity or ethnicity) is linked only to the HRP. This might be problematic for variables such as ethnicity as the HRP may belong to a different ethnic group to other members of the household. If you are interested in the ethnic group of separate members of the household, then it is better to use the Client dataset.

In this example the following variables were used to elicit background information on the respondents.

Occupational group
Some of the background information that is presented for analysis in the GHS datafile was not collected directly from the respondents. Instead, the variable is a composite of several different questions which were then put together to make a new (or derived) variable. One example is questions on occupational group where several questions about the nature of the respondent's job are combined to give one variable. This single variable is often all that is presented in the analysis files. From April 2001 the National Statistics Socio-economic Classification (NS-SEC) was introduced for all official statistics and surveys, which replaced previous classifications of social class and means that comparisons with data categorised using older occupational and social categories has to be discontinued. The GHS Household file presents three different versions of the NS-SEC classifications. For example, there is a three-class version (**hrpsec3**) comprising:

- managerial and professional occupations
- intermediate occupations
- routine and manual occupations.

There is also a five-group (**hrpsec5**) or an eight-group classification (**hrpsec8**) comprising:

- large employers and higher managerial occupations
- higher professional occupations
- lower managerial and professional occupations
- intermediate occupations
- small employers and own account workers
- lower supervisory and technical occupations
- semi-routine occupations
- routine occupations
- never worked and long-term unemployed.

The number of categories that you use depends on the level of complexity you wish to add to your data and also the substantive and theoretical interest that you bring to your research questions.

School-aged children
In the Household questionnaire, the HRP is asked to list all the people living in the household. This information is used to produce a variable for the number of school-aged children in the household, as a question about school-aged children does not actually appear in the household questionnaire. This variable is derived from other information on the questionnaire, such as number and age of dependent children and appears as variable (**schagech**) in the main datafile.

Employment status
This is presented in the datafile as the variable **hrpilo** and labelled as 'economic status'. It is a derived variable that has data in the following categories:

- not available, economic status not known
- child
- working (including unpaid)
- government scheme with employment
- government scheme at college
- unemployed (ILO definition)
- other unemployed
- permanently unable to work
- retired
- keeping house

- student
- other inactive.

Definitions for these variables are available in a separate appendix (Office for National Statistics 2007). For example, the GHS uses the International Labour Organisation (ILO) definition of unemployment. This classifies anyone as unemployed if:

> [H]e or she was out of work and had looked for work in the four weeks before interview, or would have but for temporary sickness or injury, and was available to start work in the two weeks after interview. (Office for National Statistics 2007: 4)

Household income

In the worked example shown here, household income is represented by the *usual gross weekly household income*. In addition, a range of variables are also given in the main dataset and represent both the actual and grouped weekly income for the HRP (and partner). The definition of total income for an individual refers to:

> [I]ncome at the time of the interview, and is obtained by summing the components of earnings, benefits, pensions, dividends, interest and other regular payments. Gross weekly income of employees and those on benefits is calculated if interest and dividends are the only components missing. If the last pay packet/cheque was unusual, for example in including holiday pay in advance or a tax refund, the respondent is asked for usual pay. No account is taken of whether a job is temporary or permanent. Payments made less than weekly are divided by the number of weeks covered to obtain a weekly figure. Usual gross weekly household income is the sum of usual gross weekly income for all adults in the household. (Office for National Statistics 2007: 9)

Missing data

Missing data are also an important concern and it is up to the secondary analyst to judge whether the amount of missing data jeopardises the reliability of the results. If you are working from the main dataset, the easiest way to find out how many data are missing is to run a simple frequency calculation. (If you were to analyse this in SPSS you would need to select the following sequence of commands starting on the main toolbar with **Analyse → Descriptive Statistics → Frequency** and then placing the variable of interest into the main box.) For example, for the variable gross weekly income, data were missing for a range of reasons from around 11% of households (Table 4.6).

Table 4.6 Missing responses for gross weekly income variable

	N	%
Not available	975	8
Data refused income	370	3
Data received	11,457	89
Total	**12,802**	**100**

Source: Office for National Statistics 2007

Summary

This chapter has introduced some of the practical considerations for selecting a dataset for secondary analysis. These were then illustrated by a brief worked example, which assessed the suitability of the General Household Survey for a secondary analysis of ownership of consumer durables. Of course, the key determinant of whether a dataset is suitable for secondary analysis is its fit with your research questions. Here I have tried to demonstrate some practical steps for accessing the dataset, examining the questionnaire for question wording and definitions of variables, as well as examining response rates, sampling strategies and missing information. The majority of the information needed to undertake this assessment is available in the reports that accompany the raw datasets or, in the case of aggregate data, this can usually be found in the appendices that are attached to the publication. The final decision regarding suitability of the dataset, however, lies with the researcher and their assessment of the fit between dataset and research questions.

Part  II

Part II will apply what we have learnt about locating and using secondary data by taking the reader through a series of worked examples. The aim of this is twofold. The first is to show the reader the wealth and diversity of secondary sources that can be used to answer a series of substantive research questions. The second aim is to introduce some of the data management techniques that can be helpful when analysing very large and complex datasets. Chapter 5 provides a number of short examples that use aggregate secondary data, that is, data that have already been analysed and are now presented in summary form. The examples used in Chapter 5 include an introduction to using the data management tools: CASWEB and NOMIS; the use of summary data from several government surveys; as well as government administrative data to reflect social inequalities. Chapter 6 describes the secondary analysis of raw data from two large-scale British surveys: the Youth Cohort Study and the British Social Attitudes Survey. While Chapter 7 has a more international focus, with its first example using administrative secondary data produced by California and its second providing an exploratory analysis of the PISA study.

Chapters 6 and 7 place a primary emphasis on techniques that are useful for managing large-scale datasets, in other words, they seek to encourage effective data husbandry by guiding the user through the stages needed to prepare data for analysis. Techniques that are described include accessing datasets and deleting un-needed cases and variables. The methods of analysing the data used in Chapter 6 are largely descriptive, while in Chapter 7 two regression models are developed. However, the focus on methods of analysis in these two chapters is secondary – there are many excellent books to guide novice and experienced reader alike through the arithmetic and statistical highlights of analysing numeric data. The following chapters simply present an introduction to managing the data prior to analysis, with supplementary guides to data management given in Appendices 2 and 3. Despite these relatively modest aims, effective data management or data husbandry is not to be overlooked – it is the foundation of good secondary analysis. Spending time preparing and familiarising yourself with the data rather than rushing headlong into analysis can help avoid the abstracted empiricism, button pushing or data-dredging habits that are so often criticised in numeric research.

There are several ways in which the reader may wish to use the chapters in Part II. They may be read as one might read the chapters in a conventional book: some of the substantive findings to emerge from the worked examples are actually quite interesting. Alternatively, the reader might wish to download the data and follow through the stages in preparation and analysis themselves. If you do decide to take this approach, then I suggest that you use the website that accompanies this book to help locate the datasets. Finally, the chapters may be used as a reference text when using specific datasets or management techniques. For example, if you are interested in using the British Social Attitudes Survey, a worked example is given in Chapter 6 or if you wish to download PISA, instructions appear in Chapter 7.

Sure Start and leisure habits: secondary analysis of aggregate data

This chapter describes how aggregate secondary data can be used in social research. By aggregate data we mean data that have already been analysed and that are now available in summary form. Here we use five examples to illustrate both the range of aggregate secondary data that are available to researchers and the ways in which they might be used in social research, both in their own right but also when used in combination with other approaches. Using aggregate data in this way is probably the most straightforward way of using secondary data in social research: no particular numeric expertise is required and many of the data are readily available in electronic publications or in hard copy. One of the strengths of using aggregate data in this way is their value in providing a context to in-depth work as well as enabling researchers to combine data from a range of sources. The first two examples demonstrate how to use the data-handling facilities CASWEB and NOMIS. Both facilities are introduced in Appendix 1, but this chapter takes you through the step-by-step process for retrieving your data. The third example uses the published results from several large-scale surveys to consider the leisure and lifestyle habits of adults living in the UK. Examples four and five use government social, economic, educational and health administrative data to look at inequalities in the education of looked-after children and regional social inequalities in South Wales.

Using the National Census CASWEB facility

Who lives in Sure Start areas?

This example describes the use of census data to characterise the local population of an area which is the focus of an ethnographic study. This in-depth study is concerned with examining the interactions between users and providers who are involved in one Sure Start children's centre in one English city. Sure Start is a government intervention aimed at providing integrated support for families by bringing together local childcare, early education, health and family services. Its range of pro-grammes is primarily targeted at families living in disadvantaged areas in England. Central to the Sure Start programme are the Sure Start chil-dren's centres, of which 2500 are planned by 2008. Children's centres provide multidisciplinary support to families with children under the age of 5; services include antenatal support, links with job centres as well as early learning and childcare provision (Sure Start 2007). The ethno-graphic study that is being introduced here will involve a longitudinal case study of the experiences of the practitioners and users of one chil-dren's centre in a large English city. In order to situate the study in the wider context of who might access the service in terms of their social and economic characteristics, a useful place to start is with the UK National Census data. In this example, we look at data from the 2001 National Census (the most recent at time of writing). These data are accessed using the CASWEB facility which provides aggregate data on a wide range of variables collected in the National Census. (For details on the National Census and CASWEB, see Appendix 1.)

The section that follows takes the reader through the step-by-step process for retrieving data from CASWEB. Although a large range of data are available, in this example we consider only three variables that we use to describe the area in which the Sure Start Centre is located: ethnic group, economic activity and household composition.

Retrieving data using CASWEB
CASWEB is relatively straightforward to use and step-by-step instruc-tions are provided on the screen in order to lead you through each stage in retrieving your data. The following steps outline the procedure for using CASWEB to produce data on the ethnic composition of the local Sure Start area and the wider city. The results that we retrieve from CASWEB are shown later in various tables. The CASWEB homepage can be accessed from http://casweb.mimas.ac.uk/.

Step 1
When you access the CASWEB homepage, you will be asked to log on using your ATHENS password. You will then be directed to the CASWEB homepage (Slide 5.1).

Slide 5.1 The CASWEB homepage

Step 2
Once you have successfully logged in, you will need to select the relevant census dataset – here we are interested in the 2001 Aggregate Statistics Datasets. Note the caveats about errors associated with this dataset.

Step 3
This step requires you to define your study area. You will be led through a series of stages in which you select progressively smaller geographical areas. For example: from country (e.g. England) to Government Office Region (e.g. northwest) to county or unitary authority (e.g. Greater Manchester) and so on until you reach the smallest geographical area: the *output area*. You can stop at any of these geographical areas by clicking on the **select output area** button. Slide 5.2 shows the different Government Office Regions. In this example we used data at the CAS-WEB ward level.

Step 4
Once you have selected your output level, you will confirm your selection in section **B select output geography**. You will then be taken to

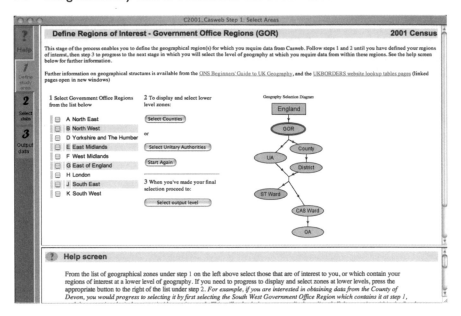

Slide 5.2 Selecting geographical regions using CASWEB

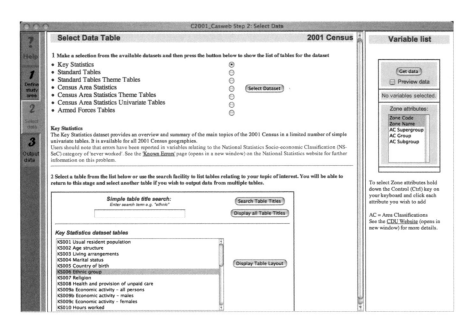

Slide 5.3 Selecting the ethnic group dataset using CASWEB

the **Select Data Table** window. This allows you to select the dataset that you are interested in. Here we are interested in ethnic group composition in the **Key Statistics** dataset; these options are shown as selected in Slide 5.3. The next step is to click on the **Display Table Layout** button.

Step 5
Slide 5.4 allows you to select the variables from the ethnic group dataset that you are interested in. Here we have selected all variables. The next step is to click on the **Add variables to data selection** button. This moves the variables across to the panel on the right-hand side – labelled as **Variable list**. The variables will appear with their numeric labels; they can be renamed using the **Rename** button. The first five variables in the right-hand panel in Slide 5.4 have been renamed.

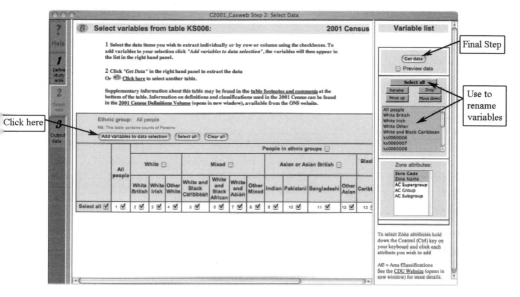

Slide 5.4 Selecting and renaming ethnic groups using CASWEB

Step 6
The final step is to retrieve the output data, which can be downloaded in Excel format. To do this you need to click on the **Get data** button. A new window will appear where you can name the new file and click the **Execute query** to export the data to a file which can be opened in Excel.

Findings

The data presented in Tables 5.1 to 5.4 were retrieved from CASWEB using the steps outlined here. It is able to provide us with some elementary contextual information about the local area that is covered by the Sure Start children's centre. Table 5.1 shows us that the majority ethnic group in the Sure Start location is Indian (63%), compared with a white British majority in the city as a whole (60%). Only around one-quarter of residents in the Sure Start area are of white British origin. The ethnic profile of the other residents of the Sure Start area suggests a predominately Asian population.

Table 5.1 Ethnic group composition, Sure Start location and city

	Sure Start location		City	
	N	%	*N*	%
White British	2555	25	169,456	60
White Irish	66	0.6	3602	1
White Other	80	0.8	5681	2
White and Black Caribbean	91	0.9	2841	1
White and Black African	10	0.1	539	0.2
White and Asian	114	1	1908	0.7
White and Other	49	0.5	1218	0.4
Indian	6504	63	72,033	26
Pakistani	125	1	4276	1
Bangladeshi	61	0.6	1926	0.7
Asian Other	411	4	5516	2
Caribbean	99	1	4610	2
African	56	0.5	3432	1
Black Other	23	0.2	553	0.2
Chinese	25	0.2	1426	0.5
Other ethnic group	28	0.2	904	0.3
Total	**10,297**	**100**	**279,921**	**100**

Source: Census 2001

Sure Start children's centres have a particular focus on improving early years' provision in disadvantaged areas. Arguably, one characteristic of a disadvantaged area is the proportion of the working-age population who are economically inactive. As we can see from Table 5.2, the proportion of economically inactive adults aged 16–74 is, at 43%, slightly higher than that for the city as a whole. Among those adults who are unemployed, the largest proportion have been unemployed long term, although the proportion of unemployed adults of all categories in the Sure Start area is similar to that of the city as a whole (Table 5.3).

Examining the composition of households in the Sure Start location

Table 5.2 Economic activity of adult population, Sure Start location and city

	Sure Start location		City	
	N	%	N	%
Economically active	4122	57	122,875	62
Economically inactive	3050	43	76,047	38
Total aged 16–74	**7172**	**100**	**198,922**	**100**

Source: Census 2001

Table 5.3 Categories of unemployed adults, Sure Start location and city

	Sure Start location		City	
	N	%	N	%
Unemployed aged 16–24	84	28	2654	33
Unemployed aged 50+	63	21	1537	19
Never worked	36	12	1070	13
Long-term unemployed	115	39	2861	35
Total unemployed	**298**	**100**	**8122**	**100**

Source: Census 2001

Table 5.4 Household composition, Sure Start location and city

	Sure Start location		City	
	N	%	N	%
One-person households	972	27	36,179	32
All pensioners	225	6	7816	7
Households with no children	333	9	14,463	13
Households with dependent children	1549	42	36,513	33
Households with no dependent children	380	10	9599	9
All students	30	0.8	1814	2
Other	169	5	4764	4
Total	**3658**	**100**	**111,148**	**100**

Source: Census 2001

suggests that, compared with the city as a whole, this area has fewer one-person households but more households with dependent children (Table 5.4).

This brief exemplar gives some indication of the types of family that might be using the Sure Start children's centre and the extent to which they are representative of the wider city. Data of this type would be very useful for providing a context to the more in-depth data that would be derived from ethnographic accounts of life at the children's centres. This sort of secondary data is also useful for providing a framework for drawing the sample for a study. For example, in the scenario just examined, if researchers wished to interview a sample of users or potential users of the children's centres, they might wish to ensure that their sample is representative of the local population. One way of doing this would be to ensure that a representative proportion of people of Indian origin were identified for inclusion in the study.

An alternative source of local area data which would be useful for providing a local context for in-depth work is the Office for National Statistics' *Neighbourhood Statistics* resource (see Appendix 1 for more details).

Using NOMIS

Many of the data produced by the large government sponsored surveys are available as raw data in huge datasets that can be complex to manipulate, especially for novice researchers. However, access to these data is facilitated by the use of electronic data management facilities similar to CASWEB, discussed earlier. In this second example, we use the NOMIS facility to look at income and employment trends among different social groups. NOMIS allows access to labour force data from a range of different sources; it is introduced in Appendix 1. In this example, we first use NOMIS to retrieve data on income trends for men and women, before using it to explore occupation patterns among different ethnic groups. The NOMIS facility homepage can be found at https://www.nomisweb.co.uk/Default.asp.

What are the recent trends in annual income between men and women?

In this first example, we consider salary gaps between men and women in the workplace. Contemporary concerns about growing achievement gaps between male and female pupils, particularly in the context of 'moral panics' about boys' underachievement in school, is often countered by evidence that suggests that despite attaining lower examination grades in school, men still earn more than women in the workplace (for example, Arnot et al. 1999). This assertion can be examined by looking at the variation in gross annual earnings between male and female full-time workers.

The dataset used to examine this variation was retrieved through NOMIS – a website that offers access to detailed and up-to-date labour market statistics from a range of sources for local areas of the UK. NOMIS is able to retrieve data in summary or more detailed format. In the analysis described here, the WIZARD QUERY option (shown in Slide 5.5) was selected. In a series of short stages, this takes you through the process of selecting a dataset and specifying your choice of geographic location, key variables and the format for presenting the data.

Slide 5.5 The NOMIS facility homepage

Selecting the **Wizard query** option allows you to select your datasets either from a list of popular datasets or from a list of all datasets that are organised by theme. In this example, the dataset used was the **Annual Survey of Hours and Earnings Workplace analysis 1998–2006** selected from **all datasets by theme** option (Slide 5.6).

The programme will then take you through the seven stages needed to define the parameters for the dataset and to export the data to an Excel file or other format. For example, Slide 5.7 shows the selection of full-time workers.

Findings
Figure 5.1 shows the variation in median gross annual earnings between male and female full-time workers in England and Wales. Full-time workers are defined here as those who work more than 30 paid hours per

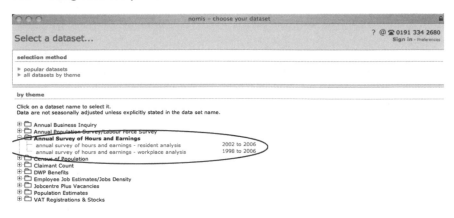

Slide 5.6 Selecting a dataset from the list of all NOMIS datasets

Slide 5.7 Selecting worker characteristics using NOMIS

week or those in teaching professions working 25 paid hours or more per week. The earnings information collected here relates to gross pay before tax, national insurance or other deductions and excludes payments in kind.

In the 8-year period for which data are available, we see male gross annual earnings increase by £6047 to £26,000 in 2006. In absolute terms, female earnings increase less over the same period from £14,740 in 1999 to £20,233 in 2006. However, female earnings do appear to be increasing at a faster rate than those of men: showing a 37% increase between 1999 and 2006, compared with 30% for men. In summary then, men in full-

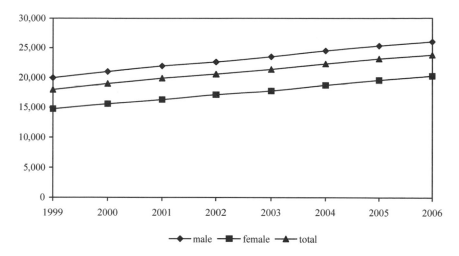

Figure 5.1 Variation in gross annual earnings, male and female full-time employees, 1999–2006

Source: Annual survey of hours and earnings, workplace analysis, 1999–2006

time employment continue to earn more than their female counterparts; however, the gap between them, in terms of median annual gross income does appear to be closing gradually. Notice however that this analysis only considers those in full-time employment; an interesting next stage would be to look at patterns of income for part-time workers.

What is the occupational class profile of the main ethnic groups in the UK?

Alongside contemporary concerns about male underachievement, we also have a 'crisis account' of the failure of students, usually boys, from various ethnic minority groups (for example, Gillborn and Youdell 2000). Although the debate in recent years has become more nuanced to focus on certain ethnic groups, particularly boys of black Caribbean or Bangladeshi origin, rather than young people of Chinese or Indian origin, for example (DfES 2003). There are also concerns that such issues as racism, low expectations, disaffection and exclusion will limit the opportunities of these young people to engage and succeed in education. One additional explanation for the presence of achievement gaps between young people from white and some ethnic minority groups emphasises the link between ethnicity and poverty (Gorard 2000; Smith 2005a). Our second demonstration of the potential of the NOMIS facility considers this assertion by using data from the Annual Population Survey to examine the relationship between employment, occupational category and ethnic group (see Appendix 1 for an introduction to this survey). The same stages were used to retrieve the data as described earlier, but the Annual Population Survey 2006 was accessed through the list of *popular datasets*. NOMIS will then take you through the six steps needed to retrieve the data.

Findings
One thing to note about the ethnic categories presented here is that they are relatively broad and do not differentiate between the different categories that exist within the broad description of 'black or black British', for example. Even so, it is apparent that there are large differences between the unemployment rate for adults of white or Indian origin and those of the other main ethnic groups. Note the relatively high unemployment rate among the Pakistani/Bangladeshi and black or black British communities and, in particular, for women of Pakistani/Bangladeshi origin (Table 5.5).

Table 5.5 Unemployment rate of 16+ age group, according to ethnic group, England and Wales

		Total	% unemployed
White	All	23,956,700	5
	Male	12,828,600	5
	Female	11,128,100	4
Non-white	All	2,435,300	12
	Male	1,394,600	12
	Female	1,040,700	11
Mixed	All	196,400	12
	Male	95,600	13*
	Female	100,900	11*
Indian	All	592,400	8
	Male	346,800	8
	Female	245,600	7
Pakistani/Bangladeshi	All	369,800	16
	Male	265,600	15
	Female	104,200	19*
Black or Black British	All	625,400	13
	Male	312,500	15
	Female	312,900	11
Other ethnic group	All	651,200	11
	Male	374,100	12
	Female	277,100	10

* Denotes 'reasonably precise' (as opposed to precise) estimates.

Source: Annual Population Survey, October 2005–September 2006

For workers aged 16 and over, the Annual Population Survey can also provide information on the occupational categories of the main ethnic groups. The data for 2006 are given in Table 5.6.

Table 5.6 Occupational categories of workers aged 16+, according to ethnic group, England and Wales

	White	Mixed	Indian	Pakistani/ Bangladeshi	Black/ Black British	Other
Managers and senior officials	15	9	16	13	8	14
Professional	13	11	20	12	10	17
Associate professional and technical	14	20	13	8	18	15
Administrative and secretarial	12	11	12	9	12	9
Skilled trades	11	8	5	7	7	8
Personal service	8	11	5	6	15	8
Sales and consumer services	7	11	10	13	9	9
Process, plant and machine operatives	7	6	8	17	7	6
Elementary occupations	11	13	11	13	14	14

Source: Annual Population Survey, October 2005–September 2006

As we can see, there are quite large variations in the occupational categories of workers from the different main ethnic groups. Fewer than 10% of workers of mixed or black/black British origin are employed as *managers and senior officials* – the largest occupational category for white workers (15%). Notice also that relatively few workers from the minority ethnic groups are employed in *skilled trades*, compared with workers who describe themselves as white. Among Pakistani and Bangladeshi workers the largest occupational category is *process, plant and machines operatives*, whereas most workers from the Indian community work in the *professions* or as *managers and senior officials* (36% in total).

Our analysis does seem to support the assertion that young people from the lowest achieving ethnic groups, in terms of academic performance, are also those who are most likely to be unemployed or, if they are in employment, are working in jobs which are likely to be lower paid. Understanding this relationship is important. Are these individuals unemployed or working in lower paid jobs because of relatively lower academic performance or is lower academic performance a consequence of growing up in poorer homes where adults may have been unemployed or in low-wage employment, for several generations? The causal patterns between the two and the reasons and consequences behind them are arguably the most important questions that social scientists seek to answer. Secondary data analysis can provide the background data on which to base such hypotheses, it can help understand how patterns develop over time or between different groups and different contexts. But it cannot establish causation – that is where the more in-depth work would begin.

Government-sponsored surveys

Leisure and lifestyle habits of UK adults

Appendix 1 lists a wide range of government-sponsored large-scale surveys each with great potential for secondary analysis. In this example, we consider the summary results from three government surveys: the 2000 and 2005 Time Use Survey, the General Household Survey and the National Survey of Culture, Leisure and Sport. Once again, we are only considering aggregate data, that is, data that have already been analysed and the results presented in summary form. Our focus is on one publication that brings together data from a wide range of surveys and other administrative sources: *Social Trends*. The data presented here are taken from the results presented in the *Social Trends* section: *Lifestyle and Social Participation*, in order to answer the question: What are the reported leisure and lifestyle habits of adults living in the UK?

Concerns over the rising trend in adult and child obesity with its consequences for one's health, as well as the food industry, the fashion and leisure industry and the economy are well documented in the media and elsewhere (for example BBC 2006). Attempts to encourage us to eat healthily and to take more exercise have become a regular concern of reality television programmes, as well as the government, which advises that adults exercise for 150 minutes each week or 30 minutes a day for 5 days a week. But how much exercise do adults in the UK undertake and what are their leisure and lifestyle habits more generally?

The 2000 Time Use Survey was the first major UK survey to monitor the amount of time spent by the population on various activities. Adults aged 16 and over in a nationally representative selection of private households were asked to keep a detailed diary of how they spent their time on a selected day during the week and at the weekend. In total, 14,100 individuals were requested to complete two time use diaries (28,200 altogether), by the end of the study 21,000 diaries had been

Table 5.7 Time spent on main activities, according to sex, 2000 and 2005

Activity	Hours and minutes per day 2000		Hours and minutes per day 2005	
	Males	Females	Males	Females
Sleep and resting	8:23	8:33	8.47	9:06
Leisure				
Watching TV and video/DVD, reading and listening to radio/music	3:17	2:52	3:13	2:51
Social life and entertainment	1:16	1:33	1:22	1:32
Hobbies and games	0:26	0:16	0:37	0:23
Sport	0:18	0:11	0:13	0:07
All leisure	**5:17**	**4:52**	**5:25**	**4:53**
Employment and study[1]	4:17	2:42	4:00	2:46
Housework and childcare	2:17	4:03	1:56	3:32
Personal care[2]	2:07	2:19	2:05	2:07
Travel	1:28	1:21	1:32	1:22
Other	0:09	0:10	0:13	0:15

Data refer to adults aged 16 and over.

1 Includes voluntary work and meetings.

2 Includes eating, drinking, washing and dressing.

Source: 2000 UK Time Use Survey (Office for National Statistics 2005: Table 13.1) and 2005 UK Time Use Survey

completed (Office for National Statistics 2004). The results from the 2000 Time Use Survey are available in summary format from the ONS Time Use Survey webpage or in publications such as *Social Trends*. In addition, the full datasets can also be downloaded free of charge from the Office for National Statistics. In 2005 a follow-up Time Use Survey was undertaken, covering many of the same topics as the original survey, which enables researchers to identify whether time use has changed over the intervening 5-year period (Lader et al. 2006).

There are some interesting differences between time spent on main activities between 2000 and 2005 (see Table 5.7). For example, women continue to spend more time on housework and childcare than men, although the amount of time spent on this activity has decreased over the last 5 years. Adults aged 16 and over also appear to be spending slightly less time doing sport than 5 years ago and certainly less than the

Table 5.8 Adult participation in a sport, game or physical activity, according to age (%)

	1987	1990/91	1996/97	2002/03
16–19	86	87	86	77
20–24	77	81	81	69
25–29	74	78	77	70
30–44	71	73	73	67
45–59	56	63	63	59
60–69	47	54	55	50
70 and over	26	31	31	30
All aged 16 and over	61	65	64	59

Participation means in the four weeks before interview.

Physical activity includes walking two miles or more for recreational purposes.

Source: General Household Survey (Office for National Statistics 2005: Table 13.8)

government's recommended 30 minutes per day. The amount of time spent on all leisure activities is similar across the 5 years; men continue to have more leisure time than women, but this could be balanced by the slightly longer time that women spend sleeping.

Data from the General Household Survey (GHS) (see Appendix 1 for more detail) can tell us something about the extent to which adults of different ages participate in a sport or other physical activity. The findings from subsequent waves of this survey can also tell us how much habits have changed over extended periods of time. Although the GHS datasets can be downloaded for further analysis, the results described here are taken from aggregate summaries of the data that appeared in *Social Trends*.

Since 1987 the percentage of adults participating in a sport, game or other physical exercise has decreased for all age groups except those aged over 45 (Table 5.8). Young people aged 16–19 remain the most active age group, although in common with overall figures, the number reporting taking regular exercise declined from 86% in 1987 to 77% in 2002/03.

When considering the type of exercise that people engage in, clear differences between gender and age begin to emerge (Table 5.9). For example, swimming, while popular for both sexes, is the most popular form of exercise reported by women, while swimming, going to the gym, cycling, outdoor football and snooker/pool/billiards are all equally popular among men. Younger men are particularly likely to take part in playing outdoor football and snooker/pool/billiards. Women of most ages enjoy similar types of activity, with going to the gym, aerobics-style exercise and swimming remaining popular through to middle age.

This example used aggregate data from three government-sponsored

Table 5.9 Top 10 sports, games and physical activities among adults, according to sex, 2005–2006 (%)

Activity	Men					Women				
	16–24	25–44	45–65	65+	All	16–24	25–44	45–64	65+	All
Swimming or diving	16	18	10	5	13	23	24	16	6	18
Health, fitness, gym	22	18	9	4	13	19	16	13	3	13
Recreational cycling	16	16	11	4	12	8	9	6	1	6
Snooker, pool, billiards	34	13	7	4	13	12	3	1	—	3
Keep fit, aerobics, dance	4	4	4	3	4	13	12	10	5	10
Outdoor football	43	14	3	—	12	5	1	1	—	1
Golf, pitch and putting	10	9	9	9	9	1	1	2	1	1
Jogging, cross-country, road running	11	10	4	—	7	6	5	2	—	3
Tenpin bowling	9	4	3	1	4	8	4	2	—	3
Darts	16	6	3	1	6	4	2	1	1	2

Physical activity excludes walking.

Estimates are based on interviews conducted over a 9-month period (mid-July 2005 to mid-April 2006).

Source: Taking part: The National Survey of Culture, Leisure and Sport, Department for Culture, Media and Sport (Office for National Statistics 2007: Table 13.13)

surveys to describe contemporary patterns in the leisure and sporting habits of adults in the UK. The results suggest that overall adults devote less time to exercise than the government recommends and that while between half and two-thirds of the adult population does enjoy some form of regular exercise, rates have fallen slightly since the 1990s. Men and women enjoy different types of exercise, with men enjoying the broadest range of activities. Swimming is popular among both sexes, regardless of age group and similar proportions of men and women visit the gym, although, perhaps unsurprisingly for anyone who has visited their local leisure centre, women are much more likely to participate in aerobics-style exercise. Interestingly, the popular female sporting activities are enjoyed by women of all ages; the only exception to this is snooker/pool/billiards, which is more popular among younger women.

The summary data presented in publications such as *Social Trends* are a useful source of information for those interested in understanding and monitoring patterns and trends in society as a whole and also for those interested in providing a context for more in-depth work. The ease with which such data can be retrieved and used makes them an ideal source of secondary data for novice researchers or those with limited skill and/or interest in exploring the raw data.

Government administrative records (part 1)

Characteristics of looked-after children

In this example we consider what government administrative records can tell us about the numbers and characteristics of children who are looked after by local authorities in the English regions. The data used here were retrieved from government administrative data made available from the Department for Children, Schools and Families (DCSF) Research & Statistics website (Slide 5.8).

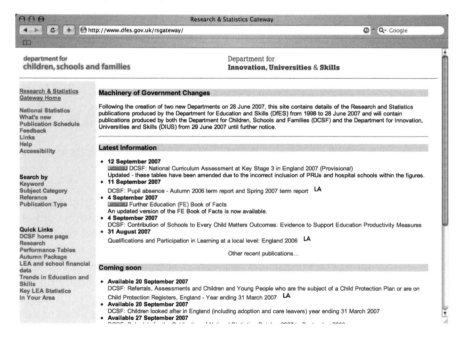

Slide 5.8 Department for Children, Schools and Families: Research & Statistics Gateway

If you click on the **Search by Keyword** option from the left-hand column, a new window will open. This will list around 200 keywords, from *A-levels* to *Youth detention centres*. In this example, the keyword **child protection** was selected allowing access to a series of publications and internet-based resources on the characteristics and provision for looked-after children. The findings presented here were taken from an internet-based resource that provided data at the regional level on the characteristics of children who were looked after by local authorities in the year ending 31 March 2006 (DfES 2007b).

Findings
A child is considered to be 'looked after' by a local authority if he or she is placed in their care by a court (under a care order) or provided with accommodation by the authority's social services department for more than 24 hours (DfES 2007b: Appendix A). In the decade between 1996 and 2006, the number of looked-after children has increased from 46 per 10,000 of the population in 1996 to 55 per 10,000 in 2006 (DfES 2007b) (see Figure 5.2).

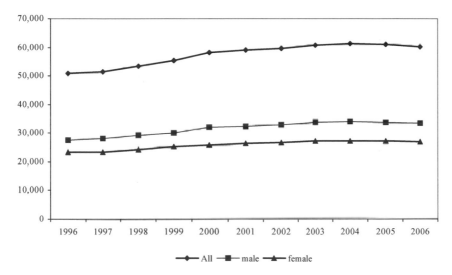

Figure 5.2 Looked-after children according to gender, 1996–2006 (England)
Source: DfES 2007b

In terms of educational benchmarks, the attainment of looked-after children lags behind that of all children in the same age group. The extent of the difference can be seen in Table 5.10. In each English region, looked-after children lag behind at the crucial foundation learning stages, for example in the Key Stage 1 reading task taken during National Curriculum year 2, when children are typically 6–7 years of age, only just

Table 5.10 Eligibility and performance of looked-after children in Key Stage 1 tasks and tests, compared with all children, 12 months ending 30 September 2006

Local authority	Looked-after children eligible for KS 1 assessments	% attaining level 2[1] or above in each task or test					
		Reading task		Writing task		mathematics task/test	
		Looked-after children	All children[2]	Looked-after children	All children[2]	Looked-after children	all children[2]
England	1700	57	84	52	81	65	90
North East	75	64	85	56	82	68	90
North West	340	56	84	49	81	65	90
Yorkshire and Humberside	200	61	83	52	80	66	89
East Midlands	105	56	85	55	83	61	91
West Midlands	225	54	83	49	80	61	89
East England	175	57	86	51	83	61	91
London	280	59	82	58	79	68	89
Southeast	195	59	85	51	82	68	92
Southwest	120	53	85	46	82	60	91

[1] Target level for age group.

[2] Includes all schools.

Source: DfES Statistical First Releases 'National Curriculum Assessments at Key Stage 1 in England, 2006 (Provisional)'

over half of all looked-after children reach minimum benchmark levels compared with over 80% of all children of the same age.

This inequality in early educational attainment extends through to the end of compulsory schooling where around one-third of looked-after children leave school with no GCSE or equivalent qualification; this figure rises to around one-quarter in the northeast of England (DfES 2007b). However, many more looked-after young people in this region actually sit for at least one GCSE examination: 81% compared with 66% of looked-after children nationally. Additionally, the highest proportion of looked-after children who reach benchmark expected levels (5+ A*-C grades at GCSE or equivalent) is also in the northeast (Table 5.11). Looked-after children are also less likely to remain in full-time education after the age of 16 and are more likely to be unemployed: 20% of looked-after children were unemployed in the September after leaving compulsory education, compared with 5% of all children (DfES 2007b); they are also more likely than their peers to be cautioned or convicted of a criminal offence (DfES 2007b).

This example has used only a small proportion of the data that are available about looked-after children on the Department for Children, Schools and Families (DCSF) website. This facility can also provide data on the type and duration of young people's placements as well as information on children who cease to be 'looked after'; many of these

Table 5.11 GCSE (or equivalent) performance of looked-after children in year 11, compared with all children

	Eligible for exam	% sitting 1+ exam	5 GCSEs (or equivalent) grades A*-C	
	Looked-after children	*Looked-after children*	*Looked-after children*	*All children*
England	5100	66	12	59
Northeast	225	81	18	57
Northwest	805	69	13	57
Yorkshire and Humberside	525	64	9	54
East Midlands	305	68	8	55
West Midlands	520	58	10	56
East of England	455	65	11	59
London	1140	65	14	58
Southeast	635	64	10	60
Southwest	440	64	12	58

Source: DfES Statistical First Release 'GCSE and Equivalent Examination Results in England 2005/06 (Revised)'

data are also available at the local authority level. Data of this nature are invaluable as a starting point for studying regional and even longitudinal patterns in society, especially when they can be combined with data from other sources, such as health and economic data.

Government administrative records (part 2)

Patterns of social, economic and educational disengagement in South Wales

This final example describes the use of secondary data from government sources to review regional inequalities and patterns of social, economic and educational disadvantage in South Wales and demonstrates the range of different sources of data that can be combined under a single topic. All the data presented here were retrieved from the National Assembly Government for Wales' statistics gateway. The focus here is on South Wales and the 12 Unitary Authorities that until 1996 comprised the old counties of Glamorgan and Gwent. This includes the cities of Cardiff and Swansea and the region known as the Valleys (Figure 5.3). The data are presented at the unitary authority (UA) level and the findings show how closely linked are the patterns of disadvantage discernible in such apparently disparate areas as education, health and the economy (Gorard et al. 2004).

1	Merthyr Tydfil
2	Caerphilly
3	Blaenau Gwent
4	Torfaen
5	Monmouthshire
6	Newport
7	Cardiff
8	Vale of Glamorgan
9	Bridgend
10	Rhondda Cynon Taff
11	Neath Port Talbot
12	Swansea

Figure 5.3 Unitary authorities of Wales

Education

Table 5.12 shows some of the indicators of attainment at Key Stage 4: the proportion of young people actually leaving education at age 16 with no qualification at all, the proportion gaining less than the equivalent of one GCSE grade G, and the proportion attaining the benchmark of five 'good' GCSEs. The general pattern suggests that scores in many of these areas

Table 5.12 Qualifications obtained by 15-year-old cohort (Key Stage 4), 2005–2006

Local authority	Number of pupils aged 15	% achieving 5+ GCSE A*-C	% achieving 5+ GCSE A*-G	% achieving no formal qualification
Wales	38,859	54	86	4
Blaenau Gwent	923	48	84	5
Bridgend	1756	51	84	3
Caerphilly	2330	46	86	5
Cardiff	3752	52	84	4
Merthyr Tydfil	803	43	81	5
Monmouthshire	951	54	86	3
Neath Port Talbot	1894	60	89	3
Newport	1845	49	84	6
Rhondda Cynon Taff	3370	48	83	5
Swansea	2834	51	83	5
Torfaen	1416	50	86	6
Vale of Glamorgan	1589	65	90	3

Source: National Assembly for Wales 2006a

Table 5.13 Number of conceptions, according to unitary authority, 2004

Local authority	All ages rate	Under 16 rate[1]	Under 18 rate[2]	Under 20 rate[3]
Blaenau Gwent	68	8	46	75
Bridgend	72	7	44	66
Caerphilly	74	9	53	76
Cardiff	66	7	45	58
Merthyr Tydfil	74	8	65	89
Monmouthshire	68	5	22	41
Neath Port Talbot	70	6	44	68
Newport	77	7	42	76
Rhondda Cynon Taff	76	13	59	83
Swansea	65	5	41	59
Torfaen	79	11	67	90
Vale of Glamorgan	67	8	37	53
Wales	**69**	**7**	**45**	**64**

[1] Rate per 1000 females aged 13–15
[2] Rate per 1000 females aged 15–17
[3] Rate per 1000 females aged 17–19
Source: National Assembly for Wales 2006b

are at or below the average for Wales as a whole; notable exceptions to this are the relatively high scores in the more affluent areas of the Vale of Glamorgan and Monmouthshire. We will see this pattern appear many times in this analysis for indicators of education and other forms of relative disadvantage.

Health
Similar patterns emerge when indicators of health are considered. Table 5.13 shows that teenage pregnancy is most common in Torfaen, Rhondda Cynon Taff, Caerphilly, Merthyr Tydfil and other valleys areas. Teenage pregnancy is proportionately quite low in more rural areas such as Monmouthshire.

Life expectancy in Wales is slightly lower than for the rest of the UK. Table 5.14 gives the breakdown for men and women, and shows that those living in Merthyr Tydfil have the lowest expectancy (72 years for men), whereas those living in Monmouthshire have the highest (82 years for women). The pattern of relative disadvantage is the same as for the indicators of educational outcome. The same pattern, unsurprisingly, also appears for the percentage who report 'not good' health (Table 5.14). This is 18% in Merthyr Tydfil and 16% in Blaenau Gwent, compared to 10% in the Vale of Glamorgan and 9% in Monmouthshire.

Table 5.14 Health-related indicators, according to unitary authority

	'Are not in good health'	'Have a limiting long-term illness'	Life expectancy[1]	
			Female	Male
Wales	**12**	**23**	**80.6**	**76.2**
Blaenau Gwent	16	28	78.4	74.2
Bridgend	14	25	79.9	75.5
Caerphilly	15	26	79.3	75.2
Cardiff	10	19	80.7	76.3
Merthyr Tydfil	18	30	78.6	74.3
Monmouthshire	9	19	82.7	78.4
Neath Port Talbot	16	29	80.4	75.2
Newport	12	22	80.4	76.0
Rhondda Cynon Taff	16	27	79.5	75.1
Swansea	13	25	80.8	75.7
Torfaen	14	25	81.1	76.3
Vale of Glamorgan	10	20	80.8	77.0

[1] Life expectancy figures are for 2003–2005.

Source: Welsh Assembly Government 2006c

Economy and housing

Economic activity rates as reported in the 2001 Census are presented in Table 5.15. The Valleys regions of Merthyr Tydfil and Blaenau Gwent have a higher proportion of economically inactive households as well as having the highest proportion of social housing. The Vale of Glamorgan and Monmouthshire are in the reverse situation.

Multiple deprivation

Having observed all these patterns, it is clear that on any coherent index of multiple deprivation the situation would be assessed as more severe in Merthyr Tydfil, Blaenau Gwent than in the Vale of Glamorgan and Monmouthshire (Table 5.16). This is what is found by ranking areas in terms of the Welsh Index of Multiple Deprivation. Indeed, among all 22 Welsh unitary authorities the deprivation indices place Merthyr Tydfil and Blaenau Gwent as the most deprived in the country whereas the Vale of Glamorgan and Monmouthshire are among the least.

As we can see, the variation between unitary authorities is often highly correlated across different indicators of disengagement. For example, attainment at Key Stage 4 is also related to the rate of teenage pregnancies, which is linked to local life expectancy. The proportion of pupils leaving school with no qualifications is related to local levels of child poverty. And so on. Although these links are familiar to anyone working in this field, we know that these links are not causal in nature. Teenage

Table 5.15 Economic activity and housing tenure (%)

	Economically active but unemployed[1]	Economically inactive[1]	Rented from local authority or registered landlord[2]
Blaenau Gwent	5	44	30
Bridgend	3	39	16
Caerphilly	4	41	21
Cardiff	3	37	19
Merthyr Tydfil	4	46	26
Monmouthshire	3	34	14
Neath Port Talbot	4	44	20
Newport	4	37	24
Rhondda Cynon Taff	4	43	16
Swansea	4	41	23
Torfaen	3	39	28
Vale of Glamorgan	3	34	13

[1] Source: Census 2001
[2] Source: Welsh Assembly Government 2004

Table 5.16 Ranking of deprivation scores

	Child poverty index rank	Overall deprivation index rank
Blaenau Gwent	2	2
Bridgend	16	11
Caerphilly	5	5
Cardiff	18	6
Merthyr Tydfil	1	1
Monmouthshire	22	22
Neath Port Talbot	11	4
Newport	3	9
Rhondda Cynon Taff	4	3
Swansea	10	12
Torfaen	7	10
Vale of Glamorgan	20	21

Higher ranking equates to greater deprivation or poverty.
Source: Welsh Index of Multiple Deprivation (NAfW) 2000

pregnancy cannot *cause* poor performance at Key Stage 4, for example, or vice versa. Neither do the links at the unitary authority level necessarily refer to the same individuals within the unitary authority. Those with poor performance in Key Stage 4 may be no more likely than any others to become pregnant as a teenager, for example. What all of these relationships imply is an underlying pattern of cause, termed variously 'deprivation', 'exclusion' or 'disengagement'. Using secondary data from multiple sources in this way can describe the inequalities that exist in our society. In doing so, it is a powerful rhetorical and analytical tool, but as we have seen here, while secondary data analysis can tell us what the patterns are, it cannot tell us why they might exist.

Summary

This chapter has taken five empirical examples of how aggregate secondary data can be used in social research. Aggregate or summary data of this type are probably the most straightforward use of secondary data. In addition to the range of official administrative data that can be accessed via government statistics gateways (see examples 4 and 5) and through publications such as *Social Trends* (see example 3), we have also introduced two online facilities, CASWEB and NOMIS, which researchers can use to produce their own summary statistics from large-scale surveys (see examples 1 and 2). As well as its accessibility and relative ease of use, one of the key benefits of data of this type is that they can allow researchers to combine data from a range of different sources. Using aggregate secondary data of this type can provide researchers with an important context for in-depth work, as well as providing a basis for drawing one's research sample or even as a research study in its own right. The next chapter will describe how the raw data from studies similar to those described here can be used in social and educational research.

6

Traffic jams and gap years: secondary analysis of survey data

This chapter provides two worked examples showing how you can use large-scale surveys to explore contemporary issues in British society. We begin by using the Youth Cohort Study to examine the gap year phenomenon, before analysing attitudes to traffic congestion and transport policies using raw data from the British Social Attitudes Survey. Each example begins with a description of guidelines for locating and accessing the dataset. Step-by-step instructions will then take you through the stages in cleaning the data and preparing them for analysis. The focus here is on deleting un-needed cases and variables and recoding variables to improve their suitability for analysis. Additional worked examples showing how to access data and use SPSS to manage the datasets effectively are given in the appendices. Appendix 2 provides a more detailed explanation of all the techniques for data management that are given in Chapters 6 and 7. If you are not very familiar with using SPSS, especially the Syntax commands, then you might wish to have a look at Appendix 2 first. Or, for complete novices, you might wish to familiarise yourself with SPSS using an introductory text (references for several excellent introductory texts are given at the end of Appendix 2).

Young people's experiences of gap years

In recent years taking a gap year appears to have become the aspiration of choice for many young people before, or sometimes after, embarking on higher education courses. It is a phenomenon that has become evident through the proliferation of websites and guides that are devoted to trip packages, survival tips, message boards and blogs, its attraction no doubt raised by high-profile gap year takers such as the Princes William and Harry. Whether it is trekking in the northern Sahara desert, mountaineering in remote parts of Patagonia, conservation projects in Tanzania and Ecuador or football coaching in Ghana, the number of people taking a gap year continues to rise. In 2005 a Mintel report valued the market at £5bn and predicted its rise to £20bn by 2010; according to STA Travel, its gap customers have increased by 11% each year, while Gapyear.com estimates that 230,000 18–24 year olds set off on a big trip each year (*Observer* 2007). But who actually takes a gap year, what do they do and what are the reasons young people give for deciding to take a year out?

Background to the study

The Youth Cohort Study (YCS) is an ideal source of information to begin answering some of these questions. The YCS is a series of surveys of young people aged 16 and upwards, which monitor 'their decisions and behaviour in making the transition from compulsory education to further or higher education, employment or another activity' (Jarvis et al. 2003: 6). Broadly, the main aim of the Youth Cohort Study is to identify and explain the factors that influence transitions after compulsory education, such as educational attainment, training opportunities and experiences at school. In addition, recent sweeps of the YCS have also started to ask young people about their intentions, motivations and experiences of taking a gap year. The YCS is a useful secondary data source for exploring the gap year phenomenon: the data are large scale, of high quality and contain a vast amount of additional data on each individual. Additionally, because those who take a gap year are still a relatively small proportion of the age cohort, collecting such information on a small group of people by other means would, at best, be time consuming and expensive. In this example, we use the 2002–2003 Youth Cohort Study (Cohort 11) to examine the following research questions related to the gap year phenomenon:

- What are the social and academic characteristics of young people who elect to take a gap year before commencing higher education?
- What are the reasons young people give for taking a gap year?
- What activities do they undertake?
- To what extent do gap year takers feel that their experiences were worthwhile?

The next section considers some of the background and technical information related to the YCS and which is needed in order to undertake this analysis. All this information is available from the user guides that accompany the Cohort 11 version of the YCS (Jarvis et al. 2003; Jarvis et al. 2006a; Phillips et al. 2005).

The YCS Cohort 11 surveyed young people who reached the end of compulsory education in summer 2001. Participants were first contacted in the spring following the end of their compulsory schooling, when they were 16–17 years of age (spring 2002, Sweep 1). Three additional sweeps were conducted over the next 3 years: Sweep 2 in spring 2003 (17–18 years of age), Sweep 3 in spring 2004 (18 and 19 years of age) and Sweep 4 in spring 2005 (19 and 20 years of age). Over the four sweeps of the YCS, three main samples of students were used: a core sample (Sweeps 1 to 4), a Connexions sample (in Sweeps 1, 2 and 3) and a higher education sample (in Sweeps 2 and 3 only). The procedure for contacting respondents in Sweep 1 was as follows: a core sample of 28,650 young people were sent a postal questionnaire with telephone interviews used to follow up non-respondents, there were also opportunities for completing the survey using the internet. Also in Sweep 1, a Connexions telephone questionnaire was administered alongside the core questionnaire to a separate sub-sample of 1535 young people, living in certain geographical locations. This makes a total of 30,185 (28,650 + 1535) young people who were approached to participate in Sweep 1 of the YCS Cohort 11. Similar procedures were used with additional questionnaires, where appropriate, in Sweeps 2–4. Sweep 2 comprised all young people who responded to the survey in Sweep 1 and who gave consent to be included in follow-up studies; this panel design whereby the same group of participants were included in subsequent sweeps of the study also determined participation in Sweeps 3 and 4.

In this example, we are particularly interested in the questions that were asked of the higher education sample. The HE sample was given a HE questionnaire alongside the core and Connexions questionnaires in Sweeps 2 and 3. The higher education questionnaire was administered by telephone to those students who had achieved at least level 2 qualifications (five or more GCSEs at grade C or above) when they were last interviewed. Where no telephone contact was possible, participants were sent a postal questionnaire. The focus of the higher education questionnaire was on plans for applying to HE, including questions about intention to take, and experience of, a gap year. Some questions were asked to all respondents, while others depended on their intention to apply for a HE place. In the YCS, 'gap year' was defined as 'a year off between getting [your] A2s (A-levels) and taking up [your] place on (a HE) course' (Jarvis et al. 2006a: 110), it did not include a year taken to study for more qualifications.

Response rates and sampling
The final response rates for the core and HE questionnaires appear in Table 6.1. In the case of the core questionnaire, these include response rates for the postal and internet questionnaires as well as those from the telephone interviews.

Table 6.1 Response rates for the Youth Cohort Study (Cohort 11, Sweeps 1–3)

	Intended N	Actual N	Response rate (%)
Sweep 1			
Core questionnaire	30185	16708	55
Sweep 2			
Core questionnaire	10184	7421	74
Higher education questionnaire	2700	2138	79
Sweep 3			
Core questionnaire	7830	5722	73
Higher education questionnaire	2138	1576	74

Sources: YCS technical manuals (Jarvis et al. 2003, 2006a; Phillips et al. 2005)

Because the questions pertaining to taking a gap year were only asked as part of the HE questionnaire, the responses can be considered to be biased towards higher attaining students who were intending to apply to HE (as the HE sample only included those young people with a level 2 qualification or higher) and not representative of the wider population. In addition, problems with non-response also leads to difficulties with the generalisability of the data; to help overcome such problems, the survey designers have introduced weights to help increase the precision of the YCS. The theory behind these weights is quite complicated, but they should be used in any analysis in order to help provide more reliable estimates of the data. More detail about weighting is given in Appendix 2. Using the weights in this analysis of the YCS is straightforward and is explained in more detail later.

Preparing the dataset

This section takes you through the stages in preparing the YCS dataset for analysis. The Youth Cohort Study can be accessed from the UK Data Archive. You will need to log in via ATHENS and register your account. An example showing how to do this for Economic and Social Data Service datasets appears in Appendix 3. Once you have found the Youth Cohort Study homepage you will see the list of datasets available for download (Slide 6.1). We have selected the most recent (Cohort 11).

Slide 6.1 Downloading the Youth Cohort Study from the UK Data Archive

Further detailed instructions for downloading datasets are given in Appendix 2.

Once you have downloaded the data you will receive a number of folders containing the SPSS dataset and additional files one of which contains the YCS user guide (file name **5452userguide**). If you open this in SPSS, you will see that the file is very large: around 50 MB with 2812 variables linked to 16,707 cases. If you are certain that you know which variables and cases you are interested in studying, it might be worthwhile to delete all un-needed variables and cases in order to make the dataset more manageable: the steps needed to do this are explained later, while more general points on using SPSS to manage your dataset effectively are given in Appendix 2.

Deleting un-needed cases
In this example, we are only interested in students who completed the higher education questionnaires. Of course, it would be very interesting to compare the characteristics of those who completed the HE questionnaire with those who did not, but that is a different study; for now we will delete all the cases which had no data for the HE questionnaires. In order to get complete data for the maximum number of cases, we only selected cases from Sweep 3. Therefore anyone who had completed the HE questionnaire in Sweep 2 but who had dropped out from Sweep 3 was not included in this analysis. The following steps were used to select

only those who responded to the Sweep 3 higher education questionnaire; all other cases were deleted.

In the **Menu Bar** of the SPSS data view window select **Data → Select Cases**. This will open a window similar to the one in Slide 6.2. As all the respondents who will have completed the HE Sweep 3 questionnaire will have been allocated a weight (variable **s3he_wt**), we use this variable to select cases for inclusion in this study. You can include cases on the basis of any criteria – it just depends on your research questions. For example, you can select all cases that responded positively to a particular question or all cases that were female and so on. Here we are selecting all cases that were included in the Sweep 3 higher education questionnaire, if they were included each case will be allocated a weight: here this is a number with a value of greater than or equal to 0.

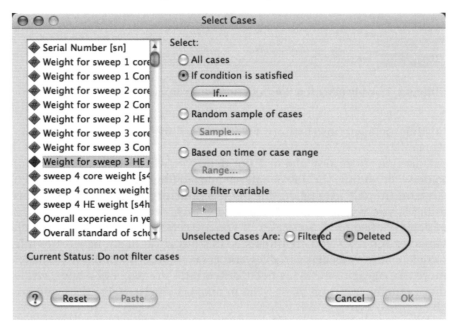

Slide 6.2 Select Cases window for the Youth Cohort Study

In order to make this selection, check the **If condition is satisfied ...** button, clicking on the **If ...** button opens a new sub-window (Slide 6.3). In the **Select Cases: If** sub-window, move the variable **Weight for sweep 3 HE module (s3he_wt)** into the **work area** box using the arrow key. Using the numbers and symbols on the keypad, enter **> = 0** and then **Continue**. This will return you to the main **Select Cases** window. To delete any cases which have not been selected, check the **Unselected Cases Are Deleted** button; if you wish to retain the unselected cases and filter them out of the analysis, the **Filtered** option will need to be selected. Finally click **OK**. See Appendix 2 for further worked examples using this technique.

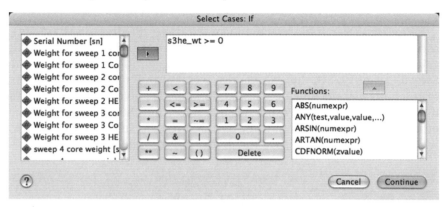

Slide 6.3 Select Cases: If sub-window

You have now instructed SPSS to select all cases which have a value for the variable **s3he_wt** which is greater than or equal to zero (> = **0**). All other cases will have no value for this variable and will not be selected. And, as instructed, all these unselected cases are then deleted.

Deleting un-needed variables
This section shows how the Syntax function can be used to delete un-needed variables from the dataset. In this example, we are only concerned with a small subgroup of all the YCS variables: those related to gap year experiences, as well as a small number of background variables. All other variables will be deleted. The variables (names highlighted in bold) that are to be retained for analysis, along with their associated questions, are listed below:

Gapyear: If you get a place on a higher education course will you take a 'gap year', that is a year off between getting your A2s (A-levels) and taking up your place on the course?
Gapone: What is the main reason why you would like to take a gap year before starting higher education?
Nowgap01: Now that you have decided to take a year off before starting a higher education course, please tell me what you've been doing so far during your gap year and if this is what you will be doing for the rest of your gap year?
Gapbal: Looking back, do you think taking a year off before starting your HE course was the right decision or do you think you should have started the course in autumn 2003?

Gapbx01: What, if any, have been the main benefits for you from taking a year off?

Gappx1: And what, if any, have been the main drawbacks for you from taking a year off?

Background variables retained included those relating to sex (**s1sex**), social group (**famsec**), school attended (**s1estab1**) and number of GCSEs gained (**s1q32a2**, renamed **nogcses**); the weighting variables for the Sweep 2 and 3 HE questionnaires were also retained. The Syntax instructions for selecting the relevant variables are given in Slide 6.4. This lists all the variables we wish to keep and instructs SPSS to delete all the others. For guidelines about using Syntax in SPSS, and further examples which use this technique, see the discussion in Appendix 2.

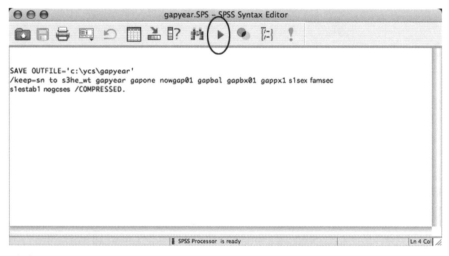

Slide 6.4 Syntax instructions for deleting variables from the YCS

If you select the text in the Syntax window and then click on the black arrow key, the programme will run. It will instruct SPSS to save only the variables listed to a new SPSS document labelled **gap year** in a file called YCS.

Using weights
When analysing questions from Sweep 3 of the YCS you will need to add the corresponding weights (**s3he_wt**), for Sweep 2 questions you will need to change to the Sweep 2 weights (**s2he_wt**).

Adding the weighting variable is straightforward: on the main **Menu Bar** go to **Data → Weight Cases**, a window titled **Weight Cases** will appear (Slide 6.5). Select the **Weight cases by frequency variable** button and use the arrow to move the weighting variable for Sweep 3 across into the **work area**. Then click **OK**. You can check that the dataset is weighted by looking for the **Weight On** label at the bottom right-hand corner of the main SPSS **Data View** screen. More information and examples of weighting cases appear in Appendix 2.

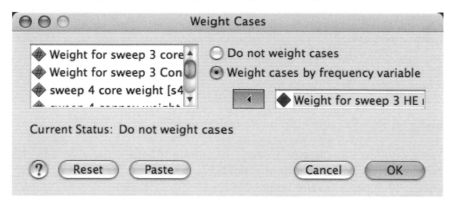

Slide 6.5 Weighting cases in the Youth Cohort Study

Recoding variables
Two other changes were made to the variables used in this example. First, the six social class categories (**famsec**) were reduced to two; in the second change, the number of GCSEs each respondent had gained (**nogcse**) was transformed into quartiles.

Recoding family social class
In the original YCS dataset, the family grouped social class (**famsec**) variable is represented by six National Statistics Socio-Economic Classification (NS-SEC) categories. Because of the relatively small number of cases in each of these six categories, for this example they were reduced from six to two: 'professional' and 'other'.

To do this use the **Recode into Different Variable** function (in the **Menu Bar** select **Transform → Recode → Into Different Variable**). This opens the window seen in Slide 6.6. The variable for family grouped social class (**famsec**) has been moved into the **work area** (labelled **Numeric variable → Output variable**). In the **Output variable** box on the right-hand side of Slide 6.6, the new variable has been named (**famcol**) and labelled (**collapsed family sec**).

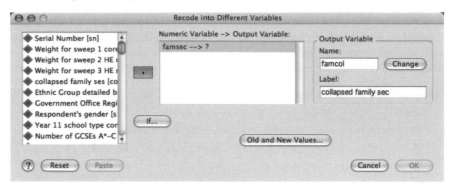

Slide 6.6 Recoding into Different Variables window

Clicking on the **Change** button will move this new variable into the **Numeric variable → Output variable** box in place of the **?**, which currently appears on the screen.

Next, click on the **Old and New Values** button to open the sub-window shown in Slide 6.7.

Slide 6.7 Recoding into Different Variables sub-window

Before recoding variables it is useful to draw up a quick table listing the old and new variables, as shown in Table 6.2. The six NS-SEC occupational categories with their original YCS codes (as labelled in the SPSS file) are listed in the table along with the new collapsed codes (which you can designate yourself).

Table 6.2 Original and new codes for recoded NS-SEC categories

NS-SEC category	Original YCS code	New collapsed code
Large employers and higher professionals	1	1
Lower professional and higher technical occupations	2	1
Intermediate	3	2
Lower supervisory occupations	4	2
Semi-routine and routine occupations	5	2
Other	6	2

In recoding this variable from six to two categories the two professional groups (originally labelled one and two) will be recoded into one group (label = 1) and the remaining four categories into another (label = 2); any missing cases in the original variable will be retained with their own codes. This can be done using the **Old Value** and then the **New Value** buttons in Slide 6.7.

For example, in the **Old Value** box, click on the **Value** button and enter the old value for *Large employers and higher professionals* (1), then in the **New Value** box click on the other **Value** button and enter the corresponding new value (also = 1). Click on the **Add** button to add the command to the **Old → New:** box. You can then repeat this for all the other variables that are to be renamed. Don't forget to also include the missing variables; this can be done by clicking on both **System- or user-missing** buttons and adding it to the **Old → New:** box (see Slide 6.7).

Once you have recoded all the variables, you can see that in the **Old → New:** box, the original variables have been given their new values (i.e. old codes 1 and 2 are now labelled 1 and old codes 3–6 are now labelled 2). Clicking **Continue** and then **OK** (in the main window) completes the analysis and the new variable (**famcol**) appears in the main dataset. The new variable should be labelled accordingly (including missing value labels) using the **variable view** window.

Recoding GCSEs into quartiles
The GCSE attainment variable (number of GCSEs A*–C obtained since the end of Sweep 1, **nogcses**) contains numbers in the range 0–13. For ease of analysis, the range was reduced to GCSE quartiles:

- quartile 1 comprising students with 6 GCSEs A*–C and fewer
- quartile 2 comprising students with 7–8 GCSEs at these grades

- quartile 3 those with 9 GCSEs
- quartile 4 those with 10 GCSEs or more.

See the British Social Attitudes Survey example later in this chapter for the steps needed to allocate and recode data into quartiles.

Findings
Once the following data management steps have been completed, it is possible to undertake some rudimentary descriptive analysis of the Youth Cohort Study. A selection of findings that attempt to answer some of the research questions posed at the start of this section are now given.

Characteristics of young people planning on taking a gap year
Sweep 2 of the YCS questioned young people when they were 17–18 years of age. For those who remained in school or college, this would be equivalent to National Curriculum year 13, which, for many students, is the final year of A-level (or equivalent) study. This section considers whether or not these young people intended to take a gap year, according to a range of background characteristics. A simple frequency analysis was undertaken with weightings used to account for non-response, the use of weightings means that in Table 6.3 the numbers of cases may vary slightly (similarly with the remaining tables in this section).

Table 6.3 Gap year intentions, according to selected background characteristics

| | | \multicolumn{7}{c}{Take gap year before starting HE course?} | | | | | | |
| | | Yes | | No | | Don't know | | Total |
		N	%	N	%	N	%	N
Occupational group	Professional	129	17	608	80	22	3	**759**
	Other	66	16	352	83	6	1	**424**
Sex	Male	81	16	414	81	15	3	**510**
	Female	115	17	546	81	13	2	**674**
School type	State non-selective	157	17	753	81	21	2	**931**
	Selective	14	13	90	85	2	2	**106**
	Independent	24	16	117	80	5	3	**146**
GCSE quartile	6 GCSEs and fewer	32	22	112	77	2	1	**146**
	7 or 8 GCSEs	45	20	176	77	6	3	**227**
	9 GCSEs	45	14	276	84	9	3	**330**
	10 + GCSEs	73	15	397	82	11	2	**481**
All respondents		195	16	961	81	28	2	**1184**

Source: Jarvis et al. 2006b

As we can see from Table 6.3, around 16% of students surveyed said that they intended to take a gap year. There is only limited evidence that certain groups of students are more likely to want to take a gap year than others. For example, there was little difference in the intentions of male and female students and students from professional or other families. The type of school one attended also appears to have a limited impact on gap year intentions, but the number of cases of students who attended selective and independent schools is small and so needs to be regarded with caution. There were differences however in the intentions of students in the different GCSE quartiles: students with the highest number of GCSE grades A*–C appeared to be the least likely to want to take a gap year.

The next section focuses on the different experiences between respondents from the two occupational groups. Differences in the experiences of the other groups were relatively small.

What reasons do young people give for taking a gap year?
When asked why they might wish to take a gap year, most (37%) young people said that they wished to take a break from study (Table 6.4). This response was more common among young people who were not from professional families, a group that was also slightly more likely to wish to take a gap year in order to earn money. Notice however, that the second largest group of responses from the 'professional' group was to do 'something else', the specific details of which are not included in the YCS data.

Table 6.4 Reasons for wanting to take a gap year, according to family occupational background

	Professional		Other		All students	
	N	%	N	%	N	%
To take a break from study	42	33	29	44	71	37
To become more independent/gain experience	5	4	5	8	10	5
To earn money	28	22	20	30	48	25
To get work experience	17	13	5	8	22	11
Something else	36	28	7	10	43	22
Total	**128**	**100**	**66**	**100**	**194**	**100**

Source: Jarvis et al. 2006b

Table 6.5 Main gap year activity, according to family occupational background

	Professional		Other		All students	
	N	%	N	%	N	%
Travelling	32	18	8	9	40	15
Working/studying abroad	7	4	4	4	11	4
Working in Britain	115	66	69	77	184	70
Training for new qualifications	5	3	1	1	6	2
Retaking examinations/ courses	4	2	3	3	7	3
Other	5	3	4	4	9	3
Voluntary work	5	3	0	0	5	2
Total	**173**	**100**	**89**	**100**	**262**	**100**

Source: Jarvis et al. 2006b

Gap year activities

Young people who actually went on a gap year were asked to list the activities they undertook during this period of time (Table 6.5). There are two potential problems with interpreting the results for this question: first, young people are likely to have undertaken more than one activity (and here they were asked to name their main activity) and, second, as this question was asked of young people who had taken a gap year, it is possible that many potential respondents were actually away taking their gap year and so were not included in the study, potentially biasing the responses against the numbers who might have gone travelling, for example, or undertaken an activity away from home. Despite these caveats, we can see that the main activity for the majority of those who took a gap year was working in Britain.

What is the main benefit of gap year?

Those who took a gap year were asked about the main benefits of the activity (see Table 6.6). For most, it seems apparent that the most beneficial part of taking a gap year was the opportunity to earn money – perhaps unsurprising given the increasing financial costs of higher education. Little difference between those from 'professional' and 'other' families was noted in the responses to this question, although a slightly higher proportion of those from 'other' occupational backgrounds found financial benefits from taking a year out.

What is the main drawback of taking a gap year?

Table 6.7 gives an indication of the main drawbacks of taking a gap year, according to the views of young people who had just taken a year out. For the majority of gap year takers, the experience was overwhelmingly

Table 6.6 Main benefit of taking a gap year

	Professional		Other		All students	
	N	%	N	%	N	%
Financial benefits/making or saving money	58	34	36	40	94	36
Get work experience/skills for future	25	15	12	13	37	14
Break from education/ studying/stress	23	13	15	17	38	15
Time to reflect/decide what to do	29	17	17	19	46	18
Travel/see world	9	5	1	1	10	4
Have fun/develop other interests	2	1	0	0	2	1
Grow up/develop life skills and experience	14	8	7	8	21	8
No benefits	2	1	1	1	3	1
Other specific answer	6	3	1	1	7	3
Other vague answer	3	2	0	0	3	1
Total	**171**	**100**	**90**	**100**	**261**	**100**

Source: Jarvis et al. 2006b

Table 6.7 Main drawbacks of taking a gap year

	Professional		Other		All students	
	N	%	N	%	N	%
Friends not around/poor social life	26	15	9	10	35	14
Falling behind peers/will finish university	12	7	12	14	24	9
Bored/out of routine/being out of education	11	6	10	11	21	8
Will be hard to go back to study/education	9	5	10	11	19	7
Didn't plan time properly/ usefully	3	2	2	2	5	2
Having to work/find work/ work hard	16	9	6	7	22	9
No drawbacks	67	40	29	33	96	37
Other specific answer	19	11	7	8	26	10
Other vague answer	1	1	1	1	2	1
Don't know	4	2	2	2	6	2
Total	**168**	**100**	**88**	**100**	**256**	**100**

Source: Jarvis et al. 2006b

positive, with no drawbacks mentioned. Those who did identify drawbacks suggested that not being around friends and having a poor social
life presented the main challenges. Again, there were only slight differences in the responses of those from 'professional' and 'other' families,
with those from the 'other' occupational groups more likely to identify
drawbacks, in particular concerns about falling behind their peers.

Section conclusion

This example has demonstrated the potential of the Youth Cohort Study
to answer questions about the characteristics and experiences of young
people who take a gap year before beginning their higher education
courses. In itself, the analysis presented here has been largely descriptive
but has shown the opportunities that large-scale surveys of this nature
present for finding out information about difficult to access groups. In the
sense that gap year students are difficult to access because they are
relatively few in number and the effort and resources needed to locate
and keep track of a representative group of these students would be
considerable. Data from the YCS presents opportunities for an interesting
study of the gap year phenomenon in its own right, for example a further
investigation of the types of activities and opportunities that students
who wish to take a gap year experience: this brief analysis suggests little
difference in the characteristics of gap year students (for example they
are just as likely to be from professional or other occupational backgrounds) but are there any other differences, for example in their
attitudes towards higher education and what about difference between
those who do and who do not wish to take a gap year? Similarly this
study is an excellent starting point for an in-depth investigation into the
challenges and experiences of young people as they make the decision to
take a gap year and the experiences they face along the way. Here the
data collected by the YCS can provide the researcher with a context for
in-depth work as well as a theoretical and methodological basis with
which they can develop their own research questions.

Attitudes to traffic congestion and transport policies

Our second example uses data from the 2004 British Social Attitudes
Survey (BSAS) (NatCen 2006) to examine the public's views on traffic
congestion and transport policy. See also Budd and Aston (2006), for a
comprehensive report on experiences of congestion and road pricing
using data from the BSAS and other large surveys, such as the British
Omnibus Survey.

Background to the British Social Attitudes Survey

The British Social Attitudes Survey is an annual survey of a representative sample of around 3600 adults aged 18 and over. Its aim is to document the opinions and attitudes of respondents on a range of social issues, including political engagement, public spending, health and the environment. Fieldwork is undertaken in respondent's home by trained interviewers; interviews last around 65 minutes and are followed by a self-completion questionnaire. The response rate for the 2004 cycle of the British Social Attitudes Survey was 57% (corresponding to 3199 productive interviews) (NatCen 2006). Technical and summary reports derived from the findings from the British Social Attitudes Survey can be obtained from the National Centre for Social Research (NatCen), which is responsible for administering the BSAS. Further links and guidelines on retrieving and accessing the BSAS datasets are given in Appendix 1.

This brief example uses data retrieved from face-to-face interviews and self-completion questionnaires that have a particular focus on transport issues. A range of contextual data about the respondent, including their sex and household income were also retained for analysis. The next section will describe the stages in retrieving, preparing and analysing the 2004 British Social Attitudes Survey (BSAS) in order to answer the following questions related to attitudes towards traffic congestion and transport policy:

- What are the characteristics of regular drivers?
- What problems do they associate with modern-day driving?
- What are their opinions on a series of potential solutions to current transport problems?

Although not considered here, the wealth of data contained in the BSAS can allow researchers to compare attitudes towards transport with many other contextual variables such as respondents' views on censorship, the welfare state, social responsibility, political affiliation and the amount of control they believe that the government should exert on people's everyday lives.

Locating the dataset

The datasets and documentation relating to the British Social Attitudes Survey can be retrieved from the Economic and Social Data Service (ESDS). The ESDS Government homepage provides a route through the **Data** link on the left-hand panel to all the surveys that are supported by ESDS Government (Slide 6.8).

Following the link for the British Social Attitudes Survey will take you to the BSAS homepage (www.esds.ac.uk/government/bsa/) and from there to the dataset download facility (Slide 6.9). From here you can

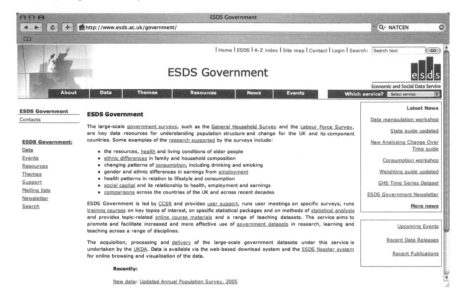

Slide 6.8 ESDS Government homepage

Slide 6.9 Downloading the British Social Attitudes Survey

explore the data online using Nesstar or download the complete datasets
and documentation to your computer, you will need an ATHENS log in
and register with the Data Archive in order to do this. If you decide to

download the dataset you have a choice of three formats: SPSS, STATA or TAB. Here we use SPSS.

Data preparation

The SPSS file containing the BSAS 2004 is a large file with 878 variables and 3199 cases. The first stage in getting the dataset ready for analysis is to delete the variables and cases that will not be relevant to this particular set of research questions.

Deleting un-needed variables
For the analysis described here only selected variables that related to transport issues, the respondents' background characteristics and data management were retained; all others were deleted. The variables kept for analysis were:

> **wtfactor**: weighting variable (see discussion later)
> **abcver:** Version A, B or C? This was needed to select cases who answered the survey questions about transport
> **rsex**: respondent's sex
> **hhincome:** how much household income last year?
> **respres**: whether respondent lived in a city, town etc.

In addition, all the variables between **transcar** and **airtrvl**, as well as those between **carwalk** and **plnuppri** were retained. There is no room here to list all the questions associated with these variables, but full details are available from NatCen (2006). For illustration, a selection of variables and questions is as follows:

> **TransCar**: Do you, or does anyone in your household, own or have the regular use of a car or a van?
> **TrfPb6U**: Now thinking about traffic and transport problems, how serious a problem **for you** is congestion on motorways?
> **Getabb5**: (What effect, if any, might this have on how much **you yourself** use the car:) ... charging £1 for every 50 miles motorists travel on motorways?
> **Getabb6**: (What effect, if any, might this have on how much **you yourself** use the car) ... making parking penalties and restrictions much more severe?

Slide 6.10 shows the Syntax instructions needed to keep these variables and delete all the others. When the text is selected, press the **run** arrow and SPSS will save the selected variables on your C: drive in a new SPSS file labelled **bsas2004**. Further information about using Syntax appears in Appendix 2. Notice in the Syntax command, rather than listing all the variables you wish to retain, if they appear in a sequence

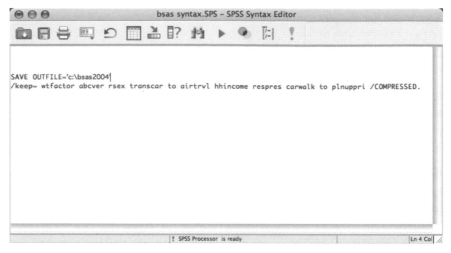

Slide 6.10 Syntax instructions for deleting variables

you can instruct SPSS to retain all the variables from X to Y (for example, **transcar** to **airtrvl**).

Deleting un-needed cases
The next step in data preparation is to delete un-needed cases. In BSAS2004, the transport questions were only asked to a subgroup of respondents, these were the respondents who participated in Version C of the interview schedule and Version C of the questionnaire. Respondents who completed Versions A and B were not asked any questions relating to transport and so can be excluded from this analysis.

Cases can be deleted using the following steps: in the **Menu Bar** select **Data → Select Cases**, the Select Cases window will open (Slide 6.11).

Select the variable named **Version A, B or C? (abcver)** and check the button **If conditions is satisfied**. This will open a new sub-window (Slide 6.12).

Move the selected variable (**abcver**) into the **work area** and using the buttons in the keypad enter = and **3**. This will tell SPSS to select all cases where the variable **abcver** is equal to 3. If you look at the labels for variable **abcver** in the **Variable View** menu of the main SPSS file, you will see that 3 is the label for Version C of the questionnaire – the one with the questions on transport.

Then press **Continue** to return to Slide 6.11.

Before clicking on **OK** to run the command, if you wish to remove the cases that you have not selected (i.e. those linked to Versions A and B of the questionnaire), then check **Unselected Cases Are Deleted** otherwise check the **Filtered** option (see Slide 6.11 again).

This should now leave you with a more manageable dataset.

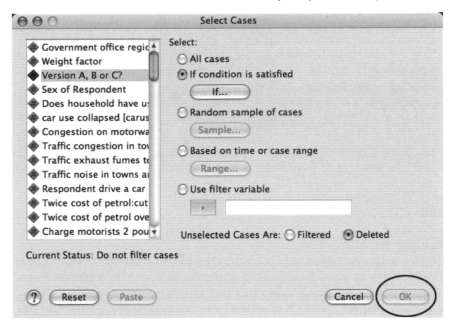

Slide 6.11 Select Cases window

Slide 6.12 Select Cases: If sub-window

Weighting cases
Weighting cases is straightforward. In the **Menu Bar** select **Data →
Weight Cases**. A window similar to Slide 6.13 will open. You will then
need to move the weighting variable (**Weight factor: wtfactor**) across
into the right-hand box. Clicking on **OK** will complete the operation and
the **Weight on** icon will appear in the bottom right-hand corner of the
main **Data View** window.

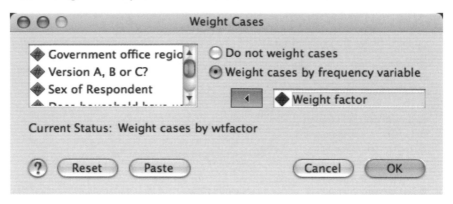

Slide 6.13 Weighting cases

Recoding variables
The final data preparation procedure used in this example was to reduce the 17 categories for household annual income (**hhincome**) to three. There are different ways to do this but here they were reduced to four income quartiles. The steps followed in order to do this are now laid out.

Step 1
Identify income quartiles. This will use the **Analyze** function to estimate the number of cases which fit into each of four income quartiles. In the **Data View** of the main SPSS window go to the **Menu Bar** and select **Analyze** → **Descriptive Statistics** → **Frequencies**. Move the variable **hhincome** into the **work area** and select the **Statistics** button. You won't need to **Display frequency tables** so you can unselect this option (Slide 6.14).

This will open a new sub-window, which you can use to specify the statistical operations you would like SPSS to perform on your data (Slide 6.15). In this window, you will need to select **Quartiles**, followed by **Continue** to return you to the main **Frequencies** window and then **OK** to run the command.

This will open the SPSS output window and the following table:

Cases	Frequency
Valid cases	898
Missing cases	171
Quartile	*Code*
25	6
50	9
75	14

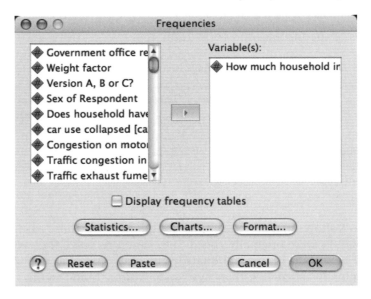

Slide 6.14 Calculating Frequencies window

Slide 6.15 Frequencies: Statistics sub-window

This table shows the codes associated with each quartile range and translates to the incomes shown in Table 6.8.

Table 6.8 Quartile ranges for household income

Quartile	Original code	Income range	New variable code
1st quartile (< 25)	1–6	Less than £14,999	1
2nd quartile (25–50)	7–9	£15,000–£22,999	2
3rd quartile (50–75)	10–14	£23,000–£43,999	3
4th quartile (75+)	15+	£44,000+	4

Table 6.8 shows that all cases in the 1st quartile (i.e. those earning less than £14,999) were originally coded 1–6. When recoded, they will now have the new code 1. The 2nd quartile (income range £15,000–22,999) were originally coded 7–9, their new code will be 2, and so on.

Step 2
Once you have established the quartile ranges, you'll need to recode the original variable (**hhincome**) into the new quartile income variables (here named **incquart**). To do this you will need to select the **Transform → Recode into Different Variable** option as shown above in the gap year example (Slides 6.6 and 6.7). See also Slides 6.16 and 6.17. Then recode the original codes with the corresponding new variable codes, as shown in Table 6.8, not forgetting to also recode the missing variables codes. This will then give you a new variable (**incquart**).

Once you have prepared your dataset for analysis, it is worth running spending a short time familiarising yourself with the data before getting down to more complex analysis. Surprising patterns and trends can

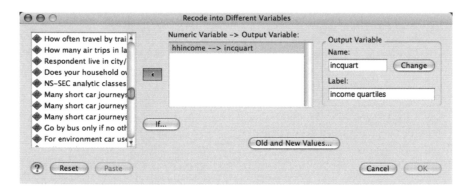

Slide 6.16 Recoding into Different Variables

Slide 6.17 Recoding in to different variables sub-window

emerge from a short time spent running a few frequencies and other descriptive analyses on the variables of interest. The next section describes some of the findings to emerge from our exploratory analysis of the British Social Attitudes Survey.

Findings

Characteristics of regular drivers
This section looks at selected characteristics of car drivers. As we can see from Table 6.9, over two-thirds of the sample report that they currently drive a car. These drivers are more likely to be male, to live outside the big cities and to come from the highest wage-earning groups.

What problems do regular drivers associate with modern-day driving?
This section examines respondents' experiences of driving in Britain today. Their comments suggest that for most, driving can be a generally negative experience. For example, only 11% of current drivers feel that congestion in towns and cities is not a problem at all (Table 6.10) and almost two-thirds think that speed cameras are mostly there to make money (Table 6.11). With regard to congestion, their experiences do not differ greatly from those who were not current drivers: around 55% of current drivers felt that congestion in towns and cities was a serious or a very serious problem, compared with 49% of respondents who weren't driving. However, they had a slightly more generous view of speed

Table 6.9 Characteristics of current drivers

Background characteristics		Do you drive a car these days?				
		Yes		No		Total
		N	%	N	%	N
Sex	Male	381	81	87	19	**468**
	Female	366	61	235	39	**601**
Residence	Big city	50	53	45	47	**95**
	Suburbs/outskirts of a big city	186	66	94	34	**280**
	Small city or town	331	72	128	28	**459**
	Country village	156	77	47	23	**203**
	Farm or home in the country	19	79	5	21	**24**
	Other	5	0.7	2	0.6	**7**
Income quartiles	1st quartile (lowest earning)	140	49	145	51	**285**
	2nd quartile	163	71	65	29	**228**
	3rd quartile	150	81	34	18	**184**
	4th quartile (highest earning)	196	97	5	3	**201**
	Total	649	72	249	28	898
All respondents		**747**	**70**	**321**	**30**	**1068**

Source: NatCen 2006

Table 6.10 Agreement with the statement that congestion in towns and cities is a problem

	Do you drive a car these days?					
	Yes		No		Total	
	N	%	N	%	N	%
A very serious problem	132	18	55	17	**187**	17
A serious problem	283	38	102	32	**385**	36
Not a very serious problem	248	33	68	21	**316**	29
Not a problem at all	85	11	97	30	182	17
Don't know	1	0.1	0	0	1	0.09
Total	**749**	**100**	**322**	**100**	**1071**	**100**

Source: NatCen 2006

cameras with around half of non-drivers agreeing or strongly agreeing that they were there mainly to make money.

What are drivers' opinions of potential solutions to current transport problems?
This final section considers drivers' views of a series of potential initiatives to reduce traffic congestion. In particular, they were asked to state the extent to which their car use would be affected by a range of financial charges and strategies to improve public transport; selected findings are

Table 6.11 Respondents' views on whether speed cameras are mostly there to make money

	Yes		No		Total	
	N	%	N	%	N	%
Agree strongly	194	32	46	19	**240**	**28**
Agree	200	33	76	31	**276**	**32**
Neutral	98	16	48	19	**146**	**17**
Disagree	96	16	65	26	**161**	**19**
Disagree strongly	22	4	11	4	**33**	**4**
Total	**610**	**100**	**246**	**100**	**856**	**100**

Do you drive a car these days?

Source: NatCen 2006

Table 6.12 Drivers' views on financial initiatives to reduce congestion

What effect, if any, might the following have on how much you use the car to get about?	**Initiative would make no difference**	
	N	%
Gradually doubling the cost of petrol over the next 10 years	728	37
Charging all motorists around £2 each time they enter or drive through a city or town centre outside London at peak times	728	42
Charging £1 for every 50 miles motorists travel on motorways	727	60
Making parking penalties and restrictions much more severe	729	58

Source: NatCen 2006

given in Tables 6.12 and 6.13 for brevity. Only the results relating to those who feel that the initiative would make no difference to their car use are presented here.

The solutions presented in Table 6.12 appear to have little potential to encourage motorists to use their car less. While doubling the cost of fuel might encourage around two-thirds of respondents to reconsider their habits, initiatives such as increasing the severity of parking penalties and restrictions would seem, from the responses given here, to be of limited use. Linking motoring sanctions with improvements in public transport did elicit more positive responses from the sample, with only around one-third claiming that linking road charges to a reduction in fares for

Table 6.13 Drivers' views on financial initiatives linked with public transport improvement

What effect, if any, might the following have on how much you use the car to get about: Charging motorists £2 for entering town centres outside London at peak times, but at the same time	Initiative would make no difference	
	N	%
Greatly improving the reliability of local public transport	727	30
Greatly improving the frequency of local public transport	727	31
Halving the fares for local public transport	727	33

Only responses from people who drive were recorded.

Source: NatCen 2006

public transport would make no difference to their behaviour (Table 6.13).

Table 6.14 shows the extent to which the respondents from the four income quartiles thought that their behaviour would change as a result of financial sanctions to limit car use. From the results it seems that financial penalties would have the same reaction from motorists regardless of their income quartile.

Finally, an alternative proposal would be to levy environmental taxes on car users. As we can see from Table 6.15, perhaps unsurprisingly, the majority of respondents disagreed with the prospect of additional taxes – a view shared among motorists as well as those who do not currently drive.

This short descriptive analysis of selected results from the British Social Attitudes Survey suggests that car drivers are more likely to be male, live outside the large cities and come from the highest income groups. For the the current driver, driving in Britain today is a fairly negative experience with few drivers regarding traffic congestion as not being a problem. Current initiatives to reduce congestion which adopt financial penalties appear to make little impact on drivers' current behaviour and this varied little among those from the most to the least wealthy groups, in terms of their annual income quartiles.

Table 6.14 Drivers' views on financial and public transport initiatives to reduce car use, according to income quartiles

What effect, if any, might charging £1 for every 50 miles motorists travel on motorways have on how much you use the car?	Initiative would make no difference		All drivers
	N	%	N
1st quartile (least wealthy)	82	59	140
2nd quartile	96	61	158
3rd quartile	82	56	146
4th quartile (most wealthy)	114	60	190
Total	374	59	634

What effect would come from charging motorists £2 for entering town centres outside London at peak times but at the same time halving the fares for local public transport?	Initiative would make no difference		All drivers
	N	%	N
1st quartile (least wealthy)	45	32	140
2nd quartile	50	32	158
3rd quartile	53	36	146
4th quartile (most wealthy)	62	33	190
Total	210	33	634

Source: NatCen 2006

Table 6.15 Respondents' views on environmental taxes on car use

	Do you drive a car these days?					
	Yes		No		Total	
	N	%	N	%	N	%
Agree	67	11	38	15	105	12
Disagree	462	75	156	61	618	71
Neutral	86	14	50	19	136	15
Can't choose	3	0.5	13	5	16	2

Source: NatCen 2006

Summary

This chapter has provided two worked examples of how secondary data analysis can be used to examine topics of contemporary social interest. It has introduced the reader to basic techniques for preparing the dataset for analysis. Techniques such as reducing the number of variables and cases are essential for preparing a large dataset for analysis and are therefore emphasised throughout this book. The analysis of the resulting datasets has been necessarily rather basic as the intention is to demonstrate how to access and manage secondary datasets rather than produce results that are of substantive or theoretical importance. In Chapter 7, we broaden our introduction to secondary datasets by considering two international sources: the PISA data and administrative data for every school in California.

7

From PISA to California: secondary analysis of international data

This final chapter in Part II introduces international sources of secondary data. We begin by using school administrative data for the US state of California to examine progress towards federal targets for qualified teachers, before using the PISA study to examine the relationship between test outcomes and student characteristics. As in Chapter 6, each example begins by locating and accessing the dataset, followed by instructions for preparing the data for analysis. Whereas in Chapter 6 the analysis was largely descriptive, here we introduce multivariate techniques, namely logistic and linear regression to model the relationship between different variables.

Improving teacher quality in California

This example describes the secondary analysis of school-level data to examine the impact of recent government policies to improve the quality of the teacher workforce in American public schools. It is taken from a recent research project, further details of which appear in Smith (2008). The quality of the teacher workforce is a subject of perennial concern in many developed countries. In 2001 the United States introduced the *No Child Left Behind* (NCLB) Act. This act has given the federal government a mandate for reform of teacher education that is unprecedented in its scale. Essentially, it demands that every teacher of core academic subjects must be deemed to be highly qualified in every subject they teach by the end of the 2005–2006 academic year. By drawing on administrative secondary data for every school in California, we examine the progress that this state is making towards meeting NCLB's mandate and also the role that teacher quality can play as a determinant of school success.

Background to No Child Left Behind

For America's public school teachers, *No Child Left Behind* means complex systems of performance and accountability measures aimed at addressing concerns over teacher quality and increasing the number of highly qualified teachers in the nation's schools. NCLB is arguably the most important piece of US educational legislation of the past 35 years. Much of the attention already given to NCLB has focused on its mandate to raise the achievement levels of all students (for example, Abedi 2004; Linn 2003; Smith 2005b). However, it also legislates for reform in the way in which teachers are trained and recruited. As it applies to teacher quality, *No Child Left Behind* has two key objectives: to ensure that every teacher is highly qualified in the subjects they teach and to reduce the barriers to becoming a teacher by 'retooling' traditional teacher education programmes and opening up alternative routes into the profession (US Department of Education 2004). Both have proven to be controversial. In addition to improving teacher quality, *No Child Left Behind* mandates for improvement in the basic skills of all students. In order to determine whether a school is meeting the requirements of NCLB for student achievement, the act requires that by 2005, states assessed performance annually in grades 3 to 8 (i.e. National Curriculum years 4 to 9) in English-language arts and mathematics and in science by 2007 (US Department of Education 2002). If students reach the required proficiency targets in these tests then the school is considered to have made 'adequate yearly progress' (AYP). If a school fails to make AYP, a series of sanctions can be administered by the school district, a situation akin to being on 'special measures' in England. The AYP status of a school is therefore crucial in determining the organisation, funding and operation of a school.

This example describes how to access and prepare two of the datasets that were used in this analysis. It then summarises some of the main findings that came from this piece of research.

Accessing the datasets

The data used to conduct this study were retrieved directly from the website of the California Department of Education. The Data and Statistics gateway on the California Department of Education website allows access to a vast source of information on Californian schools and learning support resources, including financial and student demographic data, as well as school staffing and performance information (California

Department of Education 2007). The California Basic Educational Data System (CBEDS) provides access to downloadable data files on a huge range of student and staff characteristics, at both the aggregate and school level, with some files extending back to the late 1980s. Follow the links from School Staffing or Student Demographics in order to explore further. In the main study, from which this example is drawn, the data retrieved from CBEDS included:

- *School performance data*: AYP targets, test participation and outcome data for students from different social, educational and economic groups.
- *Staff demographics*: NCLB-related data, staff certification, length of service, background characteristics.
- *Student demographics*: social, educational and economic student characteristics, school dropout rates, school graduation rates and additional NCLB-related data.

Downloading the complete datasets is relatively straightforward. Slide 7.1 shows the CBEDS information page for downloading data on school enrolments (CBEDS SIF Enrollment by school). Information about the variables contained in each file is available in the **File Structure** files. Instructions on downloading the files are available for the largest datasets; other files can be downloaded directly to your computer.

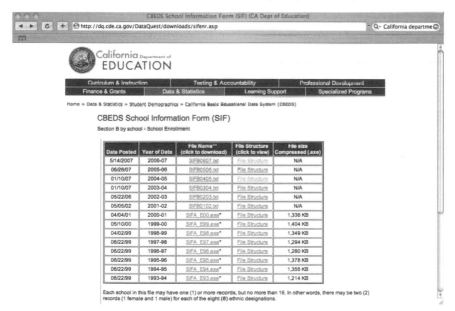

Slide 7.1 Retrieving school-level data from the California Department of Education

In addition to the raw datasets, the California Department of Education also provides access to data management tools such as DataQuest, which allows the user to retrieve summary information on a range of variables including school performance, staffing and truancy rates at progressively lower levels of aggregation from the state to the school.

Managing the data

In order to carry out the full analysis of teacher characteristics in Californian schools, data from a number of sources were collected together into one file. In this section, the steps needed to manage two of these datasets is described. Both datasets were downloaded from the **Aggregate files** section of the *Staffing Data Files* webpages in CBEDS. Dataset 1 contains school-level information on teacher credentials and experience. In this dataset un-needed variables were deleted. Dataset 2 is a larger file containing information on the profile of certificated staff such as their ethnic and educational characteristics. All variables in this file were retained and Dataset 2 was merged with Dataset 1 using the steps outlined next. In the worked example here, data for the 2005–2006 school year were used.

Preparing dataset 1: teacher credentials and experience
The file relating to teacher credentials and experience (**tchcrd05.dbf**) was downloaded and then opened in SPSS using the **File → Open → Data** command (Slide 7.2).

The **File Structure** file that accompanies the dataset (shown in the table in Slide 7.2) lists the 19 variables that are available for analysis. In this example, we will retain all 9973 cases but reduce the number of variables from 19 to eight. The variables that will be retained are:

> **CDS_CODE**: a 14-digit code to identify the county, the district, and the school
> **NUMTEACH**: number of teachers at the school
> **FULL_PCT**: percentage of teachers who have completed a teacher preparation programme and hold a preliminary, clear professional or life credential
> **UNIV_PCT**: percentage of teachers who are enrolled in a university credential programme and who are concurrently taking college coursework
> **EMER_PCT**: percentage of teachers holding emergency credentials
> **WVR_PCT**: percentage of teachers working under waivers
> **YRONE_TCH**: number of first-year teachers
> **YRTWO_TCH**: number of second-year teachers.

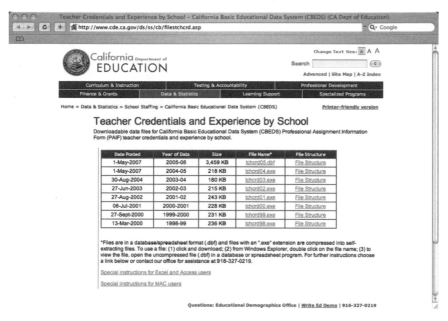

Slide 7.2 Teacher Credentials and Experience datafiles window

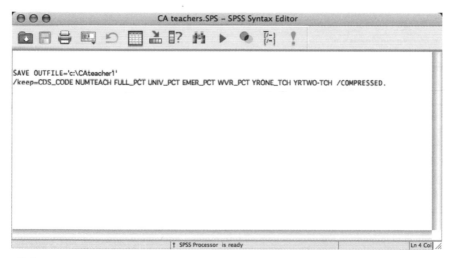

Slide 7.3 Syntax for deleting variables from Teacher Credentials and Experience dataset

The Syntax used to delete all other variables and retain the eight listed here can be found in Slide 7.3.

Highlighting the Syntax codes and clicking run will result in a new, smaller SPSS file being created. This new file was named **CAteacher1**.

Preparing dataset 2: certificated staff profile
A second dataset was also downloaded from the CBEDS Certificated Staff
Profile pages. This file contained information on the background characteristics of certificated staff (**percert05**). This file was opened in SPSS
using the same procedure as just seen and saved under the file name
CAteacher2. This new file contains 28 variables describing the following
characteristics of teachers in all California schools:

- age
- years service
- sex
- qualifications
- ethnicity
- total teachers in school.

This file was then merged with our earlier file containing the data on
teacher certification (**CAteacher1**).

Merging the two files
The steps needed to merge the two files **CAteacher1** and **CAteacher2**
are now described.

Step 1
In order to merge variables from two (or more) files, there needs to be at
least one variable that both files have in common. Here we have used the
14-digit county-district-school identification code (**CDS_CODE**) as the
variable common to both files. You will need to check that the variables
have the same *format* in both files (**CAteacher1** and **CAteacher2**) and
that both files are *sorted* in the same way, otherwise the merge will not
work. Also check that the variables are of the same type: either both
numeric or both string and that they are both of the same width or have
the same number of decimal places.

Step 2
Merging the smaller file (**CAteacher1**) into the larger file (**CAtea-
cher2**). The next step is to open the file **CAteacher2** and then in the
Menu Bar select **Data** → **Merge Files** → **Add Variables**. Use the menu
to select and then open the file **CAteacher1,** this will then open a new
window (Slide 7.4).

The variable common to both files is **cds_code**. You can see it listed in
the **Excluded Variables** work area (**cds_code> (+)**) and in the **New
Working Data File** area (**cds_code>(*)**).

Slide 7.4 Merging variables window (1)

Step 3
In the **Excluded Variables** work area, highlight the **cds_code> (+)** variable. Check the box next to **Match cases on key variables in sorted files** and then use the lower arrow key to move the **cds_code> (+)** variable into the **Key Variables** work area (Slide 7.5).

Step 4
Then click on **OK**. A warning window will appear instructing you to check that the data are sorted correctly. As you did this in **Step 1**, click **OK** to start the merge. The new variables will be added to the end of the list of variables in the file **CAteacher2**. It is worth saving this merged file under a new name.

Findings
This section provides a summary of the findings to emerge from this analysis. The dataset used in the current worked example used the most recent data available at the time of writing (for the 2005–2006 academic year). The datasets used in the original study and also used in the following section were taken from the preceding academic year.
    As we can see in Table 7.1, it is the schools in the poorest school

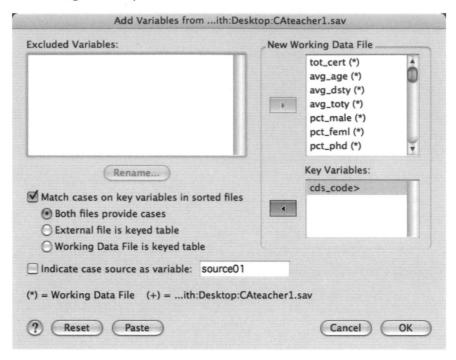

Slide 7.5 Merging variables window (2)

districts that are failing to make adequate yearly progress. (Note that district poverty quartile levels are determined by the proportion of students attending schools in the district who are eligible for free school meals.) For example, 45% of the schools in the highest poverty school

Table 7.1 School performance under NCLB, according to school district poverty quartile

	Schools making AYP		Schools not making AYP	
	N	%	N	%
1st poverty quartile (least poor)	1450	82	320	18
2nd poverty quartile	1514	70	644	30
3rd poverty quartile	1341	61	870	39
4th poverty quartile (most poor)	1233	55	1004	45
All schools	5538	66	2838	34

Source: California Department of Education 2005b

districts did not make AYP in 2004, compared with only 18% of schools in low-poverty districts.

Characteristics of California's teachers

In spring 2004, California estimated that around 52% of classes in core academic subjects were taught by 'highly qualified' teachers and gave a figure of 40% for classes in 'high-poverty' schools (Table 7.2). Estimates such as these represent a relatively low starting point from which the state has to meet its targets for compliance with *No Child Left Behind*'s highly qualified teacher requirements by 2005–2006.

Table 7.2 Number of classes in the core academic subjects being taught by 'highly qualified' teachers

School type	Total number of core academic classes	Percentage of core academic classes taught by 'highly qualified' teachers
All schools	630,647	52
High poverty schools	153,922	40
Low poverty schools	165,591	60

Source: California Department of Education 2005a: 37

Although only just over half the number of core academic classes across the state were being taught by 'highly qualified' teachers in 2004, this figure does vary slightly between schools with differing levels of success with regard to making AYP. For example, 47% of classes in schools that failed to make AYP were being taught by teachers who were NCLB compliant, compared with 54% of classes in schools that made AYP (Table 7.3). Even so, and NCLB's teacher quality targets notwith-standing, California's teachers appear to be well-trained and experienced professionals. Around 90% of teachers have teaching credentials, while over one-third hold a masters' degree or higher (Table 7.3). The pro-portion of teachers who are teaching on emergency certificates also remains quite small. Overall, the distribution of qualified teachers among schools that do not make AYP is similar to that in schools that were successful on this indicator. However, just because teachers have a degree and certification to teach does not mean that they are considered to be 'highly qualified' under NCLB – that designation depends on their additionally demonstrating sufficient content knowledge for their subject areas.

Table 7.3 Teacher qualifications in California, according to school type

	Schools making AYP		Schools not making AYP		All schools	
	N	*Mean*	*N*	*Mean*	*N*	*Mean*
Classes taught by NCLB-compliant teachers (%)	5872	54	3048	47	8920	52
Completed a teacher preparation programme (%)	5969	94	3149	89	9118	92
Teaching with emergency credentials (%)	5969	4	3149	6	9118	4
Teachers with an MA degree or higher (%)	5974	35	3155	34	9129	35

Source: California Department of Education 2005b

Characteristics of California's students

According to the California Department of Education, approximately 45% of children enrolled in kindergarten to grade 12 are Hispanic or Latino, 34% are white, 11% are Asian, Filipino or Pacific Islander, 8% are African-American and almost 1% are Native American. Together, these students speak more than 56 different languages (California Department of Education 2005b). Indeed it is students with limited English skills (here termed English learners (EL)), who are more likely to be taught in schools that do not make AYP. Schools that made AYP tested higher proportions of students from white and Asian backgrounds and fewer students from economically disadvantaged and Hispanic homes, compared with schools that failed this indicator. As we can see in Table 7.4, 66% of the learners in schools that did not make AYP came from

Table 7.4 Mean percentage of students enrolled for English-language arts tests

	Schools making AYP (N=5916) %	Schools not making AYP (N=3144) %	All schools (N=9060) %
African-American	7	11	8
Asian	8	4	7
Hispanic	34	54	41
White	44	25	37
Economically disadvantaged	46	66	53
English learners	24	37	28
SEN	10	12	11

Source: California Department of Education 2005b

economically disadvantaged homes, compared with 46% of the learners in schools that successfully met AYP targets.

Of course, testing higher proportions of certain groups of students in 'failing' schools is only really an issue if these students actually achieve lower results. Using the English-language arts test as an example, Table 7.5 shows the proportions of students from the different student groups who achieved or surpassed proficiency levels in 2004. Students from the African-American and Hispanic communities were less likely to reach minimum proficiency levels on the state literacy assessment than students from white or Asian homes. English learners, students with special educational needs and those from economically disadvantaged homes also achieved relatively low proficiency rates on this test.

Table 7.5 Mean percentage of students making English-language arts tests

	Number of schools	Students making AYP (%)
African-American	4314	30
Asian	4194	58
Hispanic	7420	29
White	6900	51
Economically disadvantaged	7599	27
English learners	6790	23
SEN	6999	16
All students	8340	39

Source: California Department of Education 2005b

Thus it seems that, on the one hand, California has a highly educated and experienced teacher workforce where, regardless of whether the school is considered to be 'failing' under *No Child Left Behind* or is located in a high-poverty school district, around one-third of teachers have at least a masters' degree and all have similar levels of teaching experience. On the other hand, higher proportions of teachers in the least wealthy school districts do not have full teacher certification, although the numbers of teachers in this category continues to fall across the state. However, and more crucially as far as the NCLB mandate for improvement is concerned, only around half of all classes were being taught by teachers who were considered to be 'highly qualified'. Although the number of these classes is lowest in high-poverty school districts, at around 42%, it is also an issue for the most wealthy districts – where around 58% of classes were taught by NCLB-compliant staff. While, to some extent, the distribution of California's teachers appears quite equitable, the distribution of certain subgroups of students does not. For example, students from the Hispanic community – the majority ethnic group in California – are overwhelmingly attending schools in the poorest school districts which, in turn, are failing to reach minimum standards under *No Child Left Behind*.

'Teacher quality' and student success

> The Teaching Commission believes that quality teachers are the critical factor in helping people overcome the damaging effects of poverty, lack of parental guidance, and other challenges. (The Teaching Commission 2004: 14)

In California, high-quality school-level data that has been collected over several years allows for a closer examination of at least one of the determinants of school success: performance in state-wide tests. By considering the influence of both teacher- and student-level variables on school outcomes, we can examine the extent to which teacher characteristics, many of which are taken as proxies of teacher quality under NCLB, can influence school outcomes at the aggregate level. The outcome measure used was the proportion of students who demonstrated that they were proficient or higher on state tests in English-language arts, although similar trends were found for the mathematics assessments. Once again, the data used in the analysis were retrieved from publicly accessible datasets on the California Department of Education Data and Statistics website (California Department of Education 2005b).

A number of linear regression models were carried out. Each considered the amount of variance in a school's test outcome that could be explained by student and teacher characteristics. Variables were selected for inclusion in the models based on the results of the descriptive analysis described earlier. Attempts were also made to include variables that contributed to the most parsimonious model. The most powerful model related the proportion of students who achieved proficiency levels or higher in the English-language arts tests to a range of student background factors, such as the proportion of students who received free school meals as well as the students' minority background and language status. The most powerful teacher-level variables were those linked to teacher characteristics, namely the proportion of female teachers and African-American teachers in a school and variables linked to teacher quality, such as the number of classes taught by NCLB-compliant teachers, the number of teachers who were certified and the number who held a masters' qualification or higher. In the final model, the student- and teacher-level variables were entered as separate blocks. As our interest here was with students' test outcomes, it makes sense that the block containing student level variables was entered into the model first, followed by a second block of teacher-level variables. The amount of variance in school examination outcomes that can be explained by the student and teacher variables and the model coefficients for the multiple linear regression analysis are given in Table 7.6.

Table 7.6 Standardised beta coefficients for proficiency in English-language arts tests

	Standardised beta coefficients	t
Block 1: student characteristics		
Constant		222.2
% Free school meal students in school	−0.6	−66.2
% English learners	0.1	9.9
Number of students in school	0.08	12.9
% Hispanic students	−0.3	−28.1
Block 2: teacher characteristics		
Constant		38.5
% free school meal students in school	−0.6	−56.9
% English learners	0.08	6.7
Number of students in school	0.1	21.6
% Hispanic students	−0.3	−29.9
% African-American teachers	−0.1	−14.0
% Female teachers	0.1	21.1
% Teachers with MA or higher	0.05	7.3
% Completed a teacher preparation programme	−0.01	−2.0
% Classes taught by NCLB-compliant teachers	0.02	2.7
Block 1: Student variables only	$R^2 = 0.69$	
Block 2: Student and teacher variables	$R^2 = 0.72$	

Table 7.6 shows that 69% of the variance in the English-language arts test outcomes can be accounted for by student-level variables, with the teacher-level variables only explaining 3% of the variance. The standardised beta coefficients give us an idea of the strength of the relationship between these variables and the test outcome. For example, the percentage of students in a school who receive free school meals has a strong negative relationship with test outcomes. This relationship is so strong that it suggests that if every other variable in this model remained the same, for every 1% increase in the number of students with free school meals, the proportion of students achieving proficiency levels or higher in the ELA test would go down by 0.6%. Similarly, for a school with a 10% increase in free school meal students, proficiency levels would fall by 6% and so on. It is also interesting to note that the teacher-level variables that have the strongest relationship with test outcomes are related to teacher characteristics, the proportion of female or African-

American teachers in a school and *not* to teacher quality, for example the proportion of teachers with a masters' degree. Variables relating to the experience of teachers and the numbers teaching on emergency certificates had no impact on the model and so were excluded from the analysis. It is important to remember that in this analysis several different models combining a range of teacher- and student-level characteristics were carried out. In each model, the results consistently provided no evidence to support the contention that student characteristics are 'less influential in predicting achievement levels than variables assessing the quality of the teaching force' (Darling-Hammond 2000). What the model does suggest is that teacher characteristics, many of which are considered to be proxies for teacher quality under *No Child Left Behind*, are less influential than student characteristics in predicting student academic outcomes.

The findings suggest that overall California has a well-qualified and highly experienced teacher workforce that is relatively equitably distributed among the states' institutions. Contrariwise, the distribution of California's students appears to be less fair, with students from poorer homes and certain ethnic backgrounds being disproportionately represented in the state's least wealthy and least successful schools. In addition, the finding that it is student background factors rather than teacher-quality characteristics that are the key determinants of school success also brings into question the extent to which requiring teachers to improve their subject content skills will really help close the achievement gaps in California's schools. With regard to the determinants of school success, here taken to be performance in high-stakes tests, it is clear that the factors most closely linked to school outcomes are not related to the quality of teachers at all. Rather, it is the *nature of the school student population* that is most likely to determine how a school performs on the state's accountability tests and, in turn, makes adequate yearly progress. This is not to say that teachers cannot make a difference to individual students, however, as this analysis has shown, at aggregate level, there is little evidence of a 'teacher effect'.

Patterns of inequality in European schools

This final example briefly considers the relationship between student characteristics and test outcomes for *PISA 2000*, in order to understand patterns of inequality in European schools. While this relationship is of important substantive interest in the field of education, its treatment here is necessarily brief – instead, our emphasis is on downloading and preparing the PISA dataset for analysis.

Accessing the PISA datasets

The results presented here are taken from a secondary analysis of the PISA study (OECD 2000a). This survey of the knowledge and skills of 15-year-old students in the principal industrialised countries is repeated on a 3-year cycle. More detail about PISA appears in Appendix 1. The first PISA study, which was conducted in 2000, covered 265,000 students from 32 countries, but this example focuses on the 74,356 pupils in 2647 schools that made up the 15 countries of the EU. In this example, we download the whole of the *PISA 2000* dataset. This file is very large and the time it takes to download can depend on your internet connection and other technical factors. If you only wish to explore a few of the PISA variables then there is an interactive data selection page (OECD 2000b), which you may find more useful. Although this worked example is with the oldest PISA datasets, the stages for downloading are the same for *PISA 2003* and *PISA 2006*. The reason why we are looking at the oldest form of PISA is simply because the UK did not meet sampling requirements for *PISA 2003* and, at the time of writing, the datasets for *PISA 2006* were not yet available for public use. Information about response rates, sampling strategies, questionnaire design for *PISA 2000* is available in the *PISA 2000* technical manual (OECD 2001).

The PISA dataset can be downloaded from the OECD PISA website (Slide 7.6). In this example, we are interested in the responses to the student questionnaire and the test scores linked with reading

Slide 7.6 Downloading the PISA 2000 datasets

achievement (the principal focus of *PISA 2000*). Instructions for down-loading the PISA dataset follow.

The first step is to visit the *PISA 2000* database website (*http://pisaweb. acer.edu.au/oecd/oecd_pisa_data_s1.html*), which appears in Slide 7.6.

You will need to select the following options if you wish to download your data into SPSS (note that it is also possible to download the data into SAS):

- *Codebooks and questionnaires*: select **Student Questionnaire** (a file of 102kB).
- *SAS control files*: leave this untouched, we are downloading into SPSS here.
- *SPSS control files*: select **SPSS control file for the student questionnaire and reading achievement data file** (a file of 38 kB).
- *Datasets in TXT formats* (compressed) and documentation: select **Student questionnaire and reading achievement data file** (a file of 46.5MB, this takes a little time to download).

Selecting these files will automatically start the download to your computer – there is no separate 'start' button that you need to press. You should now have three files:

- **PISA_2000_Student_Questionnaire.doc**: this is a word file containing the student questionnaire
- **intstud_read.sps**: this is an SPSS control file that you need to download the main dataset
- **intstud_read_v3.txt**: this is a zipped file containing the main dataset.

Once the data have been successfully downloaded you will need to open the **intstud_read.sps** file. This will be opened in SPSS as a Syntax file (Slide 7.7). Slide 7.7 shows the first section of the Syntax file that you will need to use in order to read the main dataset into SPSS.

You will now need to tell SPSS where on your computer it will need to look in order to find the main datafile (**instud_read-v3.txt**). This command appears circled on Slide 7.7. You will need to replace the **** with the file's location, for example, the C: drive folder named **PISA**.

To do this replace DATA LIST file="c:****\instud_read_v3.txt"/with DATA LIST file="c:**PISA**\instud_read_v3.txt"/.

You will then need to tell SPSS where you would like it to SAVE the dataset once it has been read as an SPSS file. If you scroll to the bottom of the **instud_read.sps** Syntax file you will find another command which has been circled in Slide 7.8.

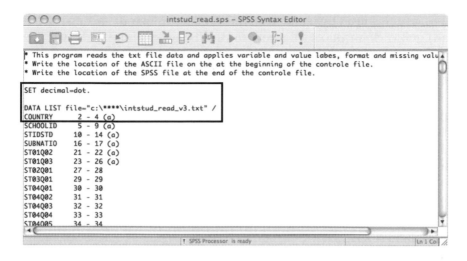

Slide 7.7 Syntax instructions for locating the PISA 2000 datafile (1)

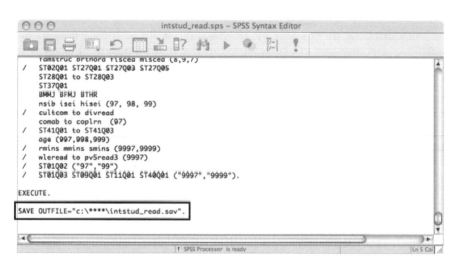

Slide 7.8 Syntax instructions for locating the new PISA 2000 SPSS datafile (2)

For example, if you wanted to save the dataset to a file called PISA2000 on your C: drive you would need to replace:

SAVE OUTFILE = ''c:****\intstud_read.sav''

with the following:

SAVE OUTFILE = ''c:\PISA2000\intstud_read.sav''

Once you have told SPSS where to find the file and then where to save it to, you just need to highlight all the Syntax commands (**Edit** → **Select all**) and click on the black arrow to run the programme. This will then open the text file (**instud_read-v3.txt**) in SPSS. Note that this is a large file with over a quarter of a million cases; it might take a little time to convert to SPSS.

Deleting un-needed cases

The *PISA 2000* dataset contain data from 43 different countries, giving 228,840 cases in total. In this example, we will limit our consideration to five European countries: Finland, France, Germany, Sweden and the UK. As we are only looking at a subgroup of the total number of countries, we will need to delete un-needed countries from our dataset. The five countries we will retain have the following codes:

Finland = 246
France = 250
Germany = 276
Sweden = 752
UK = 826

You can check these codes by viewing. We will use these codes as the basis for selecting cases to be retained in the main dataset; all cases with codes that are different from those listed will be deleted. To delete un-needed cases you will need to open the Select cases window (Slide 7.9) in the **Menu Bar** select **Data** → **Select Cases**.

Selecting the **If condition is satisfied** button opens a new window (Slide 7.10). You will now need to select cases *if* they meet certain criteria, in other words, if a country has a certain code, it will be selected.

To do this click on the **Country three-digit ISO code (country)** variable and use the arrow to move the variable into the **work area** (further information on selecting cases in this way is given in Appendix 2 and in Chapter 6).

Use the **keypad** to enter = and then place the country code in inverted commas. The reason why you need to use inverted commas is that the country codes are represented as string variables not numeric variables (you can check this by looking at the variable type in the **Variable View** window).

Once you have entered the information for the first country, you will need to separate it from the next country by the **OR** operation. This tells SPSS to select all cases if they have the value 246 OR 276 and so on. Continue this for all the countries you wish to select and then click **Continue**.

A window similar to that in Slide 7.9 will now appear. If you are sure that you have correctly selected all the cases you wish to work with, you can check the option **Unselected Cases are Deleted**, alternatively you

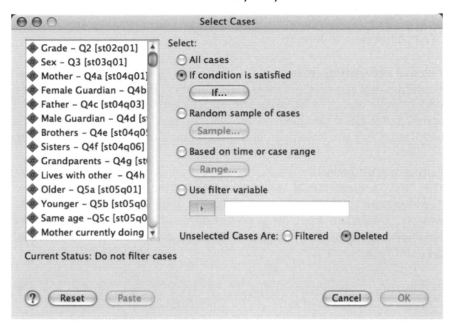

Slide 7.9 Select Cases window

Slide 7.10 Select Cases: If sub-window

can **filter** all un-needed cases by checking the **Unselected Cases are Filtered** option. Then click **OK** and the operation should run successfully and leave you with a dataset containing 28,366 cases.

Deleting un-needed variables
The original PISA dataset contains several hundred variables, in this example, we limit our analysis to only 10. Full details about the definitions of these variables and the questions that make up the indices appear

in the *PISA 2000* Manual (OECD 2001). The variables kept in this example were as follows.

Parental occupation (hisei)

Students were required to report their mothers' and fathers' occupations, which were classified according to ISCO criteria and transferred to a scale, as described by Ganzeboom and Treiman (1996). The variable is based on either the father's or mother's occupation, whichever is higher.

Family wealth (**wealth**)

The PISA index of family wealth is based on the students' responses to questionnaire items on the availability, in their own home, of a dishwasher, a room of their own, educational software and a link to the internet and the number of mobile phones, television sets, computers, cars and bathrooms they have at home.

Performance in reading examination (**pv1read**)

PISA gives two kinds of estimate for performance in reading, maths and science – a weighted likelihood estimate and a set of 'plausible' values. The plausible values are not test scores; rather, they are designed to give good estimates of parameters of student populations, instead of an estimate of individual student proficiency. As a result, the plausible values are better suited for describing the performance of a population. In this exploratory analysis, one set of plausible values is reported, although the results for the other sets of values were similar.

Academic self-concept (**scacad**)

This index was derived from students' level of agreement with the following statements: I learn things quickly in most school subjects; I am good at most school subjects; I do well in test in most school subjects.

Index of engagement in reading (**joyread**)

This index was derived from students' level of agreement with the following statements: I read only if I have to; Reading is one of my favourite hobbies; I like talking about books with other people; I find it hard to finish books; I feel happy if I receive a book as a present; For me, reading is a waste of time; I enjoy going to a bookstore or a library; I read only to get information that I need; I cannot sit still and read for more than a few minutes.

Other variables retained were student sex, the student weighting variable and the country, school and student identifiers. Slide 7.11 shows the Syntax commands for deleting the un-needed variables from the full *PISA 2000* dataset and will then save the new file as **PISA**.

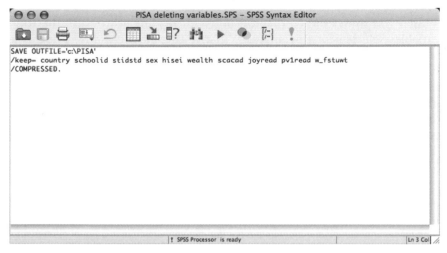

Slide 7.11 Syntax instructions for deleting variables

The *PISA 2000* dataset is now much more manageable to analyse. The next section describes some of the findings from an exploratory analysis of the relationship between reading achievement and student background characteristics.

Findings
The findings given here are for all five countries. If you wished only to focus on one country you can use the **Select cases (Data → Select cases)** or **Split file (Data → Split File)** function to analyse countries separately.

Across all five countries, female students achieved higher scores in the reading test than their male peers (Table 7.7).

Table 7.7 Mean scores for PISA 2000 reading achievement, according to sex

Country	Male	Female	All students
Finland	521 (88)	572 (84)	547 (89)
France	490 (93)	519 (87)	505 (91)
Germany	468 (111)	502 (107)	485 (110)
Sweden	498 (92)	535 (87)	516 (92)
UK	511 (102)	537 (96)	525 (100)
All countries	489 (104)	520 (98)	505 (102)

() = standard deviations.

Source: OECD 2000a

Table 7.8 shows the correlation between reading scores and the four variables selected for this analysis. In the UK and Germany, there is a relatively strong correlation between parental occupation and reading scores (around 0.4). Perhaps unsurprisingly, students who say they enjoy reading also score highly on the reading assessment: this is particularly true in the Scandinavian countries where the relationship between reading enjoyment and achievement is the strongest of all the variables considered.

Table 7.8 Correlation between reading scores and selected student variables

Country	Parental occupation	Family wealth	Academic self-concept	Engagement in reading
Finland	0.23	0.10	0.44	0.48
France	0.35	0.21	no data	0.30
Germany	0.40	0.19	0.22	0.42
Sweden	0.30	0.07	0.39	0.45
UK	0.38	0.12	0.28	0.39
All countries	0.33	0.13	0.33	0.41

Source: OECD 2000a

Notice the relatively low correlation between family wealth and the test outcome, especially when compared with the higher correlations for parental occupation. Indeed, the correlation between parental occupation and family wealth is relatively weak: 0.30, across all countries, suggesting that both variables are measuring rather different phenomena (also see Chapter 4).

The strength of the relationship between the variables across all five countries is confirmed by an exploratory multiple regression analysis (Table 7.9). Here students from higher occupational groups with high academic self-concept and who enjoy reading achieved higher scores on the *PISA 2000* reading test. However, these variables account for only

Table 7.9 Multiple regression analysis showing relationship between test outcome and student characteristics

	Standardised beta coefficients	t	Sig.
Constant		220.4	0.000
Parental occupation	0.23	33.8	0.000
Academic self-concept	0.21	29.9	0.000
Enjoyment of reading	0.37	53.7	0.000

$R^2 = 0.304$. Number = 15,853.

around 30% of the variance in test outcomes, suggesting that other variables, which were not considered in our exploratory model, may have an important role to play in influencing reading test results.

Summary

This chapter has demonstrated how international sources of secondary data can be used to model the relationship between different variables of contemporary interest in educational research. As in the preceding chapters of this part of the book, the emphasis has been on data management techniques and, in particular, taking the reader through the stages needed to download the large PISA datasets.

Part III

8

Endpiece

[Secondary data analysis] can help save time, money, career, degrees, research interests, vitality and talent, self images and myriads of data from untimely, unnecessary and unfortunate loss. (Glaser 1963: 14)

Despite these obvious plaudits, secondary data analysis is a method that is much underused in social and educational research. The approach has a long pedigree that has its roots in the early Victorian social survey movements as well as in the political arithmetic traditions of the late eighteenth century. Even so, there is limited consensus on a definition for the term, although commentators tend to agree that it involves some form of re-analysis or reporting of existing data. This flexibility with defining secondary data analysis perhaps reinforces its suitability for including any analysis that involves the reinterpretation of existing data that bring new methodological and theoretical perspectives, or that adopt the original or novel research questions and are undertaken by the original researcher or individuals new to the data. But it is also important to emphasise that the analysis of secondary data need not involve the manipulation of complex and large datasets. Indeed, much of the data that are available for secondary analysis are in the form of aggregate data – that is, data which have already been analysed and are presented in summary form. The secondary analysis of summary data is a useful technique for researchers who wish to use secondary sources to present a context for more in-depth work or who have limited experience or interest in downloading, preparing and re-analysing the larger datasets. In this way, secondary analysis is a useful complement to small-scale research and in particular research being undertaken by novice researchers perhaps as part of dissertation work at undergraduate and postgraduate level.

One of the reasons why secondary data analysis is relatively underused in social research can perhaps be attributed to the wide range of criticisms and concerns that the field attracts. As we saw in Chapter 2, numeric secondary data have been censured for reducing the complexity of social experiences to mere quantities, for being susceptible to outside control and for being 'vitiated' (Bulmer 1980: 508) with errors. In defence of secondary data, we have suggested that without them, how can social scientists describe the social work around them, posit theories and test them empirically? Official data, as reported by governments, should be used to ensure accountability and within this there is a role for social scientists in informing the collection of social data, for developing social indicators and providing theoretical justifications for the use, or exclusion, of different social categories. Numeric social data can never be error free, neither can the producers of the data prevent them from being used to make unwarranted comparisons, but neither should they be disregarded on this account, rather, they should be treated with the same amount of appropriate scepticism and attention to its limitations that we should apply to any social data: primary or secondary, numeric or qualitative.

Secondary data analysis can offer social, methodological and theoretical benefits to the researcher. Arguably, it is most effective when combined with other approaches, most notably in the new political arithmetic tradition of research where its scale aids generalisability and the numeric techniques needed for its analysis can be relatively straightforward and accessible to most social scientists, not just statisticians. The accessibility of secondary sources enables novice researchers to gain valuable experience in undertaking research in an area of their own interest, as well as presenting opportunities to publish and present their findings as independent researchers. Finally, secondary analysis also has an important role in teaching and in research methods teaching in particular, where it can be a useful tool in the teaching of statistical techniques as well as the methodologies of survey design, sampling and so on. It can enable students to undertake their own analysis of real data that are of a scale that they would be unable to replicate themselves and by encouraging students to adopt secondary analysis for at least part of their dissertation research, ethical issues can be reduced or may be avoided entirely.

In showing the usefulness of secondary data, particularly in developing research that adopts mixed methods approaches, it is hoped that this book can make some small and perhaps practical contribution to widening the use of this approach in social and educational research. It cannot be overstated, however, that the aim of this book has not been to privilege the use of one particular research method over another; it is rather a more modest attempt to argue the case for the inclusion of a relatively underused technique in the 'methodological toolbox' of the social science researcher.

Appendix 1: Sources of secondary data

This appendix provides an introduction to a small selection of the huge range of sources that are available for secondary analysis worldwide. The emphasis here is on web-based resources but many of the publications are also available through libraries. It is impossible to include every source and this appendix attempts to show the diversity of resources that are available. For researchers with an interest in international sources of secondary data, the section on archives towards the end of the chapter should provide a good starting place. This appendix deals with two principal forms of secondary data: the raw data of the large-scale datasets and data that are available in aggregate form, i.e. those that have already been analysed and are presented in summary form, often as part of a more detailed publication.

The appendix is organised into three sections. The first focuses on UK sources of secondary data and is split into seven subsections:

- administrative records
- archives and gateways
- census data
- data management tools
- longitudinal and cohort survey data
- regular survey data
- training and support.

The second section gives a brief introduction to the vast range of secondary sources that are based in the United States; it retains the same basic order as that in Section one. The final section adopts a similar approach and covers other international sources of secondary data, although the emphasis here is on international data archives and other information gateways. Active links to the secondary sources provided here are maintained through the website accompanying this book.

Section one: United Kingdom sources of secondary data

Administrative records

Data collected for administrative purposes – that is, data that are collected as part of routine administration, rather than for the basis of research – are a fruitful and easily accessible source of data for secondary analysis. For example, in the field of education and training it is possible to track patterns of applications to higher education (HE), the destinations of HE graduates, the success rates of institutions and students in further education (FE), staff and financial resources in both FE and HE, as well as applications to teacher training and performance indicators for teacher training institutions. A few examples of the sources of such data follow.

Graduate Teacher Training Registry
The Graduate Teacher Training Registry (GTTR) processes applications to postgraduate teacher training courses in Britain. It provides summary applicant statistics organised by subject and teaching sector, as well as an annual statistical report. Access is at www.gttr.ac.uk/reports.html.

Higher Education Statistical Agency
The Higher Education Statistical Agency (HESA) is the central source for collecting and disseminating statistics on higher education in the UK. Its publications and online facilities provide statistics on students, resources, finance, qualifiers, staff and destinations, as well as comparative information on the performance of institutions with regard to widening participation, student retention and teaching and learning. Data can be accessed from www.hesa.ac.uk.

Learning and Skills Council
The Learning and Skills Council (LSC) is responsible for planning and funding education and training for those not in universities in England. Data include learner numbers, work-based learning provision, success, retention and achievement rate data, as well as staff statistics dating back to 1994. LSC data are available for download in Excel format or as part of a series of *Statistical First Releases*. Access is at www.lsc.gov.uk/.

Training and Development Agency for schools
The Training and Development Agency (TDA) for schools website provides access to data on the characteristics of trainees and their chosen subjects, also spreadsheets containing detailed performance profiles of initial teacher training providers back to 1998. There is also access to the questionnaires and results of the newly qualified teacher (NQT) annual surveys. Access is at http://dataprovision.tda.gov.uk/public.

Universities and Colleges Admissions Service
The Universities and Colleges Admissions Service (UCAS) is the central service for administering admissions to British higher education institutions (HEIs). Its databases extend back to 1996 and contain statistics on applications and acceptances to HEIs; data are presented according to institution, subject, educational qualifications and student background information. Summary data can be accessed electronically and detailed annual information can be downloaded in Excel format. There is also an online statistical enquiry tool for analysing UCAS data which can be accessed by following the link to statistical services from www.ucas.com.

In addition to agencies such as those just described, government departments themselves will also collect and report a range of administrative data that are suitable for secondary analysis. The last part of this section introduces the Office for National Statistics and some of the government departments responsible for data dissemination.

Office for National Statistics
The Office for National Statistics (ONS) is responsible for overseeing the collection and publication of statistics related to the economic and social life of the UK. Its principal areas of data collection include:

* economy
* environment
* health
* labour market
* population
* society
* travel and tourism.

The ONS website provides detailed summary data on themes within its main areas of data collection through its *UK Snapshot* facility, while its *Focus On* overviews give useful summary statistics on an additional dozen topics, which can then be linked to more detailed analysis. Its *Neighbourhood Statistics* and *Census* facilities are described elsewhere in this appendix.

Government departments
Alternatively, administrative data that are useful for secondary analysis can be located directly from the different government departments; a few examples are:

* *Department for Children, Schools and Families (DCSF)*: a huge range of administrative data on examination results, class sizes, school buildings, participation and the labour market. The DCSF website is at www.dcsf.gov.uk, then follow the links from the Research & Statistics

gateway. A worked example using DCSF data to examine looked-after children is given in Chapter 5.

- *Department for Environment, Food and Rural Affairs (DEFRA)*: provides statistics on the food sector, environment, sustainable development and farm and sea fisheries: www.defra.gov.uk/evidence/statistics.htm.
- *Department of Health (DoH)*: healthcare (e.g. hospitals, mental health, NHS performance, screening and prevention), workforce (e.g. staff working across the main health and care areas), public health (e.g. smoking, drinking and drug use and abortion statistics), as well as social care and social services statistics for adults and children: www.dh.gov.uk/en/Publicationsandstatistics/Statistics/index.htm.
- *Department for Work and Pensions*: A range of summary data on disability and carers, families and children, pensioners and the working-age population can be accessed using an online tabulation tool. The site also provides access to publications linked to the Family Resources Survey and other administrative datasets: www.dwp.gov.uk/asd/statistics.asp.
- *Home Office*: crime statistics, asylum and immigration statistics are available from www.homeoffice.gov.uk/rds/.

Archives and gateways

Economic and Social Data Service
The Economic and Social Data Service (ESDS) provides an access and support gateway to a wide range of economic and social data. A key aim of the ESDS is to enhance and support the secondary analysis of such data. The ESDS operates through partnerships with organisations such as the UK Data Archive, Manchester Information and Associated Services (MIMAS) and the Cathie Marsh Centre for Survey Research (CCSR). Access to the ESDS datasets requires registration through ATHENS (see later in this appendix) but is free to academic users; commercial users may have to pay a fee. Four key areas are covered by ESDS.

ESDS Government
This is a gateway to the major government-sponsored surveys such as the Labour Force Survey (LFS) and the General Household Survey (GHS). It aims to support and facilitate the more effective use of government datasets in research and training. The following section provides more information on a selection of the individual surveys supported by ESDS and gives details on accessing the data, as well as the facilities for training and support.

ESDS International
This provides access and support for a range of international data series
and surveys including data produced by the World Bank, the Organisation for Economic Cooperation and Development (OECD), the United
Nations, Eurobarometer and the European Social Survey.

ESDS Longitudinal
This provides access and specialist support for a range of longitudinal
cohort and panel studies including the British Cohort Study and the
British Household Panel Survey.

ESDS Qualidata
This supports access to a range of qualitative datasets with a particular
emphasis on collecting and supporting digitised data resources. The service gives access to some of the classic studies of British society including
the research papers for Jackson and Marsden's work, *Education and the
Working Class* (1962).
   The homepage for the ESDS is at www.esds.ac.uk.

ESRC Question Bank
This is an information resource with a particular emphasis on quantitative survey methods. Hosted by the University of Surrey, the Question
Bank website enables users to find examples of specific data collection
questions and see them in the context within which they have been used
for data collection. It is intended to assist with the design of new survey
questionnaires, the search for data for secondary analysis and the
teaching of survey research methods. The website provides a useful
alphabetic list of topics and surveys, as well as fact sheets on data collection, computer-assisted interviewing and other techniques. Further
details are available at http://qb.soc.surrey.ac.uk/index.htm. An example
showing how questions and datasets can be identified using the Question
Bank is given in Chapter 4.

Manchester Information and Associated Services
Manchester Information and Associated Services (MIMAS) provides
data-sharing and gateway services to the UK higher education, further
education and research community. It also provides support and training
in the use of these resources. Resources include access to census datasets
and CASWEB (see later), as well as the Archives Hub, which provides
descriptions of the archives of over 150 UK universities and colleges.
MIMAS also supports the ESDS International facility. MIMAS is available
at www.mimas.ac.uk.

Mass Observation Archive
Hosted by the University of Sussex, the Mass Observation Archive
(MOA) provides access to the papers generated by the original Mass
Observation Social Research Organisation (1937 to early 1950s) and
newer material collected continuously since 1981. Further information
about the Mass Observation Archive, including information on access to
its collections, can be found at http://www.massobs.org.uk/index.htm.

UK Data Archive
The UK Data Archive curates the largest collection of digital data in the
social sciences in the UK. It is part-funded by the ESRC and is a lead
partner of the Economic and Social Data Service (ESDS). Its data catalogue provides access to over 5000 datasets for research and teaching
purposes across a range of disciplines. It is well worth accessing the UK
Data Archive and browsing through its list of datasets, just to appreciate
the variety and range of resources that are available. You will need to
register to access raw data, registration requires an ATHENS username.
The homepage for the Data Archive is at www.data-archive.ac.uk/.

Census data

National Census
In the UK, the National Census has taken place every 10 years since
1801. The census provides an invaluable source of information for
researchers on topics such as health, transport, housing, ethnic group,
education, employment and, from 2001, religion. Publications using data
derived from the census are available from numerous outlets, in particular the Office for National Statistics (www.statistics.gov.uk). But it is
also possible for individual researchers to retrieve and analyse the data
themselves. Two of the most useful tools for retrieving data from the
National Census are CASWEB and the SARs.

Census Area Statistics on the Web
Census Area Statistics on the Web (CASWEB) is a useful interface for
accessing data from the UK National Census. It provides coverage of
every national census since 1971. Data are presented in tabular form for
the range of census topics. Data can be retrieved from the country level
all the way down to the smallest level of aggregation – the output area
level which, in England and Wales, consists of around 125 households. A
worked example showing how to use CASWEB to retrieve 2001 Census
data is given in Chapter 5.
   CASWEB is available at http://www.census.ac.uk/casweb/. Users will
need an ATHENS password.

Sample of Anonymised Records
The Samples of Anonymised Records (SARs) are samples of individual-level data drawn from the UK 1991 and 2001 National Census. The data are held by the Cathie Marsh Centre for Census and Survey Research (CCSR) based at Manchester University. The SARs are extracted from national census records with individual identifiers removed to ensure confidentiality. They cover the complete range of census topics, including health, housing, education, employment, transport and demographics. The potential of the SARs should enable important empirical and theoretical advances in how we understand society at the start of the new millennium. The detailed variables collected in the most recent census will enable researchers to examine the interplay between class, education, ethnicity and religion. Comparative analyses of the 1991 and 2001 SARs will allow researchers to track changes in social mobility, social deprivation and participation in education; to help us understand, for example, the extent to which increased access to education has benefited different social and ethnic groups. The linkage of the SARs with other studies will facilitate work in topical and important areas such as family composition, workforce participation and the aging society. Similarly, the availability of equivalent SARs for other countries, in particular the USA and Canada, will also enable cross-national studies in these fields (Li 2004).

SARs data are free to academic users who will need to register through the Census Registration Service. The SARs website (http://www.ccsr.ac.uk/sars/) provides full details about SARS including how to register, access and use the datasets. A range of training datasets, teaching materials and workshops are also available.

Data management tools

In order to help users maximise their use of secondary sources, many of the datasets shown here can be retrieved and analysed using a host of different electronic data management tools. We met CASWEB, the interface for accessing data from the UK National Census, earlier. This section introduces a small selection of some others.

Neighbourhood Statistics
The Neighbourhood Statistics website provides free access to online data. Coordinated by the Office for National Statistics, it draws on social statistical data from a vast range of different sources with a particular focus on deprivation. In addition to providing access to complete datasets, it also generates summary tables that describe the characteristics of the population of a particular geographical area. The database is relatively straightforward to use. It requires the user to enter the postcode or name

of the neighbourhood and will then generate a series of summary tables providing information on areas such as education, health, crime, employment and housing. A more advanced option also exists whereby the user can select datasets from a series of topic areas including health, education, housing and indices of deprivation. This provides more detailed summary tables for a range of geographical area units such as local authority, ward or health authority. In addition, two online training modules are provided: one covering finding statistics for a particular area and the other on comparing different areas.

Further information on the Neighbourhood Statistics resource and descriptions of the types of datasets used is available through the Office for National Statistics website or at http://neighbourhood.statistics. gov.uk/dissemination/.

NOMIS: official labour market statistics
NOMIS is a web-based database of labour market statistics run by the University of Durham on behalf of the Office for National Statistics. NOMIS provides access to detailed and up-to-date labour market statistics from official sources for local areas throughout the UK. It also provides labour market and related population data for local areas from a variety of sources including: the Labour Force Survey (LFS), claimant count, Annual Business Inquiry (ABI), New Earnings Survey (NES), and the national population censuses.

Access to data is through two different online tools: the Labour Market Profiles and the Detailed Statistics. Labour Market Profiles provide summary data on factors such as employment, qualifications, benefits and earnings at local authority, ward and parliamentary constituency level. The Detailed Statistics option allows access to a fuller range of data and enables more in-depth analysis. This is a more advanced option, which enables the researcher to generate customised data tables from a range of sources including the 2001 Census and the Annual Population Survey.

The data NOMIS provides come from official government sources (mostly from National Statistics), often extending back to the 1970s. Data from non-government sources, or those preceding 1970, are not available through NOMIS. Registration is free and allows access to newsletters and alerts when new data on the labour market are released. Training courses in using NOMIS are also provided – see www.nomisweb.co.uk/ default.asp for details. A worked example using the NOMIS facility is given in Chapter 5.

Longitudinal and cohort studies

British Household Panel Survey
The British Household Panel Survey (BHPS) is carried out by the Institute for Social and Economic Research based at the University of Essex. Its objective is to provide information on household organisation, employment, income and wealth, housing, health, socioeconomic values, residential mobility, marital and relationship history, social support and individual and household demographics and so on (ESDS 2007a).

A full guide to the BHPS, including information on courses and downloads, is available at www.esds.ac.uk/longitudinal/access/bhps/L33196.asp.

National Birth Cohort Studies
The Centre for Longitudinal Studies (CLS) based at the Institute of Education London is home to three of Britain's most important national cohort studies:

- The 1958 National Child Development Study (NCDS)
- The 1970 Birth Cohort Study (BCS70)
- The Millennium Cohort Study (MCS).

The *1958 National Child Development Study* is a multidisciplinary longitudinal study whose subjects were all born during a single week in March 1958. To date there have been six attempts to trace all members of the 1958 birth cohort in order to monitor their physical, educational, social and economic development.

The *1970 Birth Cohort Study* takes as its subject babies who were born during a particular week in April 1970. During the life of the study, its focus has shifted from a mainly medical emphasis at birth to include subsequent physical, educational, social and economic development.

The *Millennium Cohort Study*: the sample for this study is slightly different from the other two birth cohort studies in that it took a selection of live births over an entire year. To date, three sweeps of this study have taken place. Its major focus is on how the life chances and prospects of these new citizens will develop in face of the challenges and opportunities offered in the new millennium.

Publications, technical reports, questionnaires, guides and guidelines for accessing the data for each of these three studies is available by following the links to each study from the CLS homepage (www.cls.ioe.ac.uk).

Regular survey data

A vast amount of data on British society are generated through survey research, often sponsored by the national government. While the links and descriptions that follow give details about how one might download and analyse the data, many of the findings from these studies are already available in summary form in publications and other bulletins. Before beginning to re-analyse an entire dataset, it is worth checking to see what is already out there. The survey descriptions presented here do provide some references to publications but it is worth looking at general publications. Of particular use are those that are published by the Office for National Statistics, such as *Social Trends* and *Living in Britain*.

Annual Population Survey
The Annual Population Survey (APS) is designed to provide better information on key social and socioeconomic variables for the interim period between the decennial national censuses. It is a relatively new survey, the first period of data collection coming in 2004. The survey comprises key variables from the Labour Force Survey and gathers information from around 65,000 households each year. Data collection is through interview with all members of the selected household who are aged 16 and above. The aim of the APS is to provide better quality data on key variables such as housing, employment, ethnicity, education and health, particularly at a local level. Results are published as part of the Office for National Statistics Neighbourhood Statistics and through NOMIS (see earlier for details of these facilities).

Accessing the Annual Population Survey datasets
Datasets and documentation linked to the APS can be accessed through the ESDS. As with many of the other datasets, users will have to register to download the complete datasets which are free to those in educational institutions. Further information is available at www.esds.ac.uk/ government/aps/.

British Crime Survey
The British Crime Survey (BCS) is one of the largest social surveys conducted in Britain. It asks respondents about their experiences of crime in the household (property crimes) and that which they themselves may have experienced (personal crimes). Since 2001 the BCS has been an annual survey of about 40,000 people aged 16 and over in England and Wales.

Accessing the British Crime Survey datasets
Questionnaires, datasets, thematic guides, analytical guides and publications that cite the BCS are all available through ESDS from
www.esds.ac.uk/government/bcs/. It is also possible to download a
teaching dataset for the 2000 BCS.

British Social Attitudes Survey
The British Social Attitudes Survey (BSAS) is a series of annual surveys
undertaken by the National Centre for Social Research (NatCen). The
aim of the series is to chart continuity and change in British social,
economic, political and moral values in relation to other changes in
society. The surveys are designed to complement other large-scale government surveys such as the General Household Survey and the Labour
Force Survey. They are administered to a sample of around 3600 individuals aged 18 or over.
    Questions can cover a diverse range of topics such as:

• charitable giving
• childcare
• civil liberties
• the countryside
• Europe
• fear of crime
• immigration
• the labour market and the workplace
• politics and governance
• the portrayal of sex and violence in the media
• religion
• transport and the environment
• welfare benefits.

Reports and publications on the British Social Attitudes Survey can
be purchased from the National Centre for Social Research
(www.natcen.ac.uk).

Accessing the British Social Attitudes Survey datasets
Datasets and documentation, including questionnaires and user guides
can be accessed through the ESDS. Users have to register for access to the
complete datasets, access is free to those in education institutions but a
charge might apply to other users. Further information on how to access
the BSA datasets and guidance for new users is available at www.
esds.ac.uk/government/bsa/. A worked example using the BSAS is given
in Chapter 6.

General Household Survey
The General Household Survey (GHS) is an annual survey of approximately 9000 private households (about 16,000 adults) in Great Britain. The main aim of the survey is to collect data for monitoring, planning and policy purposes and to present a picture of households, families and people. Data are collected on five core topics: education, employment, health, housing and population and family information. Other areas such as leisure, household burglary, smoking and drinking are also covered from time to time. Data collection is through interview with all persons over the age of 16 in the selected household.

In addition to downloading the datasets derived from subsequent years of the GHS, it is also possible to access the results in aggregate form. This can be done through the publication *Living in Britain* and the Office for National Statistics' *Results from the General Household Survey* website. For example, the results from the 2005 GHS are available in tabular form for the following variables:

• drinking
• general health and use of health services
• households, families and people
• housing and consumer durables
• marriage and cohabitation
• smoking.

Accessing the General Household Survey datasets
Datasets and documentation can be accessed through ESDS. Users have to register for access to complete datasets but some functions, for example, generating frequency tables and other descriptive data, are usually available without registration. Access to data is free to those in education institutions but a charge might apply to other users. Further information on how to access the GHS datasets is available at www.esds.ac.uk/government/ghs/datasets/ and useful guidance on getting started using the GHS is available at www.esds.ac.uk/government/ghs/starting/. A worked example that uses the GHS appears in Chapter 4.

Other GHS-related resources
Questionnaires, thematic guides, analytical guides and publications that cite the GHS are all available through ESDS at www.esds.ac.uk/government/ghs/resources/. It is also possible to download teaching datasets but you will need ATHENS registration to do this.

Labour Force Survey
The Labour Force Survey (LFS) is a quarterly survey of people aged 16 and over living in private accommodation in Great Britain. Its purpose is

to provide information on the UK labour market that can then be used to develop, manage, evaluate and report on labour market policies. The survey seeks information on respondents' personal circumstances and their labour market status at a particular point in time. The LFS has been carried out four times a year since the early 1990s and currently covers 60,000 private households. Households are interviewed face to face when first included in the survey and by telephone thereafter.

The LFS provides information on a range of variables including:

- details of current or last job
- household composition
- marital status and ethnicity
- strategies for seeking work
- usual hours worked.

The results are available for different regions with some limited coverage at the local authority district level. Further information about the LFS is available from the Office for National Statistics (www.statistics.gov.uk) or from the Economic and Social Data Service (ESDS) (www.esds.ac.uk/government/lfs/). Key results from the LFS are published monthly in the Office for National Statistics' *First Release on Labour Market Statistics*. More detailed results are published each quarter in the LFS quarterly supplement of the publication *Labour Market Trends*. A worked example using the LFS teaching dataset is given in Appendix 2.

Accessing the Labour Force Survey datasets
Datasets and documentation can be accessed through the Economic and Social Data Service. Users have to register for access to complete datasets but some functions, for example, generating frequency tables and other descriptive data, are usually available without registration. Access to data is free to those in education institutions but a charge might apply to other users. Further information on how to access the LFS datasets is available from www.esds.ac.uk/government/lfs/datasets/ and useful guidance on getting started using the LFS is available on www.esds.ac.uk/government/lfs/starting/.

Other LFS-related resources
Questionnaires, thematic guides, analytical guides and publications that cite the LFS are all available through ESDS on www.esds.ac.uk/government/lfs/resources/. It is also possible to download a teaching dataset for the 2002/2003 LFS; access is via an ATHENS account.

Office for National Statistics Omnibus Survey
The ONS Omnibus Survey is a regular multipurpose survey that is intended to provide quick answers to topics of immediate interest and

which do not require a full survey. It is conducted 12 times a year with around 1800 adults and has a turnaround time of around 14 weeks. Since it began in 1991 it has surveyed respondents on topics such as internet access, contraception, house price expectations, oral health and five pieces of fruit and vegetables.

Accessing the ONS Omnibus Survey datasets
Access to the survey is via the UK Data Archive where you can download questionnaires and the datasets. ESDS provides detailed information about the survey and links publications that summarise its findings. A good place to start is at www.esds.ac.uk/government/omnibus/.

Young People's Social Attitudes Survey
The Young People's Social Attitudes Survey (YPSAS) is an offshoot of the British Social Attitudes Survey. To date, there have been three surveys: in 1994, 1998 and 2003. The YPSA survey is designed to explore the attitudes and values of children and young people and to make comparisons with those held by adults.

The target population is young people aged 12–19 who live with BSAS respondents. In addition to demographic characteristics, topics covered include:

• friends and social networks
• fulfilment
• household tasks
• politics, citizenship and democracy
• prejudice and morality
• problems at school
• social attitudes
• views about education and work.

Accessing the Young People's Social Attitudes Survey datasets
Datasets and documentation, including questionnaires and user guides can be accessed through the ESDS. Users have to register for access to the complete datasets; access is free to those in education institutions but a fee might apply to other users. Further information on how to access the YPSAS datasets and guidance for new users is available at www.esds. ac.uk/government/bsa/. A full report from the 2003 YPSA survey is available from the Department for Children, Schools and Families (DCSF) (Park et al. 2004).

Youth Cohort Study
The Youth Cohort Study (YCS) is a series of longitudinal surveys monitoring a cohort of young people from the spring following completion of

compulsory education until they are 19 or 20 years of age. The longitudinal element of the survey enables researchers to monitor the behaviour and decisions of young people as they make the transition from compulsory education to further or higher education or to the labour market. The first wave of data collection began in 1985. To date, the most recent wave of the YCS collected data on young people who were eligible to leave compulsory education in 2001–2002. Data collection is mainly by postal questionnaire and telephone interview.

The YCS collects data on a range of variables including:

- education and qualifications
- for some cohorts, experiences of the Connexions service
- labour market experiences
- school experiences
- socio-demographic variables
- training opportunities.

In addition to downloading the YCS datasets, it is also possible to access the results in aggregate form. This is widely available through the *Statistical First Releases* published by the Department for Children, Schools and Families (www.dcsf.gov.uk).

Accessing the Youth Cohort Study datasets
Datasets and documentation can be accessed through the ESDS and the UK Data Archive. Users have to register for access to the complete datasets; access is free to those in education institutions but a charge might apply to other users. Further information on how to access the YCS datasets is available at www.data-archive.ac.uk/findingData/ycsTitles.

Other YCS-related resources
Questionnaires and user guides for the YCS are all available through the UK Data Archive. The *Statistical First Releases* also contain information on sample sizes and response rates. It is also possible to download teaching datasets from TRAMSS (Teaching Resources and Materials for Social Scientists): http://tramss.data-archive.ac.uk. Further information on TRAMMS appears later in this appendix, while a worked example using the YCS is given in Chapter 6.

Training and support

This section provides a brief overview of some of the training and support opportunities that are available in the UK to researchers interested in using numeric methods in the social sciences. In addition to the teaching datasets that accompany many of the large national surveys, there are numerous training courses, both face to face and online, catering for a broad range of skills and interests.

ATHENS

ATHENS is a management system that provides controlled access to web-based services for the UK education and health sectors. Access is through organisations such as higher education institutions, which will offer institutional access or require the user to register their details before being issued with a username and password. ATHENS allows users to access data archives, journal articles and other reference works. ATHENS does not currently support individual-level subscription. Further information about ATHENS is available from your library or resource centre or from www.athensams.net/.

Cathie Marsh Centre for Census and Survey Research

Cathie Marsh Centre for Census and Survey Research (CCSR) runs a series of short training courses in quantitative methods and data analysis. As well as introductory data analysis courses, CCSR also offers courses in longitudinal data analysis and population estimation and forecasting. Many courses are supported by ESRC training bursaries. The Centre also runs introductory workshops in using the Samples of Anonymised Records (SARs). Further details are at www.ccsr.ac.uk/.

Essex Summer School in Social Science Data Analysis and Collection

This is an annual series of one- or two-week courses held during July and August at Essex University and it attracts an international group of researchers and students. Topics deal mainly with the numeric aspects of data collection and analysis, for example, courses run in techniques such as panel data analysis, multilevel analysis and survey research methods. Financial support with tuition fees is available for some European students. Further information about courses and the application process is available at www.essex.ac.uk/methods/.

Longitudinal Data Analysis for Social Science Researchers

This programme is based at Stirling University and funded as part of the ESRC Researcher Development Initiative (www.rdi.ac.uk/). It aims to provide support and training to researchers engaged in longitudinal analysis of large secondary datasets, in particular the British Household Panel survey (BHPS). The programme offers a series of workshops and online training resources targeted at introductory levels. The website also offers links to other data sources and international datasets. More information can be found at www.longitudinal.stir.ac.uk/index.html.

Teaching Resources and Materials for the Social Sciences
Teaching Resources and Materials for the Social Sciences (TRAMSS) is a web-based resource aimed at encouraging students and other researchers to develop their methodological skills and knowledge of data resources. The site does assume a certain amount of statistical knowledge, for example, the ability to undertake a multiple regression analysis. Access to data is organised through a series of research questions based around different topic areas such as migration, youth and education. Once a theme has been selected, the links introduce the researcher to the dataset and explain the methods used to analyse the data. For example, the education theme takes the user through a multilevel modelling analysis of variation in student attainment. Access to TRAMSS is at http://tramss.data-archive.ac.uk/index.asp.

Understanding Population Trends and Processes
UPTAP is an ESRC-funded initiative designed to build capacity in secondary data analysis, promote the use of large-scale social science datasets and improve our understanding of demographic trends and processes that affect society and the population. It is coordinated by the University of Leeds and offers funding for research projects and fellowships for researchers to undertake research involving secondary data analysis. More information is available from www.uptap.net/.

Other UK-based training courses include:

- The *Centre for Applied Statistics* at Lancaster University is part of the ESRC Research Methods Programme and provides a training and support service in quantitative methods. The programme offers flexible learning web-based short-course programmes as well as hosting the TRAMSS facility. Further information is available at www.cas.lancs.ac.uk/researchmethods.html.
- *Courses in Applied Social Surveys (CASS)*: a series of short courses run by the University of Southampton covering topics in survey design and implementation, survey sampling, data collection and data analysis methods. Courses are held at different locations nationally. For more details see www.s3ri.soton.ac.uk/cass/.
- The *ESRC Oxford Spring School*: hosted by the Centre for Research Methods in the Social Sciences within the Department of Politics and International Relations at Oxford University. Further information can be found at http://springschool.politics.ox.ac.uk.

Section two: United States-based sources of secondary data

This section introduces a small selection of the huge range of secondary data sources that are available to social researchers interested in the USA. It shares the same basic organisation as Section one.

Archives and gateways

FedStats
This is a useful gateway providing access to the full range of official statistical information produced by the United States government. The site offers several possible search options including:

- *Search by topic*: the site lists over 400 topics, from adoption to field crops.
- *Search by subject area or programme*: for example, education, environment, health and transportation.
- *Search by agency*: for example the Bureau of Prisons, Office of Immigration Statistics.

Further information on *FedStats* can be found at www.fedstats.gov/.

Inter-University Consortium for Political and Social Research
The Inter-University Consortium for Political and Social Research (ICPSR) is based at the University of Michigan. According to its mission statement, its purpose is to: 'acquire and preserve social science data; provide open and equitable access to these data and to promote effective data use'. ICPSR has a network of over 500 partners worldwide. As well as undertaking research, ICPSR offers technical support to researchers in identifying data for analysis and in conducting research projects, as well as offering training in quantitative methods. Among the many thousands of archived datasets that are available for download are the data used in the seminal 1966 study by Coleman et al. (*Equality of Educational Opportunity*). Further information about ICPSR and its partner institutions is available at www.icpsr.umich.edu/ICPSR/index.html.

Roper Center for Public Opinion research
The Roper Center is a vast computer-based archive of public opinion survey research. Its aim is to promote the effective use of surveys as well as to offer research training in survey research. Its archives hold nearly 8000 US surveys and almost as many from other countries dating back to the 1930s. The many datasets that are available for download include the data and question items used in *The American Soldier* series of research. In addition the website provides guidance on using surveys and teaching resources. Further information on the Roper Center and details about its

member institutions is available at www.ropercenter.uconn.edu/.

Other useful social science gateways include:

- The *Social Science Data Collection* based at the University of California at San Diego (homepage: http://ssdc.ucsd.edu/).
- The *University of Wisconsin-Madison Center for Demography and Ecology* (homepage: www.ssc.wisc.edu/cde/library/collect.htm).

Cross-sectional surveys

The General Social Survey
The General Social Survey (GSS) is a large-scale survey of contemporary American society. To date, 26 waves of the GSS have been administered since 1972. Each wave of the survey has contained the same basic core of questions, which has enabled researchers to track key demographic, behavioural and attitudinal trends. Items include drinking behaviour, marijuana use, crime and punishment, race relations, quality of life, confidence in institutions and membership of voluntary associations. Links to datasets, documentation and training materials can be found at www.norc.org/projects/General+Social+Survey.htm.

Longitudinal studies

National Educational Longitudinal Studies Programme
The National Education Longitudinal Studies Programme (NELS) is a series of three longitudinal studies exploring the educational, vocational, and personal development of young people through school and adult life. The programme is run by the National Center for Education Statistics (NCES). There are three studies in the series: the National Longitudinal Study of the High School Class of 1972 (NLS-72), High School and Beyond (HS&B), and the National Education Longitudinal Study of 1988 (NELS-88).

- The HS&B survey included two cohorts: the 1980 senior class, and the 1980 sophomore class. Both cohorts were surveyed every 2 years through until 1986 and the 1980 sophomore class was surveyed again in 1992.
- NELS-88 started with the cohort of students who were in grade 8 in 1988; these students have been surveyed every 2 years since that time.
- The NLS-72 followed the 1972 cohort of high school seniors through until 1986 or 14 years after most of this cohort completed high school.

Data relating to these three studies can be accessed through the Data Analysis System (DAS), an application which allows users to produce basic data summaries from these and other NCES datasets. Further permissions are likely to be needed in order to access the raw data for these surveys. Links to these and other NELS surveys are available at http://nces.ed.gov/surveys/. The website also provides links to a range of other data products, publications and summary reports.

National administrative records

National Assessment of Educational Progress
The National Assessment of Educational Progress (NAEP) is a large-scale national test, used to monitor achievement trends in the United States. Also known as the *Nation's Report Card*, NAEP has been administered annually to a randomly selected sample of students aged 9, 11 and 17 since 1969. In 2003 around 10% of 9- and 11-year-old students took part in the tests. Subjects assessed include reading, mathematics, science, US history, geography and the arts. Results are available for different groups of students, in different subjects, across different regions since 1990. In addition to published reports, the NAEP Data Explorer (NDE) facility allows researchers to create tables and graphics to monitor trends in performance. The homepage for NAEP is at http://nces.ed.gov/nations reportcard/about/.

In addition to national administrative data, there is also a huge range of data available from the individual states. These data can be very comprehensive and in the field of education, can offer detail at the student or teacher level. See Chapter 7 for a worked example which uses school-level administrative data for the state of California.

Census data

United States National Census
The US Census Bureau is responsible for administering the decennial US National Census. A useful tool for exploring the US Census data is *American FactFinder*. This site allows quick access to basic demographic, social and economic data which can be searched by city, town, county, state or ZIP code. It also provides area-level data on education, income and housing. Data are available in the form of maps, tables and reports. Useful downloads also include a series of summary files containing tabulated data from the 2000 Census. A number of interactive data management tools are also available, including *Censtats* and *DataFerrett*. The US Census Bureau website also provides links to resources for teachers and training materials. These include the Census for Schools programme, which provides free teaching kits and maps. This site also provides a gateway to other census and survey data, including the *Annual Economic Surveys*, the *American Housing Survey* and the *American Community*

Survey. The main Census Bureau website is www.census.gov, which also links to *American FactFinder.*

Section three: international sources of secondary data

This section introduces international sources of data that are suitable for secondary analysis. Its emphasis is on data archives and gateways, international comparative surveys and the administrative records of international organisations such as the World Bank. Its organisation follows that of the previous two.

Administrative records

As with national sources of administrative data, international organisations also generate a vast array of data suitable for secondary analysis and are often available in aggregate form, thus are useful for studying policy goals, international performance indicators as well as providing a context for more in-depth investigations.

Afrobarometer
Afrobarometer has similarities with Eurobarometer in that it measures the social, political and economic atmosphere in Africa. It comprises a series of surveys on topics which including democracy, social capital, markets, livelihood and national identity. Further information about results, surveys, publications and data can be found at www.afrobarometer.org.

Economic Commission for Latin America and the Caribbean
The Economic Commission for Latin America and the Caribbean (ECLAC) is one of five regional commissions of the United Nations. Based in Chile, it oversees the economic and social development of the Caribbean and Latin American regions. Links to the Commission's research and statistical year books is through http://www.eclac.org/estadisticas/default.asp?idioma=IN.

Eurobarometer
Eurobarometer is a series of surveys conducted to gauge public opinion among the European Union member states. Topics include: European citizenship, health, culture, the environment, defence and so on. Eurobarometer provides a gateway to publications and reports based on Eurobarometer's surveys. Recent reports include EU citizens' views on nuclear safety, their perceptions of higher education reforms and on the role of the EU in fighting organised crime. There is also a search facility which gives access to Eurobarometer's Trends questions database. Trends

questions are asked several times a year and give a good indication of how views are evolving; there are currently over 40 trends questions in the database. The Eurobarometer facility can be explored at http://ec.europa.eu/public_opinion/index_en.htm.

Organisation for Economic Cooperation and Development
The Organisation for Economic Cooperation and Development (OECD) is a group of 30 member countries who share 'a commitment to democratic government and the market economy'. The OECD is well known for its publications and statistics covering economic and social issues including agriculture, trade, health and education. There is a huge amount of data available through the OECD website (www.oecd.org), which can be quite daunting to navigate. Data can be grouped by country, by topic or by department. This data includes e-books, annual compendia of data, individual Excel tables and so on. Selected original datasets can also be downloaded. Some data and datasets are freely available; other publications can be purchased from the OECD online store. A good place to start is with the data reports of which the following are useful examples:

- *Education at a Glance* is a publication with a specific focus on education (OECD 2006b). It provides a series of indicators on the performance of education systems and is a useful comparative resource. Data include comparative analyses of financial and human investment in education, access to education, learning conditions and educational outcomes. The publication is available through the OECD online bookstore or can be accessed electronically by subscribing institutions.
- *OECD Factbook* provides comprehensive coverage of over 100 OECD indicators including industry, foreign aid, health and the economy.
- *OECD in Figures* is a pocket databook providing summary statistics for the 30 OECD member countries on a range of topics, including demographics, economic growth and performance, unemployment, transport and the environment. *OECD in Figures* is available for free download (OECD 2005b).
- *Society at a Glance* (OECD 2006a) is similar to *Education at a Glance*, in that it provides a wide range of information on social issues including demography, family characteristics, employment, working mothers, poverty, social expenditure, healthcare expenditure, subjective well-being and suicides. The data are presented around a series of themes or indicators. For example, the *Equity Indicator* provides recent data on child poverty, social spending and income equality. A full guide to the indicators is included in the publication. The most recent edition of *Society at a Glance* can be purchased from the OECD online bookstore or accessed electronically by subscribing institutions. Selected data from previous annual publications are often available for free download.

United National Educational Scientific and Cultural Organisation (UNESCO)
The *UNESCO Institute for Statistics* provides international statistics on education, literacy, science and technology and culture and communication. It is involved in collecting, analysing and disseminating policy-relevant and timely international statistics as well as being involved in capacity building to assist member countries in improving their data collection practices. This is a great source of comparative data on initiatives to reduce inequalities in education, although it also has a huge range of publications and products in the areas of culture and communication and science and technology. The UNESCO Institute for Statistics publishes a range of annual reports, surveys and other documents covering each of its four themes. Many of these publications are available for free download. Publications include those based on:

- *Culture and communication strategies*: including reports on the international flow of cultural goods and service, the use of ICT, as well as findings from two recent international surveys on newspaper readership and radio and television broadcasting.
- *Education for all programme*: including global monitoring reports on early childhood care and education and special reports on global poverty reduction.
- *Millennium development goals indicators*: specifically progress towards ensuring universal access to primary education and promoting gender equality more widely.
- *World education indicators*: a programme to develop policy-relevant educational indicators for 19 middle-income nations, including data on finance, teachers and common education goals.

The UNESCO Institute of Statistic's homepage can be found at www.uis.unesco.org/. This gives access to the publications, surveys and other initiatives that are based around its four themes. There is also a *Data Centre* where you can request your own summary statistics and data tables based on UNESCO's four themes.

World Bank
The World Bank publishes a range of publications on global development issues; it also has links to data resources in the fields of education, gender, nutrition and population, poverty and health. Follow the Data and Research links from the World Bank homepage: www.worldbank.org/.

World Health Organisation
The Data and Statistics link from the World Health Organisation homepage (www.who.int/en/) provides access to databases and publications on a huge range of global health statistics including: obesity,

immunisation, child health, health financing, chronic diseases as well as regional statistics and global health indicators.

Archives and gateways

Australia

The *Australian Social Science Data Archive (ASSDA)* was established in 1981 in order to collect, preserve and make available data relating to social, political and economic aspects of Australian life. Datafiles are collected from organisations such as universities, market research companies and government organisations. To date ASSDA has collected over 1050 datasets; it holds the Australian population census data, as well as data from other countries within the Asia Pacific region (ASSDA 2006). More information about ASSDA's catalogue and details about how to access and use the datasets held at ASSDA are available from assda.anu.edu.au/index.html. This site also links to other useful resources such as the *Australian Consortium for Social and Political Research Inc.* and *The Australian Bureau of Statistics*.

Canada

The *Statistics Canada* website (www.statcan.ca/start.html) provides access to a huge range of statistics on the economy, society and culture of the Canadian people. Data are available in aggregate form on topics from access to healthcare to youth correction services. The site also provides links to survey questionnaires such as the *2006 Aboriginal Children's Survey* and the *2005 Survey of Financial Security*. The site also hosts the *Canadian Census data*.

China

The Chinese University of Hong Kong hosts the *Databank of Chinese Studies*, the aim of which is to make social science data for the People's Republic of China open to the academic community. A number of datasets are archived, including data from household surveys and on topics such as enterprise and reform. Many of the datasets date from the 1990s and can be found at www.usc.cuhk.edu.hk/databank.asp.

An alternative source of data on China is the *China Data Centre* hosted by the University of Michigan, USA. This site contains a wealth of data and reports including census data and publications such as the *China Statistical Yearbook* and *Monthly China Statistics*. The site also includes data that are linked to geographic information systems. Further information, including links to other sites, such as *China Data Online* can be found at www.umich.edu/~iinet/chinadata/.

Europe
The *Council of European Social Science Data Archives (CESSDA)* is an umbrella organisation for social science data archives across Europe. It provides a gateway to different types of research data including sociological surveys, longitudinal studies, opinion polls and census data. Materials include the *European Social Survey*, the *Eurobarometers* and the *International Social Survey Programme*. Users can locate datasets, as well as questions or variables within datasets, which are stored at member organisations throughout Europe. The CESSDA portal is available at http://extweb3.nsd.uib.no/cessda/home.html.

Germany
The *German Social Science Infrastructure Service (GSSIS)* is responsible for archiving data from German social survey research. In addition, it maintains databases of social science literature and research activities. As part of its data-archiving service, GSSIS provides links to data from national- and state-level elections, the *German General Social Survey* (ALLBUS) and data from other national surveys. In addition, GSSIS provides access to social data from eastern European nations and Euro-barometer. Further information can be found at www.gesis.org/en/index.htm.

Japan
The *Social Science Japan Data Archive (SSJDA)* maintains a large archive of social science data that are intended for secondary analysis. Datasets include the *Japanese General Social Survey (JGSS), National Family Research of Japan (NFRJ)* and *AsiaBarometer*. Details of the datasets and guidelines for obtaining access are available in both English and Japanese from http://ssjda.iss.u-tokyo.ac.jp/en/. The actual datasets are provided in Japanese only.

Korea
The *Korean Social Science Data Centre* collects and manages Korean and international statistical data related to the social sciences. Its database contains domestic statistics on topics such as the environment, energy, agriculture and the national census. The *Domestic Survey* database contains data collected from opinion polls and surveys undertaken by the government, universities, research institutes and other organisations. There are also links to international databases and foreign election data. Its e-stat facility is designed to help novice researchers search and analyse social science datasets as well as providing a guide to statistical tests and procedures. The website is available in Korean, English and Japanese. *The Korean Social Science Data Centre* can be accessed at ksdc.re.kr/unisql/engjap/eindex.html.

Norway
The *Norwegian Social Science Data Services (NSD)* is a source of data and of advice on data collection, research ethics and software use. It provides individual- and regional-level data, as well as data on political and other institutions. Examples of data available through NSD include ecclesiastical data on church membership, data on the resources available to higher education institutions, Norwegian survey data such as the *School Elections* data and municipal statistics gathered since 1769. Access to some of these datasets requires registration through NSD. More information is available from nsd.uib.no/english/1_2.shtml.

South Africa
The *South African Data Archive (SADA)* serves as a broker between data providers (for example, statistical agencies, government departments, opinion and market research companies and academic institutions) and the research community (SADA 2006). It is responsible for cataloguing, preserving and disseminating data such as census and household surveys, international studies, research into income and poverty, education and training and political attitudes. For further information on accessing the datasets archived at SADA and links to other South African agencies, see www.nrf.ac.za/sada/index.asp.

Surveys

European Social Survey
The European Social Survey is sponsored by the European Commission, the European Science Foundation and national funding bodies in each participating country; its focus is on understanding 'the interaction between Europe's changing institutions and the attitudes, beliefs and behaviour patterns of its diverse populations'. To date, three rounds of the survey have been carried out, with a fourth round scheduled for 2008–2009. Data collection is by face-to-face interview and topics covered include:

- education and occupation
- financial circumstances
- household circumstances
- moral and social values
- national, ethnic, religious identity
- political engagement
- social exclusion.

Background information on the European Social Survey, including publications, technical reports, training opportunities and guidelines on accessing data can be found at www.europeansocialsurvey.org.

Programme for International Student Assessment
Programme for International Student Assessment (PISA) is an international series of surveys designed to test the knowledge and skills of 15-year-old students. The first wave of PISA took place in 43 countries in 2000 with a primary focus on literacy and a secondary focus on mathematics and science. A second wave followed in 2003 with a primary focus on mathematics and a subsequent wave in 2006 with a main focus on science. In 2003 an additional domain, problem solving, was introduced. The PISA cycle is due to continue in 2009 with literacy once again being the main subject tested. In addition to testing students, PISA also collects data on their experiences and attitudes towards school and learning. In addition to this student survey, a school questionnaire is administered to school principals. Broadly, the PISA suite of questionnaires covers topics such as:

- school pedagogic practices
- school resources
- students' enjoyment of school and their experience of learning
- students' future aspirations
- students' use of computers and the internet.

Accessing PISA
PISA is coordinated by the Organisation for Economic Cooperation and Development (OECD), which also publishes a series of reports summarising the findings from the different waves of the study. While it is also possible to download the PISA datasets for analysis, the PISA website also hosts a data management facility, which allows researchers to explore data online. A worked example using PISA is given in Chapter 7. The homepage for the PISA series of studies is at www.pisa.oecd.org/.

Progress in International Reading Literacy Study
The Progress in International Reading Literacy Study (PIRLS) is a large international comparative study of the reading literacy of younger learners. It focuses on the achievement and reading experiences of 9- and 10-year-old children in over 40 countries, including England and Scotland, but not Wales and Northern Ireland. PIRLS broadly seeks to determine the reading skills of students and the extent to which their skills, habits and attitudes towards reading vary across different countries. The study includes a written test of reading comprehension and a series of questionnaires focusing on the factors associated with the development of reading literacy. *PIRLS 2001* was the first in a planned 5-year cycle of international trend studies in reading literacy. *PIRLS 2006* has a particular focus on the impact of the home environment on reading and on how parents can foster reading skills. In addition to reading comprehension

scores, PIRLS also provides information on the relationship between reading achievement and a range of contextual factors including:

- comparative data on the performance of different groups, for example boys and girls
- curriculum organisation, for example amount of instructional time spent reading
- home language
- parental involvement in reading
- the use of reading support assistants.

Accessing PIRLS

For *PIRLS 2001*, a series of reports detailing the theoretical and technical frameworks, as well as the International Results Report for the study are available online. It is also possible to download the datasets, codebooks and questionnaires. The international report on *PIRLS 2006* was made available in December 2007, with the datasets released in June 2008. All datasets and publications can be accessed from the PIRLS and TIMSS International Study Center: http://timss.bc.edu/index.html.

Trends in International Mathematics and Science Study

The Trends in International Mathematics and Science Study (TIMSS) series has been assessing international trends in mathematics and science achievement since the First International Maths and Science Study (FIMSS) in the 1960s. The number of countries participating in TIMSS continues to grow, with nearly 70 regions or countries participating in *TIMSS 2007*, including England and Scotland. The programme operates on a 4-year cycle and is aimed at two cohorts of learners aged 9 to 10 and 13 to 14. However, in an additional initiative, *TIMSS 2008* will be used to assess students in their final year of secondary school in advanced science and mathematics.

The aim of the TIMSS series of surveys is to provide information for policy development, public accountability and to address issues of equity, as well as to inform the content and quality of instruction. TIMSS uses a series of pencil-and-paper tests to assess cognitive and content domains in mathematics and science, such as problem-solving and reasoning skills, as well as knowledge of chemistry, algebra and physics. In addition to assessing these skills, TIMSS also administers background questionnaires to students, teachers and school administrators. The results from TIMSS are able to provide information on a range of factors in addition to competency in mathematics and science, these include:

- classroom activities and curriculum models
- home resources
- school resources to support mathematics and science learning

- student enjoyment of school, as well as their experience of maths and science
- teacher qualifications and pedagogic styles.

Accessing TIMSS

Publications containing the international reports, sample test items and theoretical and technical frameworks for each round of TIMSS are available online. It is also possible to download the international datasets, questionnaires and codebooks. For *TIMSS 2007*, the international report is available from December 2008. The dataset and user guide are scheduled for release in May 2009. All datasets and publications can be accessed from the TIMSS International Study Center: http://timss.bc.edu/index.html.

World Values Survey

According to the World Values Survey (WVS) homepage, it is 'a world-wide investigation of socio-cultural and political change'. Four waves of the WVS have been carried out since 1981 with interviews conducted with nationally representative samples in over 80 societies in six continents. Topics covered include:

- attitudes to society and its organisations
- attitudes towards work and family
- justification of social behaviours
- membership of voluntary organisations
- religious affiliation and practice
- views of democracy.

A huge range of publications have been generated from the results of the different waves of the WVS, details of these publications, as well as questionnaire items, reports and a useful online facility to analyse summary data are all available on the WVS website (www.worldvalues survey.org/). It is also possible to download the complete datafiles.

Appendix 2: Effective data husbandry: managing secondary datasets

When doing secondary analysis, it is likely that you will come across some very large datasets, occasionally containing millions of cases. Therefore, it is important to manage the data effectively. There are some obvious principles that apply to all datasets: saving data regularly, keeping backup files, labelling files and variables accurately and so on. However, there are also some strategies and techniques that are of particular use to the secondary analyst, such as deleting un-needed cases and variables. These techniques can make huge datasets more manageable and much less daunting for novice users.

The aim of this appendix is to take the reader through several examples of useful strategies for managing data with SPSS. While examples are also provided in the main body of Chapters 6 and 7, more detail is given here. Some of these examples will involve using the Syntax function, but most utilise the drop-down menus at the top of the SPSS screen. This appendix does assume that you have a basic knowledge of SPSS, for example, that you know where to find variables and cases and how they can be labelled. It does not, however, presume to tell you how to analyse your data – there are many excellent books that both explain statistical techniques and show you how to use SPSS to perform the analysis. Rather, this section simply hopes to pass on some useful tips for effective data husbandry.

Two example datasets are used here: the Labour Force Survey (LFS) teaching dataset and the annual data on applications and acceptances to UK higher education institutes that are produced by the Universities and Colleges Admissions Service (UCAS).

The Labour Force Survey

The Labour Force Survey (LFS) teaching dataset contains data from all four quarters of the 2002/3 LFS for respondents aged 16–65 and resident in the UK (a total of 63,559 cases and 58 variables). This is only a subset of the original datafiles, which include data on all those aged 16 and over.

You will need to register and log into the Economic and Social Science Data Service (ESDS) database using your ATHENS password. Further details on how to do this appear in Appendix 3. Once you have done this, you have a choice to explore the data using Nesstar or to download the file in your chosen format. Here we will download the data files in SPSS. Begin by accessing the LFS webpage (Slide A2.1). Then follow the **Resources** link to the teaching dataset using the left-hand menu.

Slide A2.1 Labour Force Study homepage

If you have registered correctly with ESDS, you will then be able to download the LFS teaching dataset by clicking on the **Download** button (Slide A2.2). You will be given a choice of formats: SPSS, STATA or TAB. We have chosen SPSS.

The LFS folder will include an SPSS folder with an SPSS file containing the LFS teaching dataset (file name **lfs2002**), plus a pdf containing the user guide (file name: **4736userguide** in **mrdoc** folder). Clicking on the SPSS icon will open the datafile containing 58 variables and 63,559 cases. You should now save this file to a suitable place on your computer.

Slide A2.2 Downloading the Labour Force Survey teaching dataset

The UCAS datasets

Retrieving the UCAS data is slightly more straightforward. UCAS data can be accessed without registration from the UCAS website. To do this, follow the link to **Statistical services** using the **HE staff** tab from the UCAS homepage (www.ucas.com). The Statistics online tool allows you to use data online or download the annual datasets. Full instructions for downloading the datasets are given on the screen.

Using SPSS

Before we begin, let us just remind ourselves of the main data screen in SPSS. Slide A2.3 shows the **Data View** window for the Mac version of SPSS 11, it is basically the same as the PC version, it is just that the **Menu bar** appears at the top of the screen, while on the PC version it appears below the **Title bar**.

- The **Menu bar** is located at the top of the screen. This is where the drop-down menus will appear and where you get SPSS to carry out the tasks you require.
- The **Title bar** shows the name of the SPSS file you are currently working with.

Menu Bar   Title bar   Tool bar

Slide A2.3 Data View window for Mac version of SPSS 11

- The **Tool bar** contains many shortcuts to help organise and analyse your data.
- At the bottom of the screen, we have the **Data View** and **Variable View** tabs.

If any of this is new to you, it would be worth having a look at an introductory text to using SPSS. There are several excellent books available and some suggestions appear at the end of this appendix.

Before describing some useful data management techniques, we should briefly mention the Syntax facility.

Using Syntax

A Syntax file is a file that contains commands written in SPSS' own language. The easiest way of understanding what a syntax file is, is to run a quick frequency analysis for the variable **sex**. In the **Menu bar** go to **Analyze** → **Descriptive Statistics** → **Frequency** move the variable

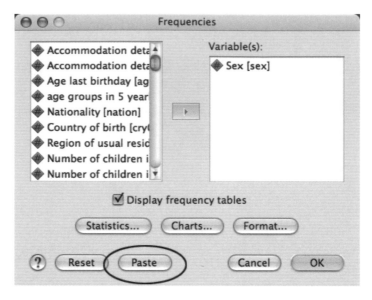

Slide A2.4 Frequencies window

sex into the **work area** using the arrow key. Then instead of clicking on **OK**, click on **Paste** (Slide A2.4).

This will open a new window called a Syntax window (Slide A2.5). The instruction that you gave SPSS through the drop-down menus (to analyse the frequencies of the variable **sex**) now appears in Syntax language which SPSS can then read. You will need to highlight the text and click on the arrow key to run this command.

Syntax is useful for several reasons.

It can cut down the time needed to run analyses. Once you have written (or pasted) the original syntax command all you need do to rerun the programme is to highlight the text and click on the black arrow (circled in Slide A2.5) and the command will run again. If you wish to run a frequency count for a different variable, rather than running through all the stages in the drop-down menus, you just delete the current variable (for example, **sex**) and type in the new variable name (for example, **age**), then highlight the text and click on the arrow key to rerun the command.

Syntax is also useful for keeping a record of any analysis that you might have done and would like to keep. For example, if you run a regression model, it can take some time to define the parameters and variables needed for the optimum model. If you do not want to lose, or to repeat, these commands, they can be pasted into a Syntax file (using the **Paste** function described earlier) and then saved.

Another use of Syntax is that it can run commands that cannot be

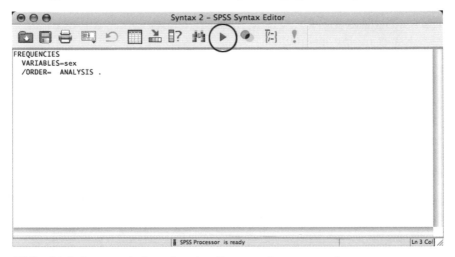

Slide A2.5 Syntax window showing Frequencies command

done easily using the drop-down menus, for example, when you need to delete variables from a large file. Rather than going through and highlighting and deleting each column of variables by hand, there is a simple Syntax command that can be used. Examples of useful Syntax commands are given throughout this appendix; where they are used it is because they tend to be more straightforward to use than the drop-down commands.

Unfortunately, there are few good books that instruct the novice user on how to write Syntax for themselves – the best guide is probably the manuals which accompany SPSS but they can be difficult to follow, especially if the user has little knowledge of computer language. The best thing to do if you come across a useful piece of Syntax is to save it and adapt it for use in future analyses. In this book, the intention is that the reader copy the Syntax commands and use them in the worked examples given here or adapt them for use with their own datasets.

Manipulating cases

This section shows you how to organise your data to take account of large numbers of cases. Many of the datasets you will come across when doing secondary analysis have thousands, even millions, of cases and it is likely that you will not wish to use them all. This section shows you how to select certain cases for analysis or, for times when you are sure that you will not need them, to delete cases from your dataset. It will also show you how to split a file so that you can analyse cases separately. The examples given here are based on the Labour Force Survey (LFS) teaching dataset (University of Manchester 2004), which was introduced at the start of this appendix.

Selecting cases

If you wished to run an analysis that included only the female respondents to the LFS, you can use the **Select Cases** option. The data for female are found in the **sex** variable and are given the code **1** (this can be checked by looking in **Variable view** and clicking on the **values** box that corresponds with the **sex** variable).

To select only female cases for analysis you will need to go to the **Menu bar** and select: **Data → Select cases**. In the **Select Cases** window, click on the **If condition is satisfied** button and then click **If ...** (Slide A2.6).

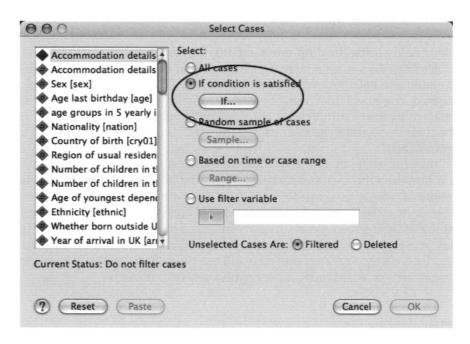

Slide A2.6 Select Cases main window

A new window will open (Slide A2.7). You will need to tell SPSS to select cases *if* they are female. To do this, click on the **Sex** variable and use the arrow in the grey box to move it into the empty **work area**. Then, using the **keypad** below this space, type **=** and **1**. Remember: female cases are labelled as 1. Then click **Continue** to go back to the original window (Slide A2.6).

Keypad   Work area

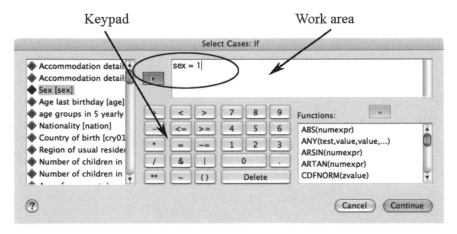

Slide A2.7 Select Cases: If sub-window

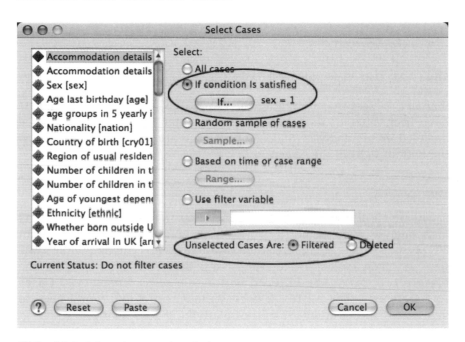

Slide A2.8 Select Cases main window

Back in the original window (Slide A2.8), you will notice that the command is to **Select cases if sex =1**. Notice also that **Unselected Cases** (i.e. those for male respondents or who have sex coded as missing) are **Filtered**. If you wish to paste this command into Syntax you just need to click **Paste**, otherwise just click **OK**.

If you have a look at the main SPSS **Data View** window, you will see

	ten96	house	sex	age	ages	nation	cry01	region	numchild	numchii1	ayfl19	ethnic
1	2	1	0	18	4	1	3	10	0	0	19	1
2	2	1	1	19	4	1	3	10	1	0	0	1
3	4	2	0	19	4	1	59	10	0	0	19	1
4	4	2	0	16	4	1	3	10	0	1	13	1
5	2	1	0	18	4	1	1	10	0	3	7	1
6	2	1	0	18	4	1	3	10	0	0	19	1
7	4	2	0	18	4	1	3	10	0	0	19	1
8	2	1	0	18	4	1	3	10	0	0	18	1
9	1	1	1	17	4	59	3	10	0	0	19	1
10	2	1	1	17	4	1	3	10	0	0	17	1
11	4	2	1	18	4	1	3	10	0	0	19	1
12	2	1	0	18	4	1	3	10	0	1	15	1
13	4	2	0	17	4	1	3	10	0	0	19	1
14	2	1	0	17	4	1	3	10	0	1	12	1
15	2	1	0	19	4	1	3	10	0	0	19	1
16	4	2	0	19	4	1	3	10	0	0	19	1
17	2	1	1	18	4	1	3	10	0	0	18	1
18	4	2	1	18	4	1	3	10	0	0	19	1
19	2	1	0	18	4	1	3	10	0	1	14	1
20	2	1	1	19	4	1	3	10	0	0	19	1

Slide A2.9 Data View window showing selected cases

that all the cases that are not female (where sex = a value other than 1) have been filtered: they have a line through them and will not be included in any analysis (Slide A2.9). Notice also the **Filter On** icon at the bottom right of the screen.

Deleting cases

If you are absolutely sure that there are cases that you will not be using in an analysis, for example, if you will only be researching women, then it is possible to delete any unwanted cases. To do this you follow the same steps as given earlier for filtering cases. But instead of selecting the **Unselected Cases Are Filtered** button you select **Unselected Cases Are Deleted** (Slide A2.10). It goes without saying, but you'll need to save a copy of the original file in case anything goes wrong.

Splitting files

Split Files is a useful alternative to the **Select Cases** function just described. It is also helpful if you wish to present and compare the results for different groups. In this example, we use the **Split Files** option to split the dataset into two groups: those who were born in the UK and those who were born outside the UK. Once we have split the file, we run a frequency analysis to find out how many of the respondents in each group were male and how many were female.

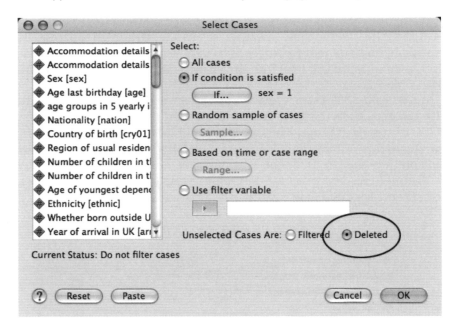

Slide A2.10 Deleting unselected cases

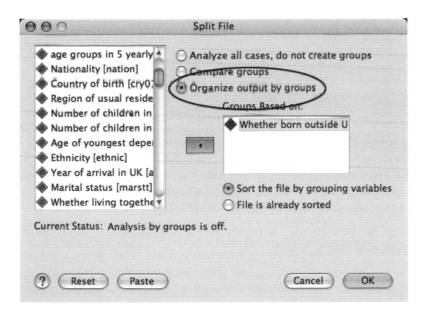

Slide A2.11 Split File window

Again, using the LFS teaching dataset, from the **Menu bar** select **Data → Split File**. In the new window select the **Organize output by groups** option and move your chosen variable (in this example: **Whether born outside UK (fb)**) into the **Groups Based on:** box. Then click **OK** (Slide A2.11).

In the main SPSS **Data View** window you will notice the icon **Split File On** appears in the bottom right of the screen.

The next stage is to run a quick analysis. In this example, we are using the frequency of male and female respondents who were born inside (and outside) the UK. To do this run **Analyze → Descriptive Statistics → Frequencies** and place the Sex (**sex**) variable into the **Variable(s)** box. Then click **OK** (Slide A2.12).

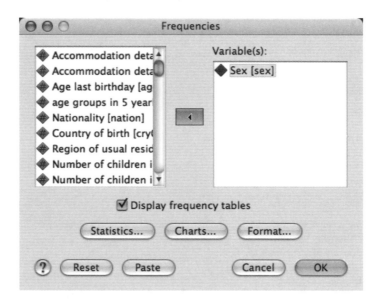

Slide A2.12 Example of analysing Frequencies

The SPSS **Output** window will then open (Slide A2.13) and present two groups of statistics: those where **Whether born outside UK = no** and those where **Whether born outside UK = yes**.

Weighting cases

The need to weight cases usually arises when certain groups of respondents have been over-selected or under-selected in the sampling process: in other words, when some groups of people are more likely to have been included in the study than others. This can bias the survey and the findings will not give a fair representation of the population from which

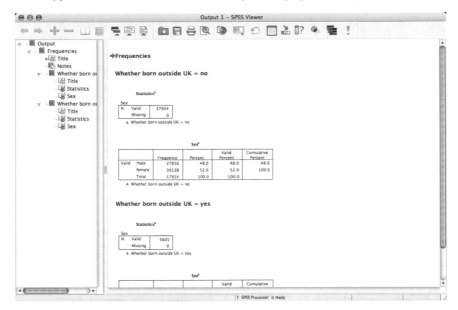

Slide A2.13 SPSS Output window for frequencies of male and female respondents, split according to birthplace

the sample was drawn. For example, surveys such as the Youth Cohort Study (YCS) are designed in order to boost the numbers of respondents from ethnic minority groups. This means that when sampling for the survey, if a school has more than 20% of students from ethnic minority groups then students are selected to participate in the survey if they have birthdays on *four* pre-selected days in every month, rather than on *three* days in every month, which is the procedure for selecting participants in other schools. Thus the school is oversampled for ethnic minority students. Similarly the data are also weighted to compensate for non-response and to bring it more in line with population estimates. If weighting did not take place, then the YCS would overestimate attainment and participation in full-time education since high attainers would be more likely to respond to the survey than those who were lower attainers and who may be more likely to be absent from school (DfES 2005).

If the researchers have an idea about which groups have been over- or underrepresented in their data, they can apply weights to the data to help account for any discrepancies. For example, if researchers know that their sample has underrepresented urban people in comparison to people who live in rural areas by a factor of two, they can correct for this by counting each urban person twice (Miller et al. 2002). Many large datasets contain weighting values that need to be used when you are analysing the dataset. Certain studies, like the YCS, contain several different weighting values which depend on the questionnaire or the sweep of the study that you are analysing. You'll need to check the manuals that accompany the surveys to find out about the weighting requirements. Adding weights to your SPSS analysis is straightforward. As the LFS teaching dataset does not require weighting, the example that follows uses the British Social Attitudes Survey dataset that we used in Chapter 6.

In the Menu Bar select **Data** → **Weight Cases**; a new window will open (Slide A2.14). Scroll down through the variable list and select the weighting variable (here it is called **wtfactor**). Select the button for **Weight cases by frequency variable** and move your weighting variable across into the empty box using the arrow key. Then click **OK**, the **Weight On** icon should appear at the bottom left of the main **Data View** screen. Further examples of weighting cases appear in Chapters 6 and 7.

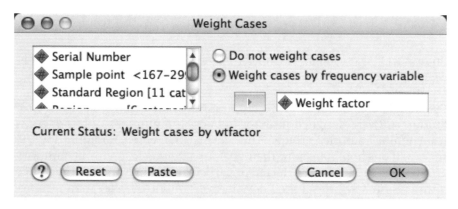

Slide A2.14 Example of weighting cases

Manipulating variables

This section takes you through some basic operations that you might wish to use when preparing your variables for analysis. We begin by describing a useful piece of Syntax for deleting un-needed variables from your file.

Deleting variables

Many of the datasets used in secondary analysis contain huge numbers of variables and it is likely that only a relatively small number will be needed for a particular analysis. Here is a useful piece of Syntax that will delete un-needed variables. Note that this operation will result in a completely new SPSS file being created; therefore you have to be careful to specify where on your computer you would like it to go.

Using the Labour Force Survey Teaching dataset as an example, suppose you wished to keep only the variables relating to income and family background and had no need for the variables concerned with government training courses, apprenticeships and so on. You can use the Syntax shown in Slide A2.15 to retain the variables that you need and delete all the others.

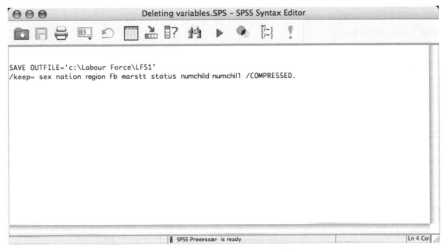

Slide A2.15 Syntax instructions for deleting variables

The first step in doing this is to be clear about which variables you wish to retain. Here, we will keep the variables that are listed along with their variable names:

- sex (**sex**)
- nationality (**nation**)
- region of residence (**region**)
- whether born outside UK (**fb**)
- marital status (**marstt**)
- economic status (**status**)
- number of children aged 0–4 (**numchild**)
- number of children aged 5–16 (**numchil1**).

The next step is to decide where on your computer you would like the new SPSS file with the reduced number of variables to be located. In this example it will be saved on the C: drive in a folder called Labour Force. This can be represented as C:\Labour Force.

To do this, open a new Syntax window: **File** → **New** →**Syntax** (Slide A2.15) and enter the commands as they appear here.

The first line of text tells SPSS the name of the new file (**LFS1**) while the second line specifies which variables are to be retained – taken from the list just given. Note that if you wish to keep several variables that are located next to each other in the main datafile then you need simply to list the first and last variable separated by the word **to**: for example keeping all the variables between **sex** and **married** you would just need to type **sex to married** into the variable line in the Syntax window. When you are happy with the Syntax command, simply highlight the text and click on the arrow key in the window's toolbar in order to run the programme.

This is a useful Syntax to keep and use with other datasets, just be sure to change the variable names and the location of the new file.

Recoding variables

Sometimes you may wish to create your own variables from ones that already exist in the original dataset. This example shows you how to reduce the number of categories in one variable by recoding them onto a completely new variable. Here we take the variable which lists eight English regions and reduces them to a single category: England. Table A2.1 lists the old and new variable codes that will be used in this transformation. It is useful to make a quick table like this before doing the recoding so that you are sure that the codes are all correct. Where necessary, you will also need to account for any missing variable codes and make sure that they are present in the new variable.

In the **Data View** window select **Transform** → **Recode** → **Into Different Variables**. A new window will appear (Slide A2.16). Move

Table A2.1 Region of usual residence, old and new variable codes

Region of usual residence	Old code h	New code value
North	1	1
Yorkshire	2	1
Northwest	3	1
East Midlands	4	1
West Midlands	5	1
East Anglia	6	1
Southeast	7	1
Southwest	8	1
Wales	9	2
Scotland	10	3
Northern Ireland	11	4

the variable **Region of usual residence** (**region**) into the **work area** box using the arrow. Then, in the **Output variable** section, you will need to select a name and label for your new variable: in this example the new variable is called **collreg** and labelled **collapsed region**. Clicking **Change** will move the new (output) variable into the work area alongside the original variable. Next step is to click on the **Old and New Values …** button.

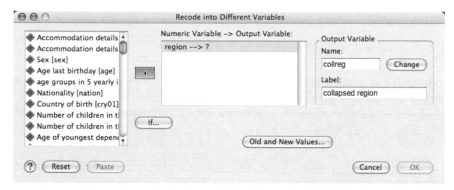

Slide A2.16 Recoding in to different variables window

This will open a new window: **Recode into Different Variables: Old and New Values** (Slide A2.17). Using the old and new values that were allocated in Table A2.1, the next step is to enter them into the grid shown in Slide A2.17. All old values in the range 1 through to 8 were recoded as 1 and then added to the **Old → New** box using the **Add**

Slide A2.17 Renaming the new variables

button, the same process was repeated for the individual values 9, 10 and 11 which were coded 2, 3 and 4 respectively. Clicking on **Continue** and then **OK** (in the new window) will result in a new variable (label: **collreg**) appearing in the **Data View** window.

It is possible to recode straight onto an existing variable using **Transform** → **Recode** → **Into Same Variables**. This can be a useful function but you need to be careful that you are absolutely sure which changes you wish to make, otherwise it is easy to lose data.

Computing new variables

Compute is a useful function, as it allows you to perform a range of mathematical operations on a numeric variable. Some of these operations can be very complex; here we use a straightforward example whereby two existing variables are added together to produce a new variable.

The LFS teaching dataset has two variables for the age of children in the household, these are:

- Number of children in the household aged 0–4 (**numchild**).
- Number of children in the household aged 5–15 (**numchil1**).

Adding these two variables together will give a new variable for the number of children in the household aged 0–15 (**totchild**).

To begin in the **Menu bar** select **Transform**→ **Compute** which will open a new window (Slide A2.18).

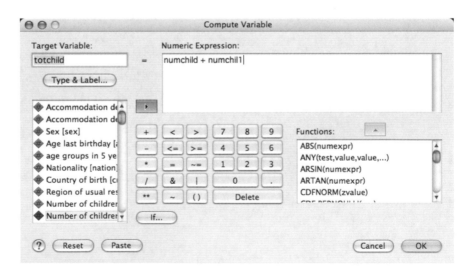

Slide A2.18 Compute Variable window

In the **Target Variable** box type in the name of the new variable (in this example, **totchild**). Note that you might wish to insert and label this variable in the main datafile before performing the **Compute** operation – this will mean that you can decide where to locate the new variable (perhaps next to the **numchild** and **numchil1** variables), otherwise SPSS will insert it at the end of the list of variables.

The next step is to move the first variable (**numchild**) into the **Numeric Expression** box, follow this with a + from the **keypad** below the box and then complete the equation by moving the second variable (**numchil1**) over. Clicking on **OK** will complete the transformation and a new variable (**totchild**) – the sum of **numchild** and **numchil1** will appear in the **Data View** window.

Other operations

Aggregating cases

Occasionally, files might contain very detailed information that might be more useful to the analyst if it was aggregated. A good example of this is a dataset that contains individual data on whether or not every pupil in a school is eligible for free school meals. This amount of data may be too detailed for the researcher's needs and it might be more useful to know how many pupils in the *school* were eligible for free school meals, rather than the status of each individual pupil. This can be done using the **Aggregate** function.

The example given here uses data on the number of applicants to undergraduate higher education courses in the UK. Applications are coordinated by the Universities and Colleges Admissions Service (UCAS), which makes data on applications and acceptances to courses freely available on its website (see Appendix 1 for more detail on this). The data for applications to courses in 2005 were downloaded as a zipped Excel file which was then opened and saved in SPSS for the purpose of this example. If you are working through this example and opening this Excel file in SPSS, then you may need to add the variable names yourself.

UCAS applications data give information on the number of applicants for different courses according to their country of domicile, sex and age and is organised into 17 different subject groups (**subgp**), which are listed in Table A2.2. Subject groups are further divided into numerous subject lines (**subln**): for example Subject Group A is further divided into subject lines, which include subjects such as preclinical medicine and dentistry.

If you have downloaded the subject dataset for 2005 from UCAS (UCAS 2007) and opened it in SPSS, you will notice that in addition to

Table A2.2 UCAS subject groups

	Subject group
A	Medicine/dentistry
B	Subjects allied to medicine
C	Biological sciences
D	Agriculture and related subjects
F	Physical sciences
G	Mathematical sciences and informatics
H/J	Engineering and technology
K	Architecture, building and planning
L/M	Social studies
N	Business and administrative studies
P	Mass communications and documentation
Q/R/T	Languages and related disciplines
V	Humanities
W	Creative arts
X	Education
Y	Combined subjects
Z	Other general and combined studies

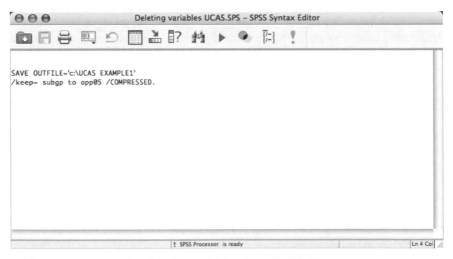

Slide A2.19 Syntax for deleting variables from UCAS files

the variables described earlier, there are also six variables relating to acceptances. As we are only interested in applications in this example, it is safe to discard these variables. This can be done either by highlighting the variables and pressing the delete key on your keyboard or by running the Syntax file (shown in Slide A2.19), which will keep all the variables that are listed and save them in a new file called **UCAS example1**.

Slide A2.20 shows the **Data View** window for the new file (named: **UCAS example1**), the variable **applications** has been renamed (**app05**). As you can see, the applicants for Group A: Medicine and Dentistry are organised by Subject Line, Domicile, Age and Sex. Thus we can see from Case 1 that 206 women aged 17 and under who were domiciled in the UK applied to read preclinical medicine in 2005.

	subgp	subin	domicile	age	sex	app05	var
1	Group A Medicine & Dentistry	A1 - Pre-clinical Medicine	A Home	17 and u	Women	206	
2	Group A Medicine & Dentistry	A1 - Pre-clinical Medicine	A Home	17 and u	Men	123	
3	Group A Medicine & Dentistry	A1 - Pre-clinical Medicine	A Home	18 yrs	Women	4198	
4	Group A Medicine & Dentistry	A1 - Pre-clinical Medicine	A Home	18 yrs	Men	3068	
5	Group A Medicine & Dentistry	A1 - Pre-clinical Medicine	A Home	19 yrs	Women	1200	
6	Group A Medicine & Dentistry	A1 - Pre-clinical Medicine	A Home	19 yrs	Men	1008	
7	Group A Medicine & Dentistry	A1 - Pre-clinical Medicine	A Home	20 yrs	Women	243	
8	Group A Medicine & Dentistry	A1 - Pre-clinical Medicine	A Home	20 yrs	Men	220	
9	Group A Medicine & Dentistry	A1 - Pre-clinical Medicine	A Home	21 yrs	Women	437	
10	Group A Medicine & Dentistry	A1 - Pre-clinical Medicine	A Home	21 yrs	Men	284	
11	Group A Medicine & Dentistry	A1 - Pre-clinical Medicine	A Home	22 yrs	Women	499	
12	Group A Medicine & Dentistry	A1 - Pre-clinical Medicine	A Home	22 yrs	Men	361	
13	Group A Medicine & Dentistry	A1 - Pre-clinical Medicine	A Home	23 yrs	Women	398	
14	Group A Medicine & Dentistry	A1 - Pre-clinical Medicine	A Home	23 yrs	Men	285	
15	Group A Medicine & Dentistry	A1 - Pre-clinical Medicine	A Home	24 yrs	Women	271	
16	Group A Medicine & Dentistry	A1 - Pre-clinical Medicine	A Home	24 yrs	Men	259	
17	Group A Medicine & Dentistry	A1 - Pre-clinical Medicine	A Home	25 to 29	Women	733	
18	Group A Medicine & Dentistry	A1 - Pre-clinical Medicine	A Home	25 to 29	Men	723	
19	Group A Medicine & Dentistry	A1 - Pre-clinical Medicine	A Home	30 to 39	Women	436	
20	Group A Medicine & Dentistry	A1 - Pre-clinical Medicine	A Home	30 to 39	Men	506	

Slide A2.20 Data View window for UCAS applications file

In this example, we want to find out how many candidates have applied to the 17 different subject groups, regardless of subject line, domicile, age and sex. To do this we will add up the number of applicants (**app05**) for each Subject Group (**subgp**). Once all the applicants for one subject group have been counted, the SPSS will break from counting and begin to count all applicants in the next subject group. The Syntax used to carry out this operation is given in Slide A2.21.

Here, we are instructing SPSS to perform an **AGGREGATE** function and to place the data into a new file, which we've called **UCAS2005**. Each time the computer reaches a new **subgp**, it will **BREAK** from counting and begin again with the next **subgp**. The new variable that we are creating is called **totapp05** (total applications in 2005) and this is created by adding together (**SUM**) all the numbers associated with the variable **app05** for each of the 17 subject groups.

To run the Syntax programme, highlight the commands and click on the arrow, a new SPSS data file, **UCAS 2005**, would be created (Slide

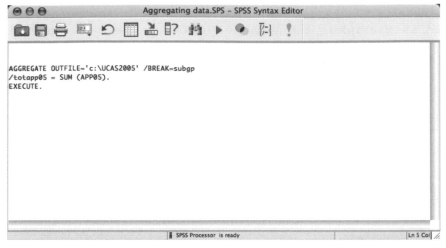

Slide A2.21 Aggregate function Syntax command

	subgp	totapp05	var	var	var	var	var	var
1	Group A Medicine & Dentistry	22039						
2	Group B Subjects allied to Medicine	41441						
3	Group C Biological Sciences	35614						
4	Group D Vet Sci,Ag & related	4703						
5	Group F Physical Sciences	14384						
6	Group G Mathematical & Comp Sci	26250						
7	Group H Engineering	22858						
8	Group J Technologies	1512						
9	Group K Architecture,Build & Plan	9103						
10	Group L Social Studies	37109						
11	Group M Law	22206						
12	Group N Business & Admin studies	55277						
13	Group P Mass Comms and Documentation	10528						
14	Group Q Linguistics, Classics & relate	12907						
15	Group R European Langs, Lit & related	4498						
16	Group T Non-European Langs and related	1439						
17	Group V Hist & Philosophical studies	15579						
18	Group W Creative Arts & Design	59547						
19	Group X Education	17307						
20	Y Combined arts	9849						

Slide A2.22 The new aggregated datafile: UCAS 2005

A2.22). If you open this file, you can see that SPSS has added together all the data in the **app05** variable for each separate subject group and that, in 2005, there were 22,039 applicants for subjects in Subject Group A: Medicine and Dentistry.

The **AGGREGATE** Syntax is a useful piece of Syntax to keep. For example, here we asked SPSS to add together (**SUM**) all the data associated with certain cases; by changing the command slightly, you can also get it to calculate mean values, just replace **SUM** with **MEAN**. There is also a very useful AGGREGATE function in the drop down menu (**Data** → **Aggregate**).

Merging data

This is a useful function for bringing together data from different datasets. This example will show you how to merge the *variables* from two different UCAS datasets: applications from 2005 (file: **UCAS 2005**) and 2006 (file: **UCAS 2006**). Note that merging *cases* follows a similar set of steps – just select the **Merge Cases** option in the drop-down menu. Before you can merge datasets, you will need to make sure that all cases are sorted in exactly the same way and that the variable names, labels and properties are identical, otherwise the command will not run successfully. In order to merge variables from two (or more) files, there needs to be at least one variable that both files have in common. In this example, the variable **subgp** will be common to both files.

This example uses the **UCAS 2005** file that was created in the previous example and contains aggregate data for the number of applicants to the 17 subject groups. This will be merged with the **UCAS 2006** file, which is also an aggregate file containing the same data as **UCAS 2005** but for the following academic year. You might wish to create the **UCAS 2006** file yourself by following the same stages as for the UCAS 2005 data that were described in the section before this.

We begin by opening the file **UCAS 2005**. In the menu toolbar, select **Data** → **Merge Files** → **Add Variables ...** . This will open a new window that will ask you to select the dataset that you wish to merge with **UCAS 2005**. In this example, the second dataset is **UCAS 2006**; you may need to browse through your datafiles to find it.

Select **UCAS 2006** and click **Open**. This will then open the window seen in Slide A2.23. This window lists all the variables that are available in the two files that we are trying to merge. The two **subgp** variables are common to both files and will form the basis of the merger.

The next step is to check the box next to **Match cases on key variables in sorted files** and leave the button marked next to **Both Files provide cases**. Then click on the variable **subgp> (+)** in the **Excluded Variables** box and use the bottom arrow to move the variable into the box marked **Key Variables**: (the other variable **subgp> (*)** which is in the **New Working Data File** box should move too). The window should then look like the one in Slide A2.24.

Then click **OK** for the merge to run. A warning window will appear asking you to check that the files are sorted in the same way – you should have checked this at the start, so click **OK**. The new variable for

Slide A2.23 Merging variables sub-window

Slide A2.24 Completed Merge Variables sub-window

university applications in 2006 (**totapp06**) should now appear in the **UCAS 2005** file, which you can then rename.

Repeating cases

There may be occasions when you might wish to retain individual-level data and merge it with data that have less detail. For example, if you have access to individual pupil-level data, you might wish to retain this and merge into the file data about the school the pupil attends. To do this, you will need to use the repeating cases function. Because individual-level data are confidential, a mock dataset is used in this example, but it should still illustrate the main principles. Two mock datasets are used: the first contains data on 19 pupils in four schools (schools 1–4). This file is called **pupil example** and comprises six variables: school identifier (**school**), pupil identifier (**student**), pupil eligibility for free school meals (**fsm**), their sex (**sex**), ethnic group (**ethnic**) and number of GCSEs grades A*–C that they achieved (**n5gcses**) (Slide A2.25).

	school	student	fsm	ethnic	sex	n5gcses
1	1	435	fsm	White Brit	female	2
2	1	436	fsm	White Brit	male	5
3	1	437	fsm	Indian	male	3
4	1	438	fsm	Indian	male	1
5	1	439	fsm	Indian	male	6
6	2	440	no fsm	Indian	female	9
7	2	441	no fsm	White Brit	female	8
8	2	442	no fsm	White Brit	female	7
9	2	443	no fsm	Indian	male	10
10	2	444	no fsm	Chinese	male	10
11	3	445	fsm	Chinese	female	9
12	3	446	fsm	White Brit	male	3
13	3	447	fsm	White Brit	female	2
14	3	448	fsm	White Brit	male	7
15	3	449	no fsm	White Brit	female	5
16	4	450	fsm	White Brit	female	8
17	4	451	no fsm	White Brit	female	3
18	4	452	no fsm	Indian	male	9
19	4	433	no fsm	Indian	male	5

Slide A2.25 Data View for pupil-level data

The second dataset is the school dataset (file name: **school example**). It comprises four variables: school identifier (**school**), school type (**stype**), school location (**location**) and percentage of pupils in school eligible for free school meals (**schfsm**).

We begin by opening the **pupil example** file. We will need to merge the school-level data from the **school example** file into the **pupil**

example file. This is done using the same stages described in the merging variables example earlier. Begin with **Data** → **Merge Files** → **Add Variables …**, then select the **school example** file from your browser and click **Open**. This will open a new window similar to Slide A2.26.

Two variables are common to both files and it is these that will be used

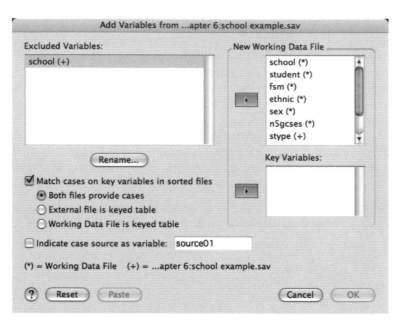

Slide A2.26 Merging variables window

to merge the two files: **school (+) and school (*)**. You will need to make sure that they are labelled and sorted identically in both files, otherwise the merge will not work.

In the **Excluded variables** box, highlight **school (+)** and check the box **Match cases on key variables in sorted files** and the button **Both files provide cases**. Then use the lower arrow key to move the high-lighted variable into the **Key Variables** box (**the school (*)** variable will move too). Then click **OK**. A warning window will ask whether your files are sorted in the same order; click **OK**. (You may also get a warning window opening in SPSS output. You just need to check that the data have been merged correctly; you can do this by skimming through them.) The new **Data View** should look like the one in Slide A2.27.

You will notice that the data from the **school example** file have only merged alongside the first pupil listed for each school. We now need to copy the school-level data so that they merge alongside each pupil in a particular school. There is a useful piece of Syntax to help you do this; it uses something called an LAG function (Slide A2.28).

Slide A2.27 Data View for merging variables

Slide A2.28 Syntax repeat variable command

The command in Slide A.28 is instructing SPSS that if the variable **school** has the same label as the variable **school** in the preceding row (**school** = lag(**school**)) then the variable **stype** will be given the same label as the variable **stype** that is in the row preceding it (**stype** = lag(**stype**)). This may become clearer if you see what happens in Slide A2.29 when the Syntax command is run.

	school	student	fsm	ethnic	sex	n5gcses	stype	location	schfsm		var	var
1	1	435	fsm	White Brit	female	2	community	city	34			
2	1	436	fsm	White Brit	male	5	community	.	.			
3	1	437	fsm	Indian	male	3	community	.	.			
4	1	438	fsm	Indian	male	1	community	.	.			
5	1	439	fsm	Indian	male	6	community	.	.			
6	2	440	no fsm	Indian	female	9	grammar	city	4			
7	2	441	no fsm	White Brit	female	8	grammar	.	.			
8	2	442	no fsm	White Brit	female	7	grammar	.	.			
9	2	443	no fsm	Indian	male	10	grammar	.	.			
10	2	444	no fsm	Chinese	male	10	grammar	.	.			
11	3	445	fsm	Chinese	female	9	community	city	18			
12	3	446	fsm	White Brit	male	3	community	.	.			
13	3	447	fsm	White Brit	female	2	community	.	.			
14	3	448	fsm	White Brit	male	7	community	.	.			
15	3	449	no fsm	White Brit	female	5	community	.	.			
16	4	450	fsm	White Brit	female	8	community	rural	12			
17	4	451	no fsm	White Brit	female	3	community	.	.			
18	4	452	no fsm	Indian	male	9	community	.	.			
19	4	433	no fsm	Indian	male	5	community	.	.			

Slide A2.29 Repeating variables Data View

SPSS has taken the **stype** variable and copied it in all the cells that have the same school code. If you change the variable name in the Syntax from **stype** to **location** and run the command, the same thing will happen for the variable **location**. You can repeat the command for the variable **schfsm**.

Useful books for analysing data with SPSS

Field, A. (2000), *Discovering Statistics using SPSS for Windows*, London: Sage.
Miller, R.L., Acton, C., Fullerton, D.A. and Maltby, J. (2002), *SPSS for Social Scientists*, Basingstoke: Palgrave Macmillan.
Mujis, D. (2004), *Doing Quantitative Research in Education with SPSS*, London: Sage.

Appendix 3: Accessing the Economic and Social Data Service

You will need to log into ESDS using your ATHENS password. If you have not already registered with ESDS, then you will need to do so by completing the registration form (Slide A3.1) and accepting the terms and conditions.

Slide A3.1 ESDS registration form

You will then receive an email with a link to the final registration page (Slide A3.2) from which you can begin to explore the ESDS site.

Slide A3.2 Final registration form

Finally, before you may download data, you will need to register a new use of data by completing the form in Slide A3.3.

Slide A3.3 Registering a new use of data form

References

Abedi, J. (2004), The No Child Left Behind Act and English-language learners: Assessment and accountability issues, *Educational Researcher*, 33(1), 4–14.

Abercrombie, N., Hill, S. and Turner, B.S. (1988), *The Penguin Dictionary of Sociology*, 2nd edn, London: Penguin Books.

Abercrombie, N., Hill, S. and Turner, B.S. (2000), *The Penguin Dictionary of Sociology*, 4th edn, London: Penguin Books.

Althaus, S.L. and Largio, D.M. (2004), When Osama became Saddam: Origins and consequences of the change in America's Public Enemy #1, *PSOnline*, October.

Arber, S. (2001), Secondary analysis of survey data, in Gilbert, N. (ed.), *Researching Social Life*, 2nd edn, London: Sage.

Archer, L. (2002), Change, culture and tradition: British Muslim girls talk about Muslim girls' post-16 'choices', *Race Ethnicity and Education*, 5(4), 359–376.

Archer, L. and Francis, B. (2005), Constructions of racism by British Chinese pupils and parents, *Race, Ethnicity and Education*, 8(4), 387–407.

Arnot, M., David, M. and Weiner, G. (1999), *Closing the Gender Gap: Postwar Education and Social Change*, Cambridge: Polity Press.

Atkinson, J.M. (1978), *Discovering Suicide*, London: Macmillan.

Avison, N.H. (1972), Criminal statistics as social indicators, in Shonfeld, A. and Shaw, S. (eds), *Social Indicators and Social Policy*, London: Heinemann.

BBC (2001), Top GCSE grades 'a fix', *BBC News online*, accessed August 2006, http://news.bbc.co.uk/1/hi/education/1505761.stm.

BBC (2002a), Exam board admits printing error, *BBC News online*, accessed August 2006, http://news.bbc.co.uk/1/hi/education/2013453.stm.

BBC (2002b), Exam board sets impossible question, *BBC News online*, accessed August 2006, http://news.bbc.co.uk/1/hi/education/2016221.stm.

BBC (2002c), Examiners knew about maths error, *BBC News online*, accessed August 2006, http://news.bbc.co.uk/1/hi/education/1771461.stm.

BBC (2006), 'Exercise could help UK economy', *BBC News online*, accessed June 2007, http://news.bbc.co.uk/1/hi/business/4855378.htm.

BBC (2007a), *Officially Ignorant?* BBC Radio 4 documentary, 22 March 2007.

BBC (2007b), Lib Dems back migrant 'amnesty', *BBC News online*, accessed September 2007, http://news.bbc.co.uk/1/hi/uk_politics/6999611.stm.

BBC (2007c), Universities to get parental info, *BBC News online*, accessed March 2007, http://news.bbc.co.uk/go/pr/fr/-/hi/education/6454073.stm.

Barretta-Herman, A. (2006), A reanalysis of the IASSW World Census 2000, *International Social Work*, 48(6), 794–808.

Bartholomew, D. (1997), Editorial: The measurement of unemployment in the UK: the position at June 2007, *Journal of the Royal Statistical Society: Series A*, 160(3), 385–388.

Bartholomew, D., Moore, P., Smith, F. and Allin, P. (1995), The measurement of unemployment in the UK, *Journal of the Royal Statistical Society, Series A*, 158(3), 363–417.

Beckett, C. (2005), The Swedish myth: The corporal punishment ban and child death statistics, *British Journal of Social Work*, 35, 125–138.

Berliner, D.C. (2002), Educational research: The hardest science of all, *Educational Researcher*, 31(8), 18–20.

Bertera, E.M. (2003), Social services for the aged in Cuba, *International Social Work*, 46(3), 313–321.

Blackwell Publishing (2005), The *Sociological Review Journal* homepage, accessed August 2007, www.blackwellpublishing.com/journal.asp?ref=0038–0261&site=1.

Boe, E., May, H., Shin, S. and Boruch, R. (2002), *Student Task Persistence in the Third International Mathematics and Science Study: A Major source of Achievement differences at the National, classroom and Student Levels*, Philadelphia, PA: University of Pennsylvania, Center for Research and Evaluation in Social Policy.

Booth, C. (1886), Occupations of the people of the United Kingdom 1801–1881, *Journal of the Statistical Society of London*, 49(2), 314–444.

British Association Study Group (1979), Does research threaten privacy or does privacy threaten research?, in Bulmer, M. (ed.), *Censuses, Surveys and Privacy*, London: Macmillan.

Brooks-Gunn, J., Phelps, E. and Elder, G.H. (1991), Studying lives through time: Secondary analyses in developmental psychology, *Developmental Psychology*, 27(6), 899–910.

Brown, M. (1998), The tyranny of the international horse race, in Slee, R., Weiner, G. and Tomlinson, S. (eds), *School Effectiveness for Whom? Challenges to the School Effectiveness and School Improvement Movements*, London: Falmer Press.

Bryman, A. (1998), Quantitative and qualitative research strategies in knowing the social world, in May, T. and Williams, M. (eds), *Knowing the Social World*, Buckingham: Open University Press.

Bryman, A. (2004), *Social Research Methods*, 2nd edn, Oxford: Oxford University Press.

Buchanan, A. and Flouri, E. (2001), Parental family structure and adult expectations of familial support in times of emotional need, *British Journal of Social Work*, 31, 133–139.

Budd, T. and Aston, J. (2006), Experiences of congestion and attitudes to road pricing, Department for Transport, accessed August 2007, www.dft.gov.uk/pgr/statistics/datatablespublications/trsnstatsatt/experiencesofcongestionandat5122.

Bulmer, M. (1979), Introduction, in Bulmer, M. (ed.), *Censuses, Surveys and Privacy*, London: Macmillan.

Bulmer, M. (1980), Why don't sociologists make more use of official statistics? *Sociology*, 14(4), 505–524.

Burkhardt, H. and Schoenfeld, A.H. (2003), Improving educational research: Toward a more useful, more influential and better-funded enterprise, *Educational Researcher*, 32(9), 3–14.

Burton, D. (2000), Secondary data analysis, in Burton, D. (ed.), *Research Training for Social Scientists*, London: Sage.

Bynner, J., Butler, N., Ferri, E., Shepherd, P. and Smith, K. (2000), *The Design and Conduct of the 1999–2000 Surveys of the National Child Development Study and the 1970 British Cohort Study*, Working Paper 1, London: Centre for Longitudinal Studies.

California Department of Education (2005a), California's Consolidated State Performance Report: Part I, accessed July 2006, www.cde.ca.gov/nclb/sr/rt/documents/usdecsprjanfinal.doc.

California Department of Education (2005b), California Basic Education Data System, accessed June 2006, www.cde.ca.gov/ds/sd/cb/.

California Department of Education (2007), California Department of Education: Data and statistics gateway, accessed September 2007, www.cde.ca.gov/ds/.

Campbell, J.P., Daft, R.L. and Hulin, C.L. (1982), *What to Study: Generating and Developing Research Questions*, Beverley Hills, CA: Sage.

Canning, R. (2000), The rhetoric and reality of professional competence-based vocational education in Scotland, *Research Papers In Education*, 15(1), 69–93.

Cohen, O. and Shnit, D. (2001), Social workers' recommendations on the non-custodial fathers' visitation rights with his pre-school children, *International Social Work*, 44(3), 311.

Coleman, J., Campbell, E., Hobson C., McPartland, J., Mood, A., Weinfeld, F. and York, R. (1966), *Equality of Educational Opportunity*, Washington, DC: US Government Printing Office.

Connor, H. (2001), Deciding for or against participation in higher education: The views of young people from lower social backgrounds, *Higher Education Quarterly*, 55(2), 202–224.

Cook, T.D. (1974), The potential and limitations of secondary evaluations, in Apple, M.W., Subkoviak, M.J. and Lufler, H.S. (eds), *Educational Evaluation: Analysis and Responsibility*, Berkeley, CA: McCutchan Publishing Corporation.

Croxford, L. (2006), *The Youth Cohort Surveys – How Good is the Evidence?* Edinburgh: Education Youth and Transitions Project.

Cutler, S.J. (1978), Instructional uses of the General Social Surveys, *Contemporary Sociology*, 7(5), 541–545.

Dale, A., Arber, S. and Procter, M. (1988), *Doing Secondary Analysis*, London: Unwin Hyman.

Darling-Hammond, L. (2000), Teacher quality and student achievement: A review of state policy evidence, *Education Policy Analysis Archives*, 8(1), January 2000.

Davies, P. (2004), Sociology and policy science: Just in time? *British Journal of Sociology*, 55(3), 447–450.

Delamont, S. (1999), Gender and the discourse of derision, *Research Papers in Education*, 14(1), 3–21.

DfES (2003), *Aiming High: Raising the Achievement of Minority Ethnic Pupils*, London: DfES.

DfES (2005), *Youth Cohort Study: The Activities and Experiences of 16 Year Olds: England and Wales, 2004*, Statistical First Release 04/2005, London: DfES.

DfES (2007a), National Curriculum Assessments at Key Stage 3 in England, 2005/ 06, SFR07/2007, accessed July 2007, www.dfes.gov.uk/rsgateway/DB/SFR/ s000711/index.shtml.

DfES (2007b), Children looked after by local authorities year ending 31 March 2006 national tables, accessed July 2007, www.dfes.gov.uk/rsgateway/DB/ VOL/v000721/index.shtml.

Dorling, D. and Simpson, S. (1993), Those missing millions: Implications for social statistics of undercount in the 1991 Census, *Radical Statistics*, 55, 14–35.

Douglas, J.D. (1967), *The Social Meanings of Suicide*, Princeton, NJ: Princeton University Press.

Driessen, G., Smit, F. and Sleegers, P. (2005), Parental involvement and educational achievement, *British Educational Research Journal*, 31(4), 509–532.

Durkheim, E. (1952), *Suicide: A Study in Sociology*, London: Routledge & Kegan Paul.

Durrant, J. (1999), Evaluating the success of Sweden's corporal punishment ban, *Child Abuse and Neglect*, 23(5), 435–448.

Edwards, A. and Protheroe, L. (2003), Learning to see in classrooms: What are student teachers learning about teaching and learning while learning to teach in schools? *British Educational Research Journal*, 29(2), 227–242.

Eisenhart, M. and Towne, L. (2003), Contestation and change in national policy on 'scientifically based' education research, *Educational Researcher*, 32(7), 31– 38.

Elashoff, J.D. and Snow, R.E. (1971), *Pygmalion Reconsidered*, Worthington, OH: Wadsworth.

ESDS (2007a), General Household Survey, Economic and Social Data Service, accessed August 2007, http://www.esds.ac.uk/government/ghs/.

ESDS (2007b), Guide to the British Household Panel Survey, accessed September 2007, www.esds.ac.uk/longitudinal/access/bhps/L33196.asp.

ESRC (2006), Economic and Social Research Council Delivery Plan 2006, accessed April 2007, www.esrc.ac.uk/ESRCInfoCentre/Images/ESRC_Delivery _Plan_06_tcm6–15443.pdf.

Fenton, S. (1996), Counting ethnicity: Social groups and official categories, in Levitas, R. and Guy, W. (eds), *Interpreting Official Statistics*, London: Routledge.

Feuer, M.J., Towne, L. and Shavelson, R.J. (2002), Scientific culture and educational research, *Educational Researcher*, 31(8), 4–14.

Fielding, N.G. and Fielding, J.L. (2000), Resistance and adaptation to criminal identity: Using secondary analysis to evaluate classic studies of crime and deviance, *Sociology*, 34(4), 671–689.

Finney, N. and Peach, E. (2004), *Attitudes towards Asylum Seekers, Refugees and Other Immigrants: A Literature Review for the Commission for Racial Equality*, London: Information Centre about Asylum and Refugees in the UK (ICAR).

FitzGibbon, C. (1996), Written response to the paper league tables and their limitations: Statistical issues in comparisons of institutional performance, *Journal of the Royal Statistical Society, Series A*, 159, 388–443.

Fletcher, T.V. and Sabers, D.L. (1995), Interaction effects in cross-national studies of achievement, *Comparative Education Review*, 39(4), 455–467.

Ganzeboom, H.B.G. and Treiman, D.J. (1996), Internationally comparable measures of occupations and status for the 1988 International Standard Classification of Occupations, *Social Science Research*, 25, 201–239.

Giddens, A. (1996), *In Defence of Sociology: Essays, Interpretations and Rejoinders*, Cambridge: Polity Press.

Gillborn, D. and Youdell, D. (2000), *Rationing Education – Policy, Practice, Reform and Equity*, Buckingham: Open University Press.

Ginn, J. and Arber, S. (2001), Pension prospects of minority ethnic groups: Inequalities by gender and ethnicity, *British Journal of Sociology*, 52(3), 519–539.

Glaser, B.G. (1962), Secondary analysis: A strategy for the use of knowledge from research elsewhere, *Social Problems*, 10, 70–74.

Glaser, B.G. (1963), Retreading research materials: The use of secondary analysis by the independent researcher, *The American Behavioural Scientist*, 6(10), 11–14.

Glass, D.V. (1950), The application of social research, *British Journal of Sociology*, 1(1), 17–30.

Glass, G.V. (1976), Primary, secondary and meta-analysis of research, *Educational Researcher*, 5(10), 3–8.

Goldstein, H. (2001), Using pupil performance data for judging schools and teachers: Scope and limitations, *British Educational Research Journal*, 27(4), 433–442.

Goldstein, H. and Spiegelhalter, D.J. (1996), League tables and their limitations: Statistical issues in comparisons of institutional performance, *Journal of the Royal Statistical Society, Series A*, 159, 388–443.

Goldthorpe, J.H., Llewellyn, C. and Payne, C. (1980), *Social Mobility and Class Structure in Modern Britain*, Oxford: Clarendon Press.

Gorard, S. (1999), Keeping a sense of proportion: The 'politician's error' in analysing school outcomes, *British Journal of Educational Studies*, 47(3), 235–246.

Gorard, S. (2000), *Education and Social Justice*, Cardiff: University of Wales Press.

Gorard, S. (2002), The role of secondary data in combining methodological approaches, *Educational Review*, 54(3), 231–237.

Gorard, S. (2005), Academies as the 'future of schooling': Is this an evidence-based policy? *Journal of Education Policy*, 20(3), 369–377.

Gorard, S. (2006), Value-added is of little value, *Journal of Educational Policy*, 21(2), 233–241.

Gorard, S., Adnett, N., May, H., Slack, K., Smith, E. and Thomas, L. (2007), *Overcoming the Barriers to Higher Education*, Staffordshire: Trentham Books.

Gorard, S., Lewis, J. and Smith, E. (2004), Disengagement in Wales: Educational, social and economic issues, *The Welsh Journal of Education*, 13(1), 118–147.

Gorard, S., Rees, G. and Salisbury, J. (1999), Reappraising the apparent under-achievement of boys at school, *Gender and Education*, 11(4), 441–454.

Gorard, S., Taylor, C. and Fitz, J. (2003b), *Schools, Markets and Choice Policies*, London: Routledge.

Gorard, S., Taylor, C., Rushforth, K. and Smith, E. (2003a), *What is the Research Capacity of the UK Education Research Community? Reconsidering the Shortage of Quantitative Skills Phenomenon*, Occasional Paper Series, Cardiff: University School of Social Sciences.

Gorard, S. and Smith, E. (2004), An international comparison of equity in education systems, *Comparative Education*, 40(1), 15–28.

Gorard, S. and Smith, E. (2006), Beyond the 'learning society': What have we learnt from widening participation research? *International Journal of Lifelong Education*, 25, 6.

Gorard, S. with Taylor, C. (2004), *Combining Methods in Educational and Social Research*, Maidenhead: Open University Press.

Gregg, P. (1994), Out for the count: A social scientist's analysis of unemployment statistics in the UK, *Journal of the Royal Statistical Society, Series A*, 157, 253–270.

GTTR (2006), *Graduate Teacher Training Registry Annual Statistical Report*, 2005 course entry, Cheltenham: GTTR.

Guardian (2007), *Councils lobby Treasury over Immigration Statistics*, 14 May, 2007.

Hakim, C. (1982a), Secondary analysis and the relationship between official and academic social research, *Sociology*, 16(1), 12–28.

Hakim, C. (1982b), *Secondary Analysis in social Research: A Guide to Data Sources and Methods with Examples*, London: Allen & Unwin.

Hakim, C. (2000), *Research Design: Successful Designs for Social and Economic Research*, 2nd edn, London: Routledge.

Halman, L. and Draulans, V. (2006), How secular is Europe? *British Journal of Sociology*, 57(2), 263–288.

Halsey, A.H. (1994), Sociology as political arithmetic, *British Journal of Sociology*, 45(3), 427–444.

Halsey, A.H., Heath, A.F. and Ridge, J.M. (1980), *Origins and Destinations: Family, Class and Education in Modern Britain*, Oxford: Clarendon Press.

Hammersley, M. (1997), Qualitative data archiving: Some reflections on its prospects and problems, *Sociology*, 31, 131–142.

Hammersley, M. (2004), A new political arithmetic to make sociology useful? Comments on a debate, *British Journal of Sociology*, 55(3), 436–446.

Hargreaves, D. H. (1996), *Teaching as a Research-based Profession: Possibilities and Prospects*, London: Teacher Training Agency.

Harrop, M. (1980), Social research and market research: A critique of a critique, *Sociology*, 14, 277–281.

Heath, S. (2000), The political arithmetic tradition in the sociology of education, *Oxford Review of Education*, 26(3&4), 314–331.

Heaton, J. (1998), Secondary analysis of qualitative data, *Social Research Update*, Guildford: Surrey University ISR.

Henry, J (2002), Watchdog's blunder list opens with 38 exam board mistakes, *Times Educational Supplement*, 19 July 2002 (accessed August 2006, www.tes.co.uk).

HESA (2006), Students in higher education institutions 2005–06, Higher Education Statistics Agency, accessed June 2007, www.hesa.ac.uk/.

HESA (2007), Destinations of leavers from higher education 2005/06: definitions, accessed June 2007, ww.hesa.ac.uk/index.php/component/option,com_datatables/task,show_file/defs,1/Itemid,121/catdex,0/disp,none/dld,dlhe0506.xls/yrStr,2005+to+2006/dfile,dlhedefs0506.htm/area,dlhe/mx,0/.

Hewson, C. (2006), *Secondary Analysis*, in Jupp, V. (ed.), *The Sage Dictionary of Research Methods*, London: Sage.

Higgins, V. (2007), Employment and the labour market: Introductory user guide, accessed June 2007, www.esds.ac.uk.

Hilton, M (2006), Measuring standards in primary English: Issues of validity and accountability with respect to PIRLS and national curriculum test scores, *British Educational Research Journal*, 32(6), 817–837.

Hindess, B. (1973), *The Use of Official Statistics in Sociology*, London: Macmillan.

Hobcraft, J. and Kiernan, K. (2001), Childhood poverty, early motherhood and adult social exclusion, *British Journal of Sociology*, 52(3), 495–517.

Hogben, L. (1939), Sir William Petty and Political Arithmetic, in *Lancelot Hogben's Dangerous Thoughts*, London: Allen & Unwin.

Huff, D. (1973), *How to Lie with Statistics*, London: Pelican Books.

Hughes, J.A., Martin, P.J. and Sharrock, W.W. (1995), *Understanding Classical Sociology: Marx, Weber and Durkheim*, London: Sage.

Husen, T. and Tujinman, A.C. (1994), Monitoring standards in education: Why and how it came about, in Tujinman, A.C. and Postlethwaite, T.N. (eds), *Monitoring Standards in Education: Papers in Honour of JP Keeves*, Oxford: Elsevier Science.

Hyman, H.H. (1972), *Secondary Analysis of Sample Surveys: Principles, Procedures and Potentialities*, London: John Wiley & Sons.

Hyman, H.H. (1978), A banquet for secondary analysts, *Contemporary Sociology*, 7(5), 545–549.

Hyman, H.H. and Reed, J.S. (1969), 'Black matriarchy' reconsidered: Evidence from secondary analysis of sample surveys, *Public Opinion Quarterly*, 33(3), 346–354.

ICPSR (2005), *European and World Values Survey Integrated Data File, 1999–2002*, Release 1, Data Collection Instruments, Michigan: Inter-University Consortium for Political and Social Research.

Jackson, B. and Marsden, D. (1962), *Education and the Working Class*, London: Routledge & Kegan Paul.

Jacob, H. (1984), *Using Published Data: Errors and Remedies*, Beverly Hills, CA: Sage.

Jarvis, L., Exley, S. and Tipping, S. (2003), *Youth Cohort Study: Survey of 16 Year Olds (Cohort 11 Sweep 1) Technical Report*, London: DfES.

Jarvis, L., Exley, S. and Tipping, S. (2006a), *Youth Cohort Study: Survey of 17 Year Olds (Cohort 11 Sweep 2) Technical Report*, London: DfES.

Jarvis, L., Exley, S., Park, A., Phillips, M., Johnson, M. and Robinson, C. (2006b), *Youth Cohort Study of England and Wales, 2002–2005 (Cohort 11 Sweeps 1 to 4)*, Colchester, Essex: UK Data Archive.

Jary, D. and Jary, J. (2000), *Collins Dictionary of Sociology*, 3rd edn, Glasgow: HarperCollins.

Jeffs, T. (1999), Are you paying attention? Education and the media, in Franklin, B. (ed), *Social Policy, the Media and Misrepresentation*, London: Routledge.

Ji, E.G. (2006), A study of the structural risk factors of homelessness in 52 metropolitan areas in the United States, *International Social Work*, 49(1), 107–117.

Joncas, M. (2003), PIRLS sampling weights and participation rates, in Martin, M.O., Mullis, I.V.S. and Kennedy, A.M. (eds), *PIRLS 2001 Technical Report*, Chestnut Hill, MA: Boston College (accessed July 2007, http://timss.bc.edu/pirls2001i/PIRLS2001_Pubs_TR.html).

Kaestle, C.F. (1993), The awful reputation of education research, *Educational Researcher*, 22(1), 23, 26–31.

Kane, T.J. and Staiger, D.O. (2002), The promise and pitfalls of using imprecise school accountability measures, *Journal of Economic Perspectives*, 16(4), 91–114.

Kellner, P. (2004), Can online polls produce accurate findings? *Journal of Marketing Research*, 46, 3–44.

Kiecolt, R.J. and Nathan, L.E. (1985), *Secondary Analysis of Survey Data*, Beverley Hills, CA: Sage.

Kitsuse, J.I. and Cicourel, A.V. (1963), A note on the use of Official Statistics, *Social Problems*, 11(2), 131–138.

Kober, N. (2002), What tests can and cannot tell us, TestTalk for leaders, Centre on Education Policy, accessed July 2006, www.cep-dc.org/testing/testtalkoctober2002.pdf.

Lader, D., Short, S. and Gershuny, J. (2006), 2005 Time use survey: How we spend our time, ONS, accessed July 2007, www.statistics.gov.uk/articles/nojournal/time_use_2005.pdf.

Lambert, P. (2002), Handling occupational information, *Building Research Capacity*, 4, 9–12.

Lauder, H., Brown, P. and Halsey, A.H. (2004), Sociology and political arithmetic: Some principles of a new policy science, *British Journal of Sociology*, 55(1), 3–22.

Lazarsfeld, P.F. (1949), The *American Soldier* – an expository review, *Public Opinion Quarterly*, 13(3), 377–404.

Lee, C. (2003), Why we need to re-think race and ethnicity in educational research, *Educational Researcher*, 32(5), 3–5.

Levitas, R. (1996), Fiddling while Britain burns? The 'measurement' of unemployment, in Levitas, R. and Guy, W. (eds), *Interpreting Official Statistics*, London: Routledge.

Li, Y. (2004), Samples of anonymized records (SARs) from the UK Census: A unique source for social science research, *Sociology*, 38(3), 553–572.

Lines, D. (2000), A disaster waiting to happen, *Times Educational Supplement*, 7 April 2000, accessed August 2006, www.tes.co.uk.

Linn, R.L. (2003), Accountability: Responsibility and reasonable expectations, *Educational Researcher*, 32(7), 3–13.

Mansell, W. and Clark, E. (2003), MPs blame ministers for A-level regrading fiasco, *Times Educational Supplement*, 18 April 2003, accessed June 2007, www.tes.co.uk.

Miles, I. and Irvine, J. (1979), The critique of official statistics, in Irvine, J., Miles, I. and Evans, J. (eds), *Demystifying Social Statistics*, London: Pluto Press.

Miliband, D. (2004), Using data to raise achievement, speech by David Miliband to the Education Network, London, 11 February 2004. Accessed 24 June 2004, www.dfes.gov.uk/speeches.

Miller, R.L., Acton, C., Fullerton, D.A. and by, J. (2002), *SPSS for Social Scientists*, Basingstoke: Macmillan.

Mosek, A. and Adler, L. (2001), The self-concept of adolescent girls in non-relative versus kin foster care, *International Social Work*, 44(2), 149–162.

Mosteller, F. and Moynihan, D.P. (1972), *On Equality of Opportunity*, papers deriving from the Harvard University faculty seminar on the Coleman Report, New York: Vintage Books.

Mullis, I.V.S., Martin, M.O., Gonzalez, E.J. and Chrostowski, S.J. (2004), *Findings from IEA's Trends in International Mathematics and Science Study at the Fourth and Eighth Grades*, Chestnut Hill, MA: Boston College.

Mullis, I.V.S., Martin, M.O., Gonzalez, E.J. and Kennedy, A.M. (2003), *PIRLS 2001 International Report: IEA's Study of Reading Literacy Achievement in Primary Schools*, Chestnut Hill, MA: Boston College.

NatCen (2005a), *Young People's Social Attitudes, 2003*, Colchester, Essex: UK Data Archive.

NatCen (2005b), *User Guide, Young People's Social Attitudes, 2003*, Colchester, Essex: UK Data Archive.

NatCen (2006), *British Social Attitudes Survey, 2004*, Colchester, Essex: UK Data Archive.

National Assembly for Wales (2006a), Statistics for Wales, accessed July 2007, www.statswales.wales.gov.uk/TableViewer/tableView.aspx?ReportId=3506.

National Assembly for Wales (2006b), Teenage conceptions in Wales 2004, Statistical Bulletin SB 78/2006, accessed July 2007, www.statswales.wales.gov.uk/tableviewer/document.aspx?FileId=805.

National Assembly for Wales (2006c), Life expectancy 2003–2005, Statistical Bulletin SB 73/2006, accessed July 2007, www.statswales.wales.gov.uk/tableviewer/document.aspx?FileId=786.

National Commission on Excellence in Education (NCEE) (1983), *A Nation at Risk*, US Department of Education, Washington, DC: US Printing Office.

Nelson, D.I. (2003), *What Explains Differences in International Performance? TIMSS Researchers Continue to Look for Answers*, Philadelphia, PA: Center for Research and Evaluation in Social Policy, University of Pennsylvania.

Neuman, W.L. (2003), *Social Research Methods: Qualitative and Quantitative Approaches*, 5th edn, Boston: Allyn & Bacon.

Newton, P.E. (2005a), The public understanding of measurement inaccuracy, *British Educational Research Journal*, 31(4), 419–442.

Newton, P.E. (2005b), Threats to the professional understanding of assessment error, *Journal of Education Policy*, 20(4), 457–483.

Nuttall, D.L. (1979), The myth of comparability, *Journal of the National Association of Inspectors and Advisers*, 11, 16–18.

Observer (2007), *Planning your Gap Year*, 24 June, 2007.

OECD (2000a), *Knowledge and Skills for Life: First Results from PISA 2000*, Paris: OECD.

OECD (2000b), PISA 2000 database, interactive data selection, accessed September 2007, http://pisaweb.acer.edu.au/oecd/oecd_pisa_data_s2.php.

OECD (2001), Manual for PISA 2000 database, accessed August 2007, www.pisa.oecd.org/dataoecd/53/18/33688135.pdf.

OECD (2002), Attracting, developing and retaining effective teachers: Design and implementation plan for the activity, accessed June 2004, www/oecd.org/dataoecd/20/36/1839878.pdf.

OECD (2005a), *PISA 2003 Technical Report*, Paris: OECD.

OECD (2005b), OECD in figures 2005: A supplement to the OECD observer, accessed March 2007, www.oecdbookshop.org/oecd/display.asp?sf1=identifiers &lang=EN&st1=012005061e1.

OECD (2006a), Society at a glance: OECD social indicators, accessed September 2007, www.oecd.org/document/24/0,3343,en_2649_201185_2671576_1_1_1_1,00.html.

OECD (2006b), Education at a glance: Homepage, accessed September 2007 from www.oecd.org/document/52/0,3343,en_2649_201185_37328564_1_1_1_1,00.html.

O'Higgins, N. (1997), *The challenge of Youth Unemployment*, Employment and Training Papers Number 7, Geneva: ILO (accessed July 2007, www.ilo.org/public/english/employment/strat/download/etp7.pdf).

Office for National Statistics (2004), The UK 2000 time use survey, accessed July 2007, www.statistics.gov.uk/TimeUse/default.asp.

Office for National Statistics (2005), *Census 2001, General Report for England and Wales*, Basingstoke: Palgrave Macmillan.

Office for National Statistics (2006), The Labour Force Survey: General Information, accessed August 2007, http://www.statistics.gov.uk/StatBase/Source.asp?vlnk=358&More=Y.

Office for National Statistics (2007), Social and Vital Statistics Division, *General Household Survey, 2005*. Colchester, Essex: UK Data Archive.

Olson, L. and Viadero, D. (2002), Law mandates scientific base for research, *Education Week*, 21(1), 14–15.

Papasolomontos, C. and Christie, T. (1998), Using national surveys: A review of secondary analysis with special reference to education, *Educational Research*, 40(3), 295–310.

Park, A., Phillips, M. and Johnson, M. (2004), *Young People in Britain: The Attitudes and Experiences of 12–19 year olds*, DfES Research Report 564, London: DfES.

Payne, G., Williams, M. and Chamberlain, S. (2004), Methodological pluralism in British sociology, *Sociology*, 38(1), 153–163.

Payne, J. (2003), The impact of part-time jobs in years 12 and 13 on qualification achievement, *British Educational Research Journal*, 29(4).

Phillips, M., Johnson, M., Robinson, C. and Tipping, S. (2005), *Youth Cohort Study: Survey of 18 and 19 Year Olds (Cohort 11 Sweeps 3 and 4), Technical Report*, London: DfES.

Porter, T.M. (1995), *Trust in Numbers: The Pursuit of Objectivity in Science and Public Life*, Princeton, NJ: Princeton University Press.

Post, D. (2003), Hong Kong higher education, 1981–2001: Public policy and re-emergent social stratification, *Oxford Review of Education*, 29(4), 545–570.

Power, S. and Rees, G. (2006), *Making sense of changing Times and Changing Places: The Challenges of the New Political Arithmetic of Education*, paper presented at the British Educational Research Association Annual Conference, University of Warwick, 6–9 September 2006.

Prais, S. J. (2003), Cautions on OECD's recent educational survey (PISA), *Oxford Review of Education*, 29(2), 139–163.

Propper, C. and Wilson, D. (2003), The use and usefulness of performance measures in the public sector, *Oxford Review of Economic Policy*, 19(2), 250–267.

QCA (2002), Public examinations: Views on maintaining standards over time. A summary of the MORI/CDELL project in Spring 2002, accessed August 2006, www.qca.org.uk.

RAE (2001a), Education Panel RAE 2001: Overview report, accessed May 2007, www.hero.ac.uk/rae/overview/docs/UoA68.pdf.

RAE (2001b), Social work panel RAE 2001: Overview report, accessed May 2007, www.hero.ac.uk/rae/overview/docs/UoA41.pdf.

RAE (2001c), Briefing note 11: Additional information for fields for UoA68 (education) submissions, accessed May 2007, www.hero.ac.uk/rae/Pubs/briefing/note11.htm.

RAE (2008), Research assessment exercise 2008, accessed May 2007, www.rae.ac.uk.

Ravitch, D. (1995), *National Standards in American Education*, Washington, DC: The Brookings Institution.

Rew, L., Koniak-Griffin, D., Lewis, M.A., Miles, M. and O'Sullivan, A. (2000), Secondary data analysis: New perspectives for adolescent research, *Nursing Outlook*, 48, 223–229.

Rhoades, K. (2003), *Errors in standardized Tests: A Systematic Problem*, Boston, MA: National Board on Educational Testing and Public Policy.

Riddell, S., Tinklin, T. and Wilson, A. (2005), New Labour, social justice and disabled students in higher education, *Educational Research Journal*, 31(5), 623–643.

Riedel, M. (2000), *Research Strategies for secondary Data: A Perspective for Criminology and Criminal Justice*, Thousand Oaks, CA: Sage.

Rodda, C. (2005), Economics for international students, accessed July 2007, www.cr1.dircon.co.uk/TB/3/unemployment.htm.

Rosenthal, R. and Jacobsen, L. (1968), *Pygmalion in the Classroom: Teacher Expectation and Pupils' Intellectual Development*, New York: Holt, Rinehart & Winston.

Royal Statistical Society (1991), Official statistics: Counting with confidence, *Journal of the Royal Statistical Society, Series A*, 154, 23–44.

Royal Statistical Society (2005), Performance indicators: Good, bad and ugly, *Journal of the Royal Statistical Society, Series A*, 168, 1–27.

Royal-Dawson, L. (2005), *Is Teaching Experience a Necessity for Markers of Key Stage 3 English?* London: Qualifications and Curriculum Authority.

Sales, E., Lichtenwalter, S. and Fevola, A. (2006), Secondary analysis in social work research education: Past, present and future promise, *Journal of Social Work Education*, 42(3), 543–558.

Schagen, I. and Hutchinson, D. (2006), Comparisons with PISA and TIMSS – we could be the man with two watches, *Education Journal*, 101, 34–35.

Schutt, R.K. (2006), *Investigating the Social World: The Process and Practice of Research*, 5th edn, London: Sage.

Schutt, R.K. (2007), *The Blackwell Encyclopaedia of Sociology*, Volume III, Ritzer, G. (ed.), Oxford: Blackwell.

Sharma, Y. (2002), Short, sharp 'schock' wakes Germany up, *The Times Education Supplement*, 27 September 2002.

Shirahase, S. (2001), Women and class structure in contemporary Japan, *British Journal of Sociology*, 52(3), 391–408.

Simpson, G. (1952), *Introduction*, in Durkheim, E. (1952), *Suicide: A Study in Sociology*, London: Routledge & Kegan Paul.

Slater, J. (2001), Cultures in a class of their own, *Times Educational Supplement*, 14 December 2001 (accessed December 2001, www.tes.co.uk).

Slavin, RE. (1989), PET and the pendulum: Faddism in education and how to stop it. *Phi Delta Kappan*, 70, 752–758.

Slavin, R. (2002), Evidence-based educational policies: Transforming educational practice and research, *Educational Researcher*, 31(7), 15–21.

Smith, E. (2002), *Understanding Underachievement: An Investigation into the Achievement of Secondary School Students*, PhD thesis, Cardiff: Cardiff University.

Smith, E. (2003), Understanding underachievement: An investigation into the differential achievement of secondary school pupils, *British Journal of Sociology of Education*, 24(5), 575–586.

Smith, E. (2005a), *Analysing Underachievement in Schools*, London: Continuum.

Smith, E. (2005b), Raising standards in American schools: The case of No Child Left Behind, *Journal of Educational Policy*, 20(4), 507–524.

Smith, E. (2007), Considering the experiences of 'underachieving' and 'over-achieving' students, *International Journal of Research and Method in Education*, 30(1), 19–32.

Smith, E. (2008), Raising standards in American schools? Problems with improving teacher quality, *Teaching and Teacher Education*.

Smith, E. and Gorard, S. (2007), Who succeeds in teacher training? *Research Papers in Education*, 19(4), 465–482.

Smith, E., Gorard, S. and Furlong, J. (2004), *Factors Supporting high-quality in ITT: Phase I, in-depth data analysis*, London: Teacher Training Agency.

Smith, H.W. (1981), *Strategies of Social Research: The Methodological Imagination*, 2nd edn, Englewood Cliffs, NJ: Prentice-Hall.

Smith, M.S. (1972), *Equality of Educational Opportunity: The Basic Findings Reconsidered*, in Mosteller, F. and Moynihan, D.P. (eds), *On Equality of Opportunity: Papers deriving from the Harvard University Faculty Seminar on the Coleman Report*, New York: Vintage Books.

Smithers, R. (2001), Inquiry into exam grade inflation claims, *Education Guardian*, accessed August 2006, http://education.guardian.co.uk.

Sobal, J. (1981), Teaching with secondary data, *Teaching Sociology*, 8(2), 149–170.

Sparrow, N. and Curtice, J. (2004), Measuring the attitudes of the general public via internet polls: An evaluation, *International Journal of Market Research*, 46(1), 23–44.

Strand, S. (2002), Pupils' mobility, attainment and progress during Key Stage 1: A study in cautious interpretation, *British Educational Research Journal*, 28(1), 63–78.

Sure Start (2007), Sure Start homepage, accessed August 2007, www.sure start.gov.uk/aboutsurestart/.

Taylor and Francis Group (2007), *Oxford Review of Education Journal* homepage, accessed August 2007, www.tandf.co.uk/journals/titles/03054985.asp.

Teaching Commission (2004), Teaching at risk: A call to action, accessed July 2006, www.theteachingcommission.org/press/FINAL_Report.pdf.

Thomas, R. (1996), Statistics as organizational products, *Sociological Review Online*, 1(3), 1–13 (accessed June 2007, www.socresonline.org.uk/socresonline/1/3/5.html).

Tomlinson, P. (2002), *Inquiry into A-level Standards: Final Report*, London: DfES.

Tooley, J. with Darby, D. (1998), *Educational Research: A Critique*, London: Office for Standards in Education.

Torrance, H. (2006), Globalizing empiricism: What, if anything, can be learned from International comparisons of Educational Achievement?, in Lauder, H., Brown, P., Dillabough, J. and Halsey, A.H. (eds), *Education, Globalisation and Social Change*, Oxford: Oxford University Press.

UCAS (2006), Universities Central Admissions Service, accessed June 2007, www.ucas.ac.uk/figures/ucasdata/socio/index.html.

UCAS (2007), Universities and Colleges Admissions Service, annual datasets: Subject dataset 2005 and 2006, accessed August 2007, http://www.ucas.com/figures/ads.html.

University of Manchester (2004), Cathie Marsh Centre for Census and Survey Research. ESDS Government, *Labour Force Survey, 2002: Teaching Dataset*, 2nd edn, Office for National Statistics, Social Survey Division, Northern Ireland Statistics and Research Agency, Central Survey Unit, Colchester, Essex: UK Data Archive.

US Department of Education (2002), No Child Left Behind: Executive summary, accessed June 2004, www.ed.gov/nclb/overview/intro/presidentplan/page_pg3.html.

US Department of Education (2004), *Meeting the Highly Qualified Teachers Challenge: The Secretary's Second Annual Report on Teacher Quality*, US Department of Education, Washington, DC: US Government Printing Office.

Van de Werfhorst, H., Sullivan, A. and Cheung, S.Y. (2003), Social class, ability and choice of subject in secondary and tertiary education in Britain, *British Educational Research Journal*, 29(1), 41–62.

Vulliamy, G. and Webb, R. (2001), The social construction of school exclusion rates: Implications for evaluation methodology, *Educational Studies*, 27(3), 358–370.

Wardell, F., Lishman, J. and Whalley, L.J. (2000), Who volunteers? *British Journal of Social Work*, 30, 227–248.

Warmington, P. and Murphy, R. (2004), Could do better? Media depictions of UK educational assessment results, *Journal of Educational Policy*, 19(3), 285–299.

Webb, E.J., Campbell, D.T., Schwartz, R.D. and Sechrest, L. (1966), *Unobtrusive Measures: Nonreactive Measures in the Social Sciences*, Chicago, IL: Rand McNally & Company.

Welsh Assembly Government (2001), Communities First baseline health and care social justice and equality statistics, accessed July 2007, www.statswales.wales.gov.uk/TableViewer/tableView.aspx?ReportId=3584.

Welsh Assembly Government (2004), Digest of Welsh local area statistics,

Chapter 5: The natural and built environment, accessed August 2007, http://new.wales.gov.uk/topics/statistics/publications/dwlas2004/?lang=en.

White, P. and Smith, E. (2005), What can PISA tell us about teacher shortages? *The European Journal of Education*, 40(1), 93–112.

Wiles, P. (2004), Policy and sociology, *British Journal of Sociology*, 55(1), 31–34.

Williams, R.M. (1989), The *American Soldier*: An assessment several wars later, *Public Opinion Quarterly*, 53, 155–174.

Williams, T., Williams, K., Kastberg, D. and Jocelyn, L. (2005), Achievement and affect in OECD nations, *Oxford Review of Education*, 31(4), 517–545.

Yaish, M. (2001), Class structure in a deeply divided society: Class and ethnic inequality in Israel, 1974–1991, *British Journal of Sociology*, 52(3), 409–439.

Index

A TEACHER'S GUIDE TO CLASSROOM RESEARCH
FORTH EDITION

David Hopkins

- How do we conduct classroom research?

- Why is classroom research valuable to teachers and schools?

- How does classroom research contribute to teaching, learning and school transformation?

The fourth edition of this bestselling book is a practical guide for teachers that wish to conduct research in their classrooms and for schools that wish to improve their practice. Classroom research, as described in this book, will enable teachers to enhance their own or their colleagues' teaching, to test the assumptions of educational theory in practice and to implement and evaluate whole school developments.

Comprehensively revised and updated, changes to the new edition include:

- A major re-working of the last four chapters

- Comprehensive description of how to conduct classroom research

- Two new chapters on analyzing and reporting research

- Updated case study examples and cameos

- The contribution of teacher research in enhancing personalized learning and school transformation

The book also explores models of teaching and learning; methods for collecting, analyzing and reporting data; and the ways in which classroom research can be published and linked to the curriculum, teaching and staff development.

Contents: *Preface to the fourth edition - Acknowledgements - A teacher's guide to classroom research - Classroom research in action - Why classroom research by teachers? - Action research and classroom research by teachers - Developing a focus - Principles of classroom observation - Methods of observation in classroom research - Data gathering - Analysing classroom research data - Reporting classroom research - Teaching and learning as the heartland of classroom research - Teacher research, the creation of professional learning communities and the transformation of schooling - Appendix: Ethics for classroom research - References - Index.*

2008   240pp
978-0-335-22174-5   (Paperback)   978-0-335-22175-2   (Hardback)

ACTION RESEARCH
A Methodology for Change and Development

Bridget Somekh

This book presents a fresh view of action research as a methodology uniquely suited to researching the processes of innovation and change. Drawing on twenty-five years' experience of leading or facilitating action research projects, Bridget Somekh argues that action research can be a powerful systematic intervention, which goes beyond describing, analyzing and theorizing practices to reconstruct and transform those practices.

The book examines action research into change in a range of educational settings, such as schools and classrooms, university departments, and a national evaluation of technology in schools. The opening chapter presents eight methodological principles and discusses key methodological issues. The focus then turns to action research in broader contexts such as 'southern' countries, health, business and management, and community development. Each chapter thereafter takes a specific research project as its starting point and critically reviews its design, relationships, knowledge outcomes, political engagement and impact.

Action Research is important reading for postgraduate students and practitioner researchers in education, health and management, as well as those in government agencies and charities who wish to research and evaluate change and development initiatives. It is also valuable for pre-service and in-service training of professionals such as teachers, nurses and managers.

Contents: *Introduction - Agency, change and the generation of actionable knowledge - Doing action research differently - Action research from the inside: A teacher's experience - Action research and radical change in schools - Action research for organizational development in higher education - Action research in a partnership between regional companies and a university - Action research in the evaluation of a national programme - Action research and innovative pedagogies with ICT - Reflections on the process of writing this book and its purposes - References - Index.*

2005   243pp
978-0-335-21658-1 (Paperback)   978-0-335-21659-8 (Hardback)

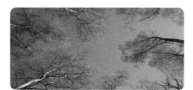